Arthur Gilman

The Story of Rome

From the Earliest Times to the End of the Republic

Arthur Gilman

The Story of Rome
From the Earliest Times to the End of the Republic

ISBN/EAN: 9783742811363

Manufactured in Europe, USA, Canada, Australia, Japa

Cover: Foto ©ninafisch / pixelio.de

Manufactured and distributed by brebook publishing software (www.brebook.com)

Arthur Gilman

The Story of Rome

The Story of the Nations

THE
STORY OF ROME

FROM THE EARLIEST TIMES TO THE END
OF THE REPUBLIC

BY

ARTHUR GILMAN, M.A.

AUTHOR OF "A HISTORY OF THE AMERICAN PEOPLE," EDITOR OF "THE POETICAL
WORKS OF GEOFFREY CHAUCER," ETC.

NEW YORK
G. P. PUTNAM'S SONS
LONDON : T. FISHER UNWIN
1895

COPYRIGHT BY
G. P. PUTNAM'S SONS
1885

PREFACE.

It is proposed to rehearse the lustrous story of Rome, from its beginning in the mists of myth and fable down to the mischievous times when the republic came to its end, just before the brilliant period of the empire opened.

As one surveys this marvellous vista from the vantage-ground of the present, attention is fixed first upon a long succession of well-authenticated facts which are shaded off in the dim distance, and finally lost in the obscurity of unlettered antiquity. The flesh and blood heroes of the more modern times regularly and slowly pass from view, and in their places the unsubstantial worthies of dreamy tradition start up. The transition is so gradual, however, that it is at times impossible to draw the line between history and legend. Fortunately for the purposes of this volume it is not always necessary to make the effort. The early traditions of the Eternal City have so long been recounted as truth that the world is slow to give up even the least jot or tittle of them, and when they are disproved as fact, they must be told over and over again as story.

Roman history involves a narrative of social and political struggles, the importance of which is as wide as modern civilization, and they must not be passed over without some attention, though in the present volume they cannot be treated with the thoroughness they deserve. The story has the advantage of being to a great extent a narrative of the exploits of heroes, and the attention can be held almost the whole time to the deeds of particular actors who successively occupy the focus or play the principal parts on the stage. In this way the element of personal interest, which so greatly adds to the charm of a story, may be infused into the narrative.

It is hoped to enter to some degree into the real life of the Roman people, to catch the true spirit of their actions, and to indicate the current of the national life, while avoiding the presentation of particular episodes or periods with undue prominence. It is intended to set down the facts in their proper relation to each other as well as to the facts of general history, without attempting an incursion into the domain of philosophy.

A. G.

CAMBRIDGE, *September*, 1885.

CONTENTS.

I.

ONCE UPON A TIME 1–15

The old king at Troy, 1—Paris, the wayward youth, 2—Helen carried off, 2—The war of ten years, 2—Æneas, son of Anchises, goes to Italy, 4—His death, 4—Fact and fiction in early stories, 5—How Milton wrote about early England, 5—How Æneas was connected with England, 6—Virgil writes about Æneas, 7—How Livy wrote about Æneas, 7—Was Æneas a son of Venus? 8—Italy, as Æneas would have seen it, 8—Greeks in Italy, 9—How Evander came from Arcadia, 9—How Æneas died, 10—Thirty cities rise, 11—Twins and a she-wolf, 12—Trojan names in Italy, 13—How the Romans named their children and themselves, 14.

II.

HOW THE SHEPHERDS BEGAN THE CITY . 16–38

Augury resorted to, 16—Romulus and Remus on two hills, 17—Vultures determine a question, 17—Pales, god of the shepherds, 18—Beginning the city, 19—Celer killed, 20—An asylum, 20—Bachelors want wives, 21—A game of wife-snatching, 22—Sabines wish their daughters back, 22—Tarpeia on the hill, 23—A duel between two hills, 24—Two men named Curtius, 25—Women interfere for peace, 26—Where did Romulus go? 27—Society divided by Romulus, 28—Numa Pompilius chosen king, 29—Laws of religion given the people, 30—Guilds established, 31—The year divided into months, 32—Tullus Hostilius king, 33—Six brothers fight, 34—Horatia killed, 36—Ancus Martius king, 37—The wooden bridge, 38.

III.

HOW CORINTH GAVE ROME A NEW DYNASTY . 39–47

Magna Græcia, 39—Cypselus, the democratic politician, 40—Demaratus goes to Tarquinii, 41—Etruscan relics, 42—Lucomo's cap lifted, 42—Lucomo changes his name, 43—A Greek king of Rome, 43—A circus and other great public works, 44—A light around a boy's head, 46—Servius Tullius king, 46—How the kingdom passed from the Etruscan dynasty, 47.

IV.

THE RISE OF THE COMMONS 48–57

A king of the plebeians, 48—A league with Latin cities, 48—A census taken, 48—The Seven Hills, 49—Classes formed among the people, 50—Assemblies of the people, 50—How ace means one, 51—Heads of the people, 51—Armor of the different classes, 51—A Lustration or *Suovetaurilia*, 54—What is a lustrum? 54—Servius divides certain lands, 55—A wicked husband and a naughty wife, 55—King Servius killed, 56—Sprinkled with a father's blood, 57.

V.

HOW A PROUD KING FELL 58–68

A tyrant king, 58—The mysterious Sibyl of Cumæ comes to sell books, 59—The head found on the Capitoline, 59—A serpent frightens a king, 60—A serious inquiry sent to Delphi, 60—A hollow stick filled with gold helps a young man, 62—A good wife spinning, 62—A terrible oath, 63—The Tarquins banished, 63—A republic takes the place of the kingdom, 64—The first of the long line of consuls, 64—The good Valerius, 65—The god Silvanus cries out to some effect, 65—Lars Porsena of Clusium and what he tried to do, 66—Horatius the brave, 66—Rome loses land, 67—A dictator appointed, 67—Castor and Pollux help the army at Lake Regillus, 67—Caius Marcius wins a crown, 68—Appius Claudius comes to town, 68.

VI.

THE ROMAN RUNNYMEDE 69-79

The character of the Romans, 69—Traits of the kings, 70—Insignificance of Latin territory, 71—Occupations, 71—Art backward, 71—A narrow religion, 72—Who were the *populus Romanus?* 73—Patricians oppress the people, 73—Wrongs of Roman money-lending, 74—How a debtor flaunted his rags to good purpose, 75—Appius Claudius defied, 76—A secession to the Anio, 77—Apologue of the body and its members, 78—Laws of Valerius re-affirmed, 78—Tribunes of the people appointed, 79—Peace by the treaty of the Sacred Mount, 79.

VII.

HOW THE HEROES FOUGHT FOR A HUNDRED YEARS 80-97

Coriolanus fights bravely, 80—He enrages the plebeians, 81—Women melt the strong man's heart, 82—Plebeians gain ground, 82—Agrarian laws begin to be made, 83—Cassius, who makes the first, undermined, 84—The family of the Fabii support the commons, 85—A black day on the Cremara, 85—Cincinnatus called from his plow, 86—The Æquians subjugated, 87—What a conquest meant in those days, 87—The Aventine Hill given to the commons, 88—The ten men make ten laws and afterwards twelve, 89—The ten men become arrogant, 90—How Virginia was killed, 91—Appius Claudius cursed, 91—The second secession of the plebeians, 92—The third secession, 92—The commons make gains, 93 Censors chosen, 93—The wonderful siege of Veii, 94—How a tunnel brings victory, 95—Camillus the second founder of Rome, 96—How the territory was increased, but ill omens threaten, 97.

VIII.

A BLAST FROM BEYOND THE NORTH WIND . 98-110

What the Greeks thought when they shivered, 98—A warlike people come into notice, 99—Brennus leads the barbarians to victory, 100—A voice from the temple of Vesta,

100—Tearful Allia, 101—The city alarmed and Camillus called for, 102—How the sacred geese chattered to a purpose, 103—Brennus successful, but defeated at last, 104—A historical game of scandal, 106—Camillus sets to work to make a new city, 107—Camillus honored as the second founder of Rome, 108—Manlius less fortunate, 108—Poor debtors protected by a law of Stolo, 109—A plague comes to Rome, and priests order stage-plays to be performed, 110—The floods of the Tiber come into the circus, 110.

IX.

HOW THE REPUBLIC OVERCAME ITS NEIGHBORS, 111–125

Alexander the Great strides over Persia, 111—Suppose he had attacked Rome? 112—The man with a chain, and the man helped by a crow, 113—How the Samnites came into Campania, 114—The memorable battle of Mount Gaurus, 114—How Carthage thought best to congratulate Rome, 115—Debts become heavy again, 115—How Decius Mus sacrificed himself for the army, 116—Misfortune at the Caudine Forks, 117—A general muddle, in which another Mus sacrifices himself, 118—Another secession of the commons, 119—An agrarian law and an abolition of debts, 119—What the wild waves washed up, 119—Pyrrhus, King of Epirus, takes a lofty model, 120—How Cineas asked hard questions, 121—Blind Appius Claudius stirs up the people, 122—Maleventum gets a better name, 123—Ptolemy Philadelphus thinks best to congratulate Rome, 123—How the Romans made roads, 124—The classes of citizens, 125.

X.

AN AFRICAN SIROCCO 126–148

How an old Bible city sent out a colony, 126—Carthage attends strictly to its own business, 127—Sicily a convenient place for a great fight, 128—The Mamertines not far from Scylla and Charybdis, 129—Ancient war-vessels and how they were rowed, 130—The prestige of Carthage on the water destroyed, 132—Xanthippus the Spartan helps the Carthaginians, 132—The horrible fate of noble Regulus, 133—Hamilcar, the man of lightning, comes to view, 133—Gates of the temple of Janus closed the second time, 134—A perfidious queen overthrown, 135—Two Gauls and two Greeks buried alive, 136—Hannibal hates Rome, 137—Rome and Carthage fight the second time, 138—Scipio and Fabius the Delayer fight for Rome, 139—Hannibal crosses the Alps, 140—The terrible rout at Lake Trasimenus, 142—A business man beaten, 143—Syracuse falls and Archimedes dies, 144—Fabius takes Tarentum, 145—A great victory at the Metaurus, 146—War carried to Africa and closed at Zama, 147—Hannibal a wanderer, 148.

XI.

THE NEW PUSHES THE OLD—WARS AND CONQUESTS 149–166

Tumultuous women stir up the city, 149—What the Oppian Law forbade, 150—Cato the Stern opposes the women, 152—The women find a valorous champion, 153—How did the matrons establish their high character? 154—Two parties look at the growing influence of ideas from Greece, 156—What were those influences? 158—How Rome coveted Eastern conquests, 159—How Flamininus fought at the Dog-heads, 160—How the Grecians cried for joy at the Isthmian games, 161—Great battles at Thermopylæ and Magnesia, and their results, 162—Philopœmen, Hannibal, and Scipio die, 163—The battle of Pydna marks an era, 164—Greece despoiled of its works of art, 165—Cato wishes Carthage destroyed, 165—Numantia destroyed, 166—The slaves in Sicily give trouble, 166.

XII.

A FUTILE EFFORT AT REFORM . . 167–184

Scipio gives away his daughter, 167—Tiberius Gracchus serves the state, 168—Romans without family altars or tombs, 169—Cornelia urges Gracchus to do somewhat for the state, 170—Gracchus misses an opportunity, 171—Another son of Cornelia comes to the front, 172—The younger Gracchus builds roads and makes good laws, 173—Drusus undermines the reformer, 174—Office looked upon as a means of getting riches, 175—Marius and Sulla appear, 175—Jugurtha fights and bribes, 176—Metellus, the general of integrity, 178—Marius captures Jugurtha, 180—A shadow falls upon Rome, 181—A terrible battle at Vercellæ, 182—The slaves rise again, 183—The Domitian law restricts the rights of the senate, 183—The ill-gotten gold of Toulouse, 184.

XIII.

SOCIAL AND CIVIL WARS 185-197

The agrarian laws of Appuleius, 185—Luxury increases and faith falls away, 186—Rome for the Romans, 186—Another Drusus appears, 187—The brave Marsians menace Rome, 187—Ten new tribes formed, 188—A war with Mithridates of Pontus, 189—Marius and Sulla struggle and Marius goes to the wall, 190—Sulla besieges Athens, 191—Sulla threatens the senate, 192—The capitol burned, 193—A battle at the Colline Gate, 193—Proscription and carnage, 194—Sulla makes laws and retires to see the effect, 195—A *congiarium*, 196—A grand funeral and a cremation, 197.

XIV.

THE MASTER-SPIRITS OF THIS AGE . . 198-213

Tendency towards monarchy, 198—Sertorius and his white fawn, 199—Crassus and his great house, 200—Cicero, the eloquent orator, 202—Verres, the great thief, 203—How Verres ran away, 204—Catiline the Cruel, 205—Cæsar, the man born to rule, 206—Looking for gain in confusion, 207—Lepidus flees after the fight of the Mulvian bridge, 208—How the two young men caused gladiators to fight, 209—What Spartacus did, 210—Six thousand crosses, 211—Pompey overawes the senate, 212.

XV.

PROGRESS OF THE GREAT POMPEY . . 214-230

Pompey the principal citizen, 214—Crassus feeds the people

at ten thousand tables, 216—How the pirates caught Cæsar, and how Cæsar caught the pirates, 217—Gabinius makes a move, 218—The Manilian law sets Pompey further on, 219—Mithridates fights and flees, 220—Times of treasons, stratagems, and spoils, 221—Catiline plots, 222—The sacrilege of Clodius, 223—Cæsar pushes himself to the front, 224—The last agrarian law, 226—Cæsar's success in Gaul, 227—Vercingetorix appears, 228—Cæsar's conquests, 229.

XVI.

HOW THE TRIUMVIRS CAME TO UNTIMELY ENDS 231–254

Pompey builds a theatre, 231—Crassus must make his mark, 232—Cato against Cæsar, 234—Curio helps Cæsar, 235—Solemn jugglery of the pontiffs, 236—Curio warm enough, 237—At the Rubicon, 238—Crossing the little river, 240—Pompey stamps in vain, 241—Cato flees from Rome, 242—Metellus stands aside, 243—Pompey killed, 244—*Veni, vidi, vici*, 245—Honors and plans of Cæsar, 246—The calendar reformed, 247—Cæsar has too much ambition, 248—'T was one of those coronets, 249—The Ides of March, 250—Antony, the actor, 251—Antony the chief man in Rome, 252—What next? 254.

XVII.

HOW THE REPUBLIC BECAME AN EMPIRE . 255–270

How Octavius became a Cæsar, 255—Agrippa and Cicero give him their help, 256—Octavius wins the soldiers, and Cicero launches his Philippics, 257—Antony, Lepidus, and Octavius become Triumvirs, 258—Their first work a bloody one, 259—Cicero falls, 260—Brutus and Cassius defeated at Philippi, 261—Antony forgets Fulvia, 262—Antony and Octavius quarrel and meet for discussion at Tarentum, 264—How Horace travelled to Brundusium, 265—The duration of the Triumvirate extended five years, 266—Cleopatra beguiles Antony a second time, 267—The great battle off Actium, 268—Octavius wins complete power, and a new era begins, 270—The Republic ends, 270.

XVIII.

SOME MANNERS AND CUSTOMS OF THE ROMAN
 PEOPLE 271–291

 How did these people live? 271—The first Roman house, 272—The vestibule and the dark room, 274—The dining-room and the parlor, 276—Rooms for pictures and books, 277—Cooking taken out of the atrium, 278—How the houses were heated and lighted, 279—Life in a villa, 280—The extravagance of the pleasure villa, 281—When a man and a woman had agreed to marry, 282—How the bride dressed and what the groom did, 283—The wife's position and work, 284—The *stola* and the *toga*, 285—Foot-gear from *soccus* to *cothurnus*, 286—Breakfast, luncheon, and dinner, 288—The formal dinner, 289—How the Romans travelled, and how they sought office, 290—The law and its penalties, 291.

XIX.

THE ROMAN READING AND WRITING . . 292–312

 Grecian influence on Roman mental culture, 292—Text-books, 293—Cato and Varro on education, 294—Dictation and copy-books, 295—The early writers, 295—Fabius Pictor, 297—Plautus, 297—Terence, 298—Atellan plays, 298—Cicero's works, 299—Varro's works, 300—Cæsar and Catullus, 302—Lucretius, 303—Ovid and Tibullus, 304—Sallust, 305—Livy, 306—Horace, 307—Cornelius Nepos, 308—Virgil and his works, 309—Life at the villa of Mæcenas, 311.

XX.

THE ROMAN REPUBLICANS SERIOUS AND
 GAY 312–332

 The will of the gods sought for, 312—The first temples, 313—Festivals in the first month, 314—Vinalia and Saturnalia, 314—Fires of Vulcan and Vesta, 315—Matronly and family services, 316—No mythology at first, 317—Colleges of priests needed, 318—An incursion of Greek philosophers, 319—Games of childhood, 320—Checkers and other games of chance, 321—The people cry for games, 322—Games in

PAGE

the circus, 323—The amphitheatre invented, 325—Men and beasts fight, 326—Funeral ceremonies, 326—Charon paid, 327—The mourning procession, 329—Inurning the ashes, 329—The columbarium, 330—The Roman May-day, 331— Change from rustic simplicity to urban orgies, 332.

INDEX 333

LIST OF ILLUSTRATIONS.

	PAGE
MAP OF THE ROMAN EMPIRE	1
MAP OF ANCIENT ROME	332
VIEW OF THE COLOSSEUM AND PORTION OF MODERN ROME	*Frontispiece*
THE PLAIN OF TROY IN MODERN TIMES	3
ROMAN GIRLS WITH A STYLUS AND WRITING-TABLET	23
A ROMAN ALTAR	31
MONUMENT OF THE HORATII AND THE CURIATII	35
MOUTH OF THE CLOACA MAXIMA AT THE TIBER, AND THE SO-CALLED TEMPLE OF VESTA	45
ROMAN SOLDIERS, COSTUMES AND ARMOR	53
THE RAVINE OF DELPHI	61
THE CAPITOL RESTORED	105
ROMAN STREET PAVEMENT	125
A PHŒNICIAN VESSEL (TRIREME)	126
A ROMAN WAR-VESSEL	131
HANNIBAL	137
TERENCE, THE LAST ROMAN COMIC POET	141
PUBLIUS CORNELIUS SCIPIO AFRICANUS	145
A ROMAN MATRON	151
ROMAN HEAD-DRESSES	155
GLADIATORS AT A FUNERAL	157
ACTORS' MASKS	159
A ROMAN MILE-STONE	173
IN A ROMAN STUDY	177

xvi LIST OF ILLUSTRATIONS.

	PAGE
PLAN OF A ROMAN CAMP IN THE TIME OF THE REPUBLIC	179
POMPEY (CNEIUS POMPEIUS MAGNUS)	203
CAIUS JULIUS CÆSAR	207
GLADIATORS	211
TRIUMPHAL PROCESSION OF A ROMAN GENERAL	213
INTERIOR OF A ROMAN HOUSE	215
A ROMAN POETESS	219
THE FORUM ROMANUM IN MODERN TIMES	225
AN ELEPHANT IN ARMOR (SEE PAGE 122)	233
ITALIAN AND GERMAN ALLIES, COSTUMES AND ARMOR	239
INTERIOR OF THE FORUM ROMANUM	253
MARCUS TULLIUS CICERO	259
CLEOPATRA'S SHOW SHIP	263
ANCIENT STATUE OF AUGUSTUS	269
THE HOUSE-PHILOSOPHER (SEE PAGE 277)	273
DINING-TABLE AND COUCHES	275
COVERINGS FOR THE FEET	285
ARTICLES OF THE ROMAN TOILET	287
RUINS OF THE COLOSSEUM, SEEN FROM THE PALATINE HILL	324
A COLUMBARIUM	330

THE STORY OF ROME.

I.

ONCE UPON A TIME.

ONCE upon a time, there lived in a city of Asia Minor, not far from Mount Ida, as old Homer tells us in his grand and beautiful poem, a king who had fifty sons and many daughters. How large his family was, indeed, we cannot say, for the story-tellers of the olden time were not very careful to set down the actual and exact truth, their chief object being to give the people something to interest them. That they succeeded well in this respect we know, because the story of this old king and his great family of sons and daughters has been told and retold thousands of times since it was first related, and that was so long ago that the bard himself has sometimes been said never to have lived at all. Still, somebody must have existed who told the wondrous story, and it has always been attributed to a blind poet, to whom the name Homer has been given.

The place in which the old king and his great family lived was Ilium, though it is better known as Troja or Troy, because that is the name that the

Roman people used for it in later times. One of the sons of Priam, for that was the name of this king, was Paris, who, though very handsome, was a wayward and troublesome youth. He once journeyed to Greece to find a wife, and there fell in love with a beautiful daughter of Jupiter, named Helen. She was already married to Menelaus, the Prince of Lacedæmonia (brother of another famous hero, Agamemnon), who had most hospitably entertained young Paris, but this did not interfere with his carrying her off to Troy. The wedding journey was made by the roundabout way of Phœnicia and Egypt, but at last the couple reached home with a large amount of treasure taken from the hospitable Menelaus.

This wild adventure led to a war of ten years between the Greeks and King Priam, for the rescue of the beautiful Helen. Menelaus and some of his countrymen at last contrived to conceal themselves in a hollow wooden horse, in which they were taken into Troy. Once inside, it was an easy task to open the gates and let the whole army in also. The city was then taken and burned. Menelaus was naturally one of the first to hasten from the smoking ruins, though he was almost the last to reach his home. He lived afterwards for years in peace, health, and happiness with the beautiful wife who had cost him so much suffering and so many trials to regain.

Among the relatives of King Priam was one Anchises, a descendant of Jupiter, who was very old at the time of the war. He had a valiant son, however, who fought well in the struggle, and the story of his

THE PLAIN OF TROY IN MODERN TIMES.

deeds was ever afterwards treasured up among the most precious narratives of all time. This son was named Æneas, and he was not only a descendant of Jupiter, but also a son of the beautiful goddess Venus. He did not take an active part in the war at its beginning, but in the course of time he and Hector, who was one of the sons of the king, became the most prominent among the defenders of Troy. After the destruction of the city, he went out of it, carrying on his shoulders his aged father, Anchises, and leading by the hand his young son, Ascanius, or Iulus, as he was also called. He bore in his hands his household gods, called the Penates, and began his now celebrated wanderings over the earth. He found a resting-place at last on the farther coast of the Italian peninsula, and there one day he marvellously disappeared in a battle on the banks of the little brook Numicius, where a monument was erected to his memory as "The Father and the Native God."

According to the best accounts, the war of Troy took place nearly twelve hundred years before Christ, and that is some three thousand years ago now. It was before the time of the prophet Eli, of whom we read in the Bible, and long before the ancient days of Samuel and Saul and David and Solomon, who seem so very far removed from our times. There had been long lines of kings and princes in China and India before that time, however, and in the hoary land of Egypt as many as twenty dynasties of sovereigns had reigned and passed away, and a certain sort of civilization had flourished for two or three thousand years, so that the great world was not so young at that time as one might at first think. If only there had been books and newspapers in those olden days, what revelations they would make to us now ! They would tell us exactly where Troy was, which some of the learned think we do not know, and we might, by their help, separate fact from fiction in the immortal poems and stories that are now our only source of information. It is not for us to say that that would be any better for us than to know merely what we do, for poetry is elevating and entertaining, and stirs the heart ; and who could make poetry out of the columns of a newspaper, even though it were as old as the times of the Pharaohs? Let us, then, be thankful for what we have, and take the beginnings of history in the mixed form of truth and fiction, following the lead of learned historians who are and long have been trying to trace the true clue of fact in the labyrinth of poetic story with which it is involved.

When the poet Milton sat down to write the history of that part of Britain now called England, as he expressed it, he said : " The beginning of nations, those excepted of whom sacred books have spoken, is to this day unknown. Nor only the beginning, but the deeds also of many succeeding ages, yes, periods of ages, either wholly unknown or obscured or blemished with fables." Why this is so the great poet did not pretend to tell, but he thought that it might be because people did not know how to write in the first ages, or because their records had been lost in wars and by the sloth and ignorance that followed them. Perhaps men did not think that the records of their own times were worth preserving when they reflected how base and corrupt, how petty and perverse such deeds would appear to those who should come after them. For whatever reason, Milton said that it had come about that some of the stories that seemed to be the oldest were in his day regarded as fables; but that he did not intend to pass them over, because that which one antiquary admitted as true history, another exploded as mere fiction, and narratives that had been once called fables were afterward found to "contain in them many footsteps and reliques of something true," as what might be read in poets "of the flood and giants, little believed, till undoubted witnesses taught us that all was not feigned." For such reasons Milton determined to tell over the old stories, if for no other purpose than that they might be of service to the poets and romancers who knew how to use them judiciously. He said that he did not intend even to stop to argue and debate disputed questions, but, "imploring divine assistance," to relate," with plain and lightsome brevity," those things worth noting.

After all this preparation Milton began his history of England at the Flood, hastily recounted the facts to the time of the great Trojan war, and then said that he had arrived at a period when the narrative could not be so hurriedly dispatched. He showed how the old historians had gone back to Troy for the beginnings of the English race, and had chosen a great-grandson of Æneas, named Brutus, as the one by whom it should be attached to the right royal heroes of Homer's poem. Thus we see how firm a hold upon the imagination of the world the tale of Troy had after twenty-seven hundred years.

Twenty-five or thirty years before the birth of Christ there was in Rome another poet, named Virgil, writing about the wanderings of Æneas. He began his beautiful story with these words: " Arms I sing, and the hero, who first, exiled by fate, came from the coast of Troy to Italy and the Lavinian shore." He then went on to tell in beautiful words the story of the wanderings of his hero,—a tale that has now been read and re-read for nearly two thousand years, by all who have wished to call themselves educated ; generations of school-boys, and school-girls too, have slowly made their way through the Latin of its twelve books. This was another evidence of the strong hold that the story of Troy had upon men, as well as of the honor in which the heroes, and descent from them, were held.

In the generation after Virgil there arose a graphic writer named Livy, who wrote a long history of Rome, a large portion of which has been preserved to our own day. Like Virgil, Livy traced the origin of the Latin people to Æneas, and like Milton, he re-told the ancient stories, saying that he had no intention of affirming or refuting the traditions that had come down to his time of what had occurred before the building of the city, though he thought them rather suitable for the fictions of poetry than for the genuine records of the historian. He added, that it was an indulgence conceded to antiquity to blend human things with things divine, in such a way as to make the origin of cities appear more venerable. This principle is much the same as that on which Milton wrote his history, and it seems a very good one. Let us, therefore, follow it.

In the narrative of events for several hundred years after the city of Rome was founded, according to the early traditions, it is difficult to distinguish truth from fiction, though a skilful historian (and many such there have been) is able, by reading history backwards, to make up his mind as to what is probable and what seems to belong only to the realm of myth. It does not, for example, seem probable that Æneas was the son of the goddess Venus; and it seems clear that a great many of the stories that are mixed with the early history of Rome were written long after the events they pretend to record, in order to account for customs and observances of the later days. Some of these we shall notice as we go on with our pleasant story.

We must now return to Æneas. After long wanderings and many marvellous adventures, he arrived, as has been said, on the shores of Italy. He was not able to go rapidly about the whole country, as we are in these days by means of our good roads and other modes of communication, but if he could have done this, he would have found that he had fallen upon a land in which the inhabitants had come, as he had, from foreign shores. Some of them were of Greek origin, and others had emigrated from countries just north of Italy, though, as we now know that Asia was the cradle of our race, and especially of that portion of it that has peopled Europe, we suppose that all the dwellers on the boot-shaped peninsula had their origin on that mysterious continent at some early period.

If Æneas could have gone to the southern part of Italy,—to that part from which travellers now take the steamships for the East at Brindisi, he would have found some of the emigrants from the North. If he had gone to the north of the river Tiber, he would have seen a mixed population enjoying a greater civilization than the others, the aristocracy of which had come also from the northern mountains, though the common people were from Greece or its colonies. These people of Greek descent were called Etruscans, and it has been discovered that they had advanced so far in civilization, that they afterwards gave many of their customs to the city of Rome when it came to power. A confederacy known as the "Twelve Cities of Etruria" became famous afterwards, though no one knows exactly which the twelve were. Probably they changed from time to time ; some that belonged to the union at one period, being out of it at another. It will be enough for us to remember that Veii, Clusium, Fidenæ, Volsinii, and Tarquinii were of the group of Etruscan cities at a later date.

The central portion of the country to which Æneas came is that known as Italia, the inhabitants of which were of the same origin as the Greeks. It is said that about sixty years before the Trojan war, King Evander (whose name meant good man and true) brought a company from the land of Arcadia, where the people were supposed to live in a state of ideal innocence and virtue, to Italia, and began a city on the banks of the Tiber, at the foot of the Palatine Hill. Evander was a son of Mercury, and he found that the king of the country he had come to was Turnus, who was also a relative of the immortal gods. Turnus and Evander became fast friends, and it is said that Turnus taught his neighbors the art of writing, which he had himself learned from Hercules, but this is one of the transparent fictions of the story. It may be that he taught them music and the arts of social life, and gave them good laws. What ever became of good Evander we do not know.

The king of the people among whom Æneas landed was one Latinus, who became a friend of his noble visitor, giving him his daughter Lavinia to wife, though he had previously promised her to Turnus. Æneas named the town in which he lived Lavinium, in honor of his wife. Turnus was naturally enraged at the loss of his expected bride, and made war upon both Æneas and Latinus. The Trojan came off victorious, both the other warriors being killed in the struggle. Thus for a short time, Æneas was left sole king of all those regions, with no one to dispute his title to the throne or his right to his wife; but the pleasure of ruling was not long to be his, for a short time after his accession to power, he was killed in battle on the banks of the Numicius, as has already been related. His son Ascanius left the low and unhealthy site of Lavinium, and founded a city on higher ground, which was called Alba Longa (the long, white city), and the mountain on the side of which it was, the Alban mountain. The new capital of Ascanius became the centre and principal one of thirty cities that arose in the plain, over all of which it seemed to have authority. Among these were Tusculum, Præneste, Lavinium, and Ardea, places of which subsequent history has much to say.

Ascanius was successful in founding a long line of sovereigns, who reigned in Alba for three hundred years, until there arose one Numitor who was dispossessed of his throne by a younger brother named Amulius. One bad act usually leads to another, and this case was no exception to the rule, for when Amulius had taken his brother's throne, he still feared that the rightful children might interfere with the enjoyment of his power. Though he supported Numitor in comfort, he cruelly killed his son and shut his daughter up in a temple. This daughter was called Silvia, or, sometimes, Rhea Silvia. Wicked men are not able generally to enjoy the fruits of their evil doings long, and, in the course of time, the daughter of the dethroned Numitor became the mother of a beautiful pair of twin boys, (their father being the god of war, Mars,) who proved the avengers of their grandfather. Not immediately, however. The detestable usurper determined to throw the mother and her babes into the river Tiber, and thus make an end of them, as well as of all danger to him from them. It happened that the river was at the time overflowing its banks, and though the poor mother was drowned, the cradle of the twins was caught on the shallow ground at the foot of the Palatine Hill, at the very place where the good Evander had begun his city so long before.

There the waifs were found by one of the king's shepherds, after they had been, strangely enough, taken care of for a while by a she-wolf, which gave them milk, and a woodpecker, which supplied them with other food. Faustulus was the name of this shepherd, and he took them to his wife Laurentia, though she already had twelve others to care for. The brothers, who were named Romulus and Remus, grew up on the sides of the Palatine Hill to be strong and handsome men, and showed themselves born leaders among the other shepherds, as they attended to their daily duties or fought the wild animals that troubled the flocks.

The grandfather of the twins fed his herds on the Aventine Hill, nearer the river Tiber, just across a little valley, and a quarrel arose between his shepherds and those of Faustulus, in the course of which Remus was captured and taken before Numitor. The old man thus discovered the relationship that existed between him and the twins who had so long been lost. In consequence of the discovery of their origin, and the right to the throne that was their father's, they arose against their unworthy uncle, and with the aid of their followers, put him to death and placed Numitor in supreme authority, where he rightfully belonged. The twins had become attached to the place in which they had spent their youth, and preferred to live there rather than to go to Alba with their royal grandfather. He therefore granted to them that portion of his possessions, and there they determined to found a city.

Thus we have the origin of the Roman people. We

see how the early traditions " mixed human things with things divine," as Livy said had been done to make the origin of the city more respectable ; how Æneas, the far-back ancestor, was descended from Jupiter himself, and how he was a son of Venus, the goddess of love. How Romulus and Remus, the actual founders, were children of the god of war, and thus naturally fitted to be the builders of a nation that was to be strong and to conquer all known peoples on earth. The effort to ascribe to their nation an origin that should appear venerable to all who believed the stories of the gods and goddesses, was remarkably successful, and there is no doubt that it gave inspiration to the Roman people long after the worship of those divinities had become a matter of form, if not even of ridicule.

This was not all that was done, however, to establish the faith in the old stories in the minds of the people. In some way that it is not easy to explain, the names of the first heroes were fixed upon certain localities, just as those of the famous British hero, King Arthur, have long been fixed upon places in Brittany, Cornwall, and Southern Scotland. We find at a little place called Metapontem, the tools used by Epeus in making the wooden horse that was taken into Troy. The bow and arrows of Hercules were preserved at Thurii, near Sybaris ; the tomb of Philoctetes, who inherited these weapons of the hero, was at Macalla, in Bruttium, not far from Crotona, where Pythagoras had lived ; the head of the Calydonian Boar was at Beneventum, east of Capua, and the Erymanthian Boar's tusks were at Cumæ, cele-

brated for its Sibyl; the armor of Diomede, one of
the Trojan heroes, was at Luceria, in the vicinity of
Cannæ; the cup of Ulysses and the tomb of Elpenor were at Circei, on the coast; the ships of
Æneas and his Penates were at Lavinium, fifteen
miles south of Rome; and the tomb of the hero
himself was at a spot between Ardea and Lavinium,
on the banks of the brook Numicius. Most men are
interested in relics of olden times, and these, so many
and of such great attractiveness, were doubtless
strong proofs to the average Roman, ready to think
well of his ancestors, that tradition told a true story.

As we read the histories of other nations than our
own, we are struck by the strangeness of many of
the circumstances. They appear foreign (or " out-
landish," as our great-grandparents used to say), and
it is difficult to put ourselves in the places of the
people we read of, especially if they belong to
ancient times. Perhaps the names of persons and
places give us as much trouble as any thing. It
seems to us, perhaps, that the Romans gave their
children too many names, and they often added to
them themselves when they had grown up. They
did not always write their names out in full; sometimes they called each other by only one of them,
and at others by several. Marcus Tullius Cicero was
sometimes addressed as " Tullius," and is often mentioned in old books as " Tully "; and he was also
" M. Tullius Cicero." It was as if we were to write
" G. Washington Tudela," and call Mr. Tudela familiarly " Washington." This would cause no con-

fusion at the time, but it might be difficult for his descendants to identify "Washington" as Mr. Tudela, if, years after his death, they were to read of him under his middle name only. The Greeks were much more simple, and each of them had but one name, though they freely used nicknames to describe peculiarities or defects. The Latins and Etruscans seem to have had at first only one name apiece, but the Sabines had two, and in later times the Sabine system was generally followed. A Roman boy had, therefore, a given name and a family name, which were indispensable; but he might have two others, descriptive of some peculiarity or remarkable event in his life—as " Scævola," left-handed; " Cato," or " Sapiens," wise; " Coriolanus," of Corioli. " Appius Claudius Sabinus Regillensis " means Appius of the Claudian family of Regillum, in the country of the Sabines. " Lucius Cornelius Scipio Africanus " means Lucius, of the Cornelian family, and of the particular branch of the Scipios who won fame in Africa. These were called the *prænomen* (forename), *nomen* (name), *cognomen* (surname), and *agnomen* (added name).

II.

HOW THE SHEPHERDS BEGAN THE CITY.

THE proverbs says that Rome was not built in a day. It was no easy task for the twins to agree just where they should even begin the city. Romulus thought that the Palatine Hill, on which he and his brother had lived, was the most favorable spot for the purpose, while Remus inclined no less decidedly in favor of the Aventine, on which Numitor had fed his flocks. In this emergency, they seem to have asked counsel of their grandfather, and he advised them to settle the question by recourse to augury,* a practice of the Etrurians with which they were probably quite familiar, for they had been educated, we are told, at Gabii, the largest of the towns of Latium, where all the knowledge of the region was known to the teachers.

Following this advice, the brothers took up positions at a given time on the respective hills, surrounded by their followers; those of Romulus being

* Augury was at first a system of divining by birds, but in time the observation of other signs was included. At first no plebeians could take the auspices, as they seem to have had no share in the divinities whose will was sought, but in the year 300, B.C., the college of augurs, then comprising four patricians, was enlarged by the admission of five plebeians. The augurs were elected for life.

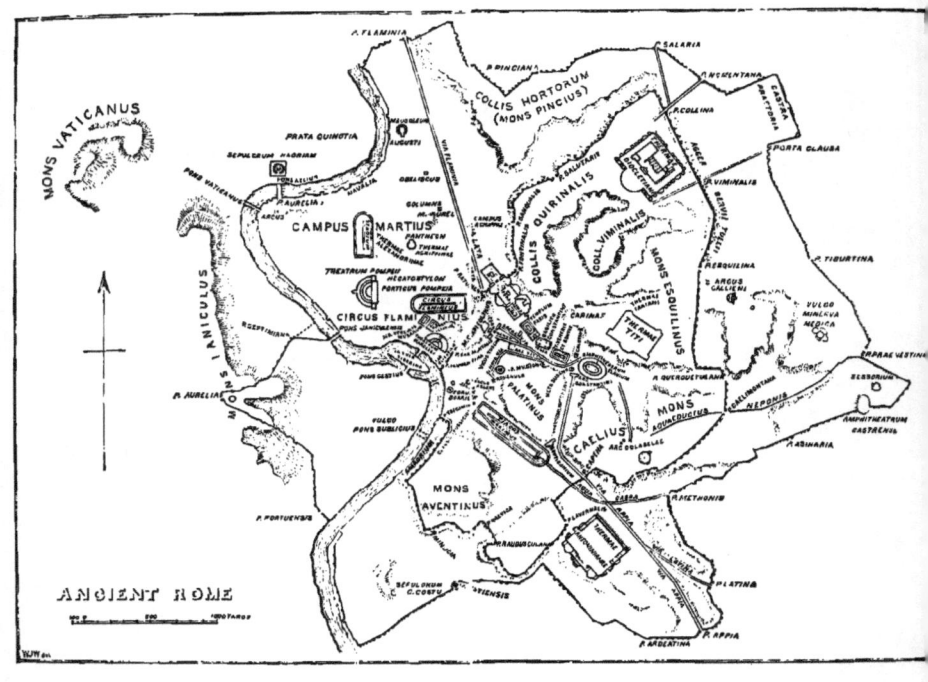

known as the Quintilii, and those of Remus as the Fabii. Thus, in anxious expectation, they waited for the passage of certain birds which was to settle the question between them. We can imagine them as they waited. The two hills are still to be seen in the city, and probably the two groups were about half a mile apart. On one side of them rolled the muddy waters of the Tiber, from which they had been snatched when infants, and around them rose the other elevations over which the "seven-hilled" city of the future was destined to spread. From morning to evening they patiently watched, but in vain. Through the long April night, too, they held their posts, and as the sun of the second day rose over the Cœlian Hill, Remus beheld with exultation six vultures swiftly flying through the air, and thought that surely fortune had decided in his favor. The vulture was a bird seldom seen, and one that never did damage to crops or cattle, and for this reason its appearance was looked upon as a good augury. The passage of the six vultures did not, however, settle this dispute, as Numitor expected it would, for Romulus, when he heard that Remus had seen six, asserted that twelve had flown by him. His followers supported this claim, and determined that the city should be begun on the Palatine Hill. It is said that this hill, from which our word palace has come, received its name from the town of Pallantium, in Arcadia, from which Evander came to Italy.

The twenty-first of April was a festal day among the shepherds, and it was chosen as the one on which the new city should be begun (753 B.C.). In the morning of the day, it was customary, so they say, for the country people to purify themselves by fire and smoke, by sprinkling themselves with spring water, by formal washing of their hands, and by drinking milk mixed with grape-juice. During the day they offered sacrifices, consisting of cakes, milk, and other eatables, to Pales, the god of the shepherds. Three times, with faces turned to the east, a long prayer was repeated to Pales, asking blessings upon the flocks and herds, and pardon for any offences committed against the nymphs of the streams, the dryads of the woods, and the other deities of the Italian Olympus. This over, bonfires of hay and straw were lighted, music was made with cymbal and flute, and shepherds and sheep were purified by passing through the flames. A feast followed, the simple folk lying on benches of turf, and indulging in generous draughts of their homely wines, such, probably, as the visitor to-day may regale himself with in the same region. Towards evening, the flocks were fed, the stables were cleansed and sprinkled with water with laurel brooms, and laurel boughs were hung about them as adornments. Sulphur, incense, rosemary, and fir-wood were burned, and the smoke made to pass through the stalls to purify them, and even the flocks themselves were submitted to the same cleansing fumes.

The beginning of a city in the olden time was a serious matter, and Romulus felt the solemnity of the acts in which he was about to engage. He sent men to Etruria, from which land the religious customs of the Romans largely came, to obtain for him the minute details of the rites suitable for the occasion.

At the proper moment he began the Etrurian ceremonies, by digging a circular pit down to the hard clay, into which were cast with great solemnity some of the first-fruits of the season, and also handfuls of earth, each man throwing in a little from the country from which he had come. The pit was then filled up, and over it an altar was erected, upon the hearth of which a fire was kindled. Thus the centre of the new city was settled and consecrated. Romulus then harnessed a white cow and a snow-white bull to a plow with a brazen share, and holding the handle himself, traced the line of the future walls with a furrow (called the pomœrium *), carrying the plow over the places where gates were to be left, and causing those who followed to see that every furrow as it fell was turned inwards toward the city. As he plowed, Romulus uttered the following prayer:

> *Do thou, Jupiter, aid me as I found this city; and Mavors* [that is, Mars, the god of war and protector of agriculture], *my father, and Vesta, my mother, and all other, ye deities, whom it is a religious duty to invoke, attend; let this work of mine rise under your auspices. Long may be its duration; may its sway be that of an all-ruling land; and under it may be both the rising and the setting of the day.*

It is said that Jupiter sent thunder from one side

---

* *Pomœrium* is composed of *post*, behind, and *murus*, a wall. The word is often used as meaning simply a boundary or limit of jurisdiction. The *pomœrium* of Rome was several times enlarged.

of the heavens and lightnings from the other, and that the people rejoiced in the omens as good and went on cheerfully building the walls. The poet Ovid says that the work of superintending the building was given to one Celer, who was told by Romulus to let no one pass over the furrow of the plow. Remus, ignorant of this, began to scoff at the lowly beginning, and was immediately struck down by Celer with a spade. Romulus bore the death of his brother "like a Roman," with great fortitude, and, swallowing down his rising tears, exclaimed : " So let it happen to all who pass over my walls ! "

Plutarch, who is very fond of tracing the origin of words, says that Celer rushed away from Rome, fearing vengeance, and did not rest until he had reached the limits of Etruria, and that his name became the synonym for quickness, so that men swift of foot were called *Celeres* by the Romans, just as we still speak of " celerity," meaning rapidity of motion. Thus the walls of the new city were laid in blood.

In one respect early Rome was like our own country, for Plutarch says that it was proclaimed an asylum to which any who were oppressed might resort and be safe ; but it was more, for all who had incurred the vengeance of the law were also taken in and protected from punishment. Romulus is said to have erected in a wood a temple to a god called Asylæus, where he " received and protected all, delivering none back—neither the servant to his master, the debtor to his creditor, nor the murderer into the hands of the magistrate ; saying it was a privileged place, and they could so maintain it by an order of the holy oracle ; insomuch that the city grew presently very populous." It was men, of course, who took advantage of this asylum, for who ever heard of women who would rush in great numbers to such a place? Rome was a colony of bachelors, and some of them pretty poor characters too, so that there did not seem to be a very good chance that they could find women willing to become their wives. Romulus, like many an ardent lover since, evidently thought that all was fair in love and war, and, after failing in all his efforts to lead the neighboring peoples to allow the Roman men to marry their women, he gave it out that he had discovered the altar of the god Consus, who presided over secret deliberations,—a very suitable divinity to come up at the juncture,—and that he intended to celebrate his feast.

Consus was honored on the twenty-first of August, and this celebration would come, therefore, just four months after the foundation of the city. There were horse and chariot races, and libations which were poured into the flames that consumed the sacrifices. The people of the country around Rome were invited to take part in the novel festivities, and they were nothing loth to come, for they had considerable curiosity to see what sort of a city had so quickly grown up on the Palatine Hill. They felt no solicitude, though perhaps some might have thought of the haughtiness with which they had refused the offers of matrimony made to their maidens. Still, it was safe, they thought, to attend a fair under the protection of religion, and so they went,—they and their wives and their daughters.

citadel to them if each soldier would give his bracelet to her. This was promised, and as each entered he threw his golden ornament upon the poor maiden, until she fell beneath the weight and died, for they wished to show that they hated treachery though willing to profit by it. Her name was fixed upon the steep rock of the Capitoline Hill from which traitors were in after years thrown.

We now have the Sabines on one hill and the Romans on another, with a swampy plain of small extent between them, where the forum was afterward built. The Romans wished to retake the Capitoline Hill (which was also called the Hill of Saturn), and a battle was fought the next day in the valley. It is said that two men began the fight, Mettus Curtius, representing the Sabines, and Hostus Hostilius, the Romans, and that though the Roman was killed, Curtius was chased into the swamp, where his horse was mired, and all his efforts with whip and spur to get him out proving ineffectual, he left the faithful beast and saved himself with difficulty. The swamp was ever after known as *Lacus Curtius*, and this story might be taken as the true origin of its name (for *lacus* in Latin meant a marsh as well as a lake), if it were not that there are two other accounts of the reason for it. One story is that in the year 362 B.C.—that is, some four centuries after the battle we have just related, the earth in the forum gave way, and all efforts to fill it proving unsuccessful, the oracles were appealed to. They replied that the spot could not be made firm until that on which Rome's greatness was based had been cast into the chasm, but that then the state would prosper. In the midst of the doubting that followed this announcement, the gallant youth, Curtius, came forward, declaring that the city had no greater treasure than a brave citizen in arms, upon which he immediately leaped into the abyss with his horse. Thereupon the earth closed over the sacrifice. This is the story that Livy prefers. The third is simply to the effect that while one Curtius was consul, in the year 445 B.C., the earth at the spot was struck by lightning, and was afterwards ceremoniously enclosed by him at the command of the senate. This is a good example of the sort of myth that the learned call *ætiological*—that is, myths that have grown up to account for certain facts or customs. The story of the carrying off of the Sabine women is one of this kind, for it seems to have originated in a desire to account for certain incidents in the marriage ceremonies of the Romans. We cannot believe either, though it is reasonable to suppose that some event occurred which was the basis of the tradition told in connection with the history of different periods. We shall find that, in the year 390, all the records of Roman history were destroyed by certain barbarians who burned the city, and that therefore we have tradition only upon which to base the history before that date. We may reasonably believe, however, that at some time the marshy ground in the forum gave way, as ground often does, and that there was difficulty in filling up the chasm. A grand opportunity was thus offered for a good story-teller to build up a romance, or to touch up the early history

citadel to them if each soldier would give his bracelet to her. This was promised, and as each entered he threw his golden ornament upon the poor maiden, until she fell beneath the weight and died, for they wished to show that they hated treachery though willing to profit by it. Her name was fixed upon the steep rock of the Capitoline Hill from which traitors were in after years thrown.

We now have the Sabines on one hill and the Romans on another, with a swampy plain of small extent between them, where the forum was afterward built. The Romans wished to retake the Capitoline Hill (which was also called the Hill of Saturn), and a battle was fought the next day in the valley. It is said that two men began the fight, Mettus Curtius, representing the Sabines, and Hostus Hostilius, the Romans, and that though the Roman was killed, Curtius was chased into the swamp, where his horse was mired, and all his efforts with whip and spur to get him out proving ineffectual, he left the faithful beast and saved himself with difficulty. The swamp was ever after known as *Lacus Curtius*, and this story might be taken as the true origin of its name (for *lacus* in Latin meant a marsh as well as a lake), if it were not that there are two other accounts of the reason for it. One story is that in the year 362 B.C.—that is, some four centuries after the battle we have just related, the earth in the forum gave way, and all efforts to fill it proving unsuccessful, the oracles were appealed to. They replied that the spot could not be made firm until that on which Rome's greatness was based had been cast into the chasm, but that then the state would prosper. In the midst of the doubting that followed this announcement, the gallant youth, Curtius, came forward, declaring that the city had no greater treasure than a brave citizen in arms, upon which he immediately leaped into the abyss with his horse. Thereupon the earth closed over the sacrifice. This is the story that Livy prefers. The third is simply to the effect that while one Curtius was consul, in the year 445 B.C., the earth at the spot was struck by lightning, and was afterwards ceremoniously enclosed by him at the command of the senate. This is a good example of the sort of myth that the learned call *ætiological*—that is, myths that have grown up to account for certain facts or customs. The story of the carrying off of the Sabine women is one of this kind, for it seems to have originated in a desire to account for certain incidents in the marriage ceremonies of the Romans. We cannot believe either, though it is reasonable to suppose that some event occurred which was the basis of the tradition told in connection with the history of different periods. We shall find that, in the year 390, all the records of Roman history were destroyed by certain barbarians who burned the city, and that therefore we have tradition only upon which to base the history before that date. We may reasonably believe, however, that at some time the marshy ground in the forum gave way, as ground often does, and that there was difficulty in filling up the chasm. A grand opportunity was thus offered for a good story-teller to build up a romance, or to touch up the early history with an interesting tale of heroism. The temptation to do this would have been very strong to an imaginative writer.

The Sabines gained the first advantage in the present struggle, and it seemed as though fortune was about to desert the Romans, when Romulus commended their cause to Jupiter in a prayer in which he vowed to erect an altar to him as Jupiter Stator—that is, "Stayer," if he would stay the flight of the Romans. The strife was then begun with new vigor, and in the midst of the din and carnage the Sabine women, who had by this time become attached to their husbands, rushed between the fierce men and urged them not to make them widows or fatherless, which was the sad alternative presented to them. "Make us not twice captives!" they exclaimed. Their appeal resulted in peace, and the two peoples agreed to form one nation, the ruler of which should be alternately a Roman and a Sabine, though at first Romulus and Tatius ruled jointly. The women became thus dearer to the whole community, and the feast called Matronalia was established in their honor, when wives received presents from their husbands and girls from their lovers.

Romulus continued to live on the Palatine among the Romans, and Tatius on the Quirinal, where the Sabines also lived. Each people adopted some of the fashions and customs of the other, and they all met for the transaction of business in the Forum Romanum, which was in the valley of the Curtian Lake, between the hills. For a time this arrangement was carried on in peace, and the united nation grew in numbers and power. After five years, however, Tatius was slain by some of the inhabitants of Lavinium, and Romulus was left sole ruler until his death.

Under him the nation grew still more rapidly, and others were made subject to it, all of which good fortune was attributed to his prowess and skill. Romulus became after a while somewhat arrogant. He dressed in scarlet, received his people lying on a couch of state, and surrounded himself with a body of young soldiers called *Celeres*, from the swiftness with which they executed his orders. It was a suspicious fact that all at once, at a time when the people had become dissatisfied with his actions, Romulus disappeared (717 B.C.). Like Evander, he went, no one knew where, though one of his friends presented himself in the forum and assured the people under oath that one day, as he was going along the road, he met Romulus coming toward him, dressed in shining armor, and looking comelier than ever. Proculus, for that was the friend's name, was struck with awe and filled with religious dread, but asked the king why he had left the people to bereavement, endless sorrow, and wicked surmises, for it had been rumored that the senators had made away with him. Romulus replied that it pleased the gods that, after having built a city destined to be the greatest in the world for empire and glory, he should return to heaven, but that Proculus might tell the Romans that they would attain the height of power by exercising temperance and fortitude, in which effort he would sustain them and remain their propitious god Quirinus.

An altar was accordingly erected to the king's honor, and a festival called the Quirinalia was annually celebrated on the seventeenth of February, the day on which he is said to have been received into the number of the gods.

Romulus left the people organized into two great divisions, Patricians and Clients: the former being the *Populus Romanus*, or Roman People, and possessing the only political rights; and the others being entirely dependent upon them. The Patricians were divided into three tribes—the Romans (*Ramnes*), the Etruscans (*Luceres*), and the Sabines (*Tities*, from Tatius). Another body, not yet organized, called Plebeians, or Plebs, was composed of inhabitants of conquered towns and refugees. These, though not slaves, had no political rights. Each tribe was divided into ten Curiæ, and the thirty Curiæ composed the *Comitia Curiata*, which was the sovereign assembly of the Patricians, authorized to choose the king and to decide all cases affecting the lives of the citizens. A number of men of mature age, known as the *Patres*, composed the Senate, which Romulus formed to assist him in the government. This body consisted of one hundred members until the union with the Sabines, when it was doubled, the Etruscans not being represented until a later time. The army was called a Legion, and was composed of a contribution of a thousand foot-soldiers and a hundred cavalry (*Equites*, Knights) from each tribe.

A year passed after the death of Romulus before another king was chosen, and the people complained that they had a hundred sovereigns instead of one, because the senate governed, and that not always with justness. It was finally agreed that the Romans should choose a king, but that he should be a Sabine. The choice fell upon Numa Pompilius, a man learned in all laws, human and divine, and two ambassadors were accordingly sent to him at his home at Cures, to offer the kingdom to him. The ambassadors were politely received by the good man, but he assured them that he did not wish to change his condition; that every alteration in life is dangerous to a man; that madness only could induce one who needed nothing to quit the life to which he was accustomed; that he, a man of peace, was not fitted to direct a people whose progress had been gained by war; and that he feared that he might prove a laughing-stock to the people if he were to go about teaching them the worship of the gods and the offices of peace when they wanted a king to lead them to war. The more he declined, the more the people wished him to accept, and at last his father argued with him that a martial people needed one who should teach them moderation and religion; that he ought to recognize the fact that the gods were calling him to a large sphere of usefulness. These arguments proved sufficient, and Numa accepted the crown. After making the appropriate offerings to the gods, he set out for Rome, and was met by the populace coming forth to receive him with joyful acclamations. Sacrifices were offered in the temples, and with impressive ceremonies the new authority was joyfully entrusted to him (715 B.C.).

As Romulus had given the Romans their warlike

customs, so now Numa gave them the ceremonial laws of religion ; but before entering upon this work, he divided among the people the public lands that Romulus had added to the property of the city by his conquests, by this movement showing that he was possessed of worldly as well as of heavenly wisdom. He next instituted the worship of the god Terminus, who seems to have been simply Jupiter in the capacity of guardian of boundaries. Numa ordered all persons to mark the limits of their lands by consecrated stones, and at these, when they celebrated the feast of Terminalia, sacrifices were to be offered of cakes, meal, and fruits. Moses had done something like this hundreds of years before, in the land of Palestine, when he wrote in his laws: " Thou shalt not remove thy neighbor's landmark, which they of old time have set, in thine inheritance which thou shalt inherit, in the land that the Lord thy God giveth thee." He had impressed it upon the people, repeating in a solemn religious service the words: " Cursed be he that removeth his neighbor's landmark," to which all the people in those primitive times solemnly said " Amen ! " You will find the same sentiment repeated in the Proverbs of Solomon. When Romulus had laid out the pomœrium, he made the outline something like a square, and called it *Roma Quadrata*, that is " Square Rome," but he did not direct the landmarks of the public domain to be distinctly indicated. The consecration of the boundaries undoubtedly made the people consider themselves more secure in their possessions, and consequently made the state itself more stable.

GUILDS ESTABLISHED. 31

In order to make the people feel more like one body and think less of the fact that they comprised persons belonging to different nations, Numa instituted nine guilds among which the workmen were distributed. These were the pipers, carpenters, goldsmiths, tanners, leather-workers, dyers, potters,

A ROMAN ALTAR

smiths, and one in which all other handicraftsmen were united. Thus these men spoke of each other as members of this or that guild, instead of as Etruscans, Romans, and Sabines.

Human sacrifices were declared abolished at this

time; the rites of prayer were established; the temple of Janus was founded (which was closed in time of peace and open in time of war); priests were ordained to conduct the public worship, the Pontifex Maximus* being at the head of them, and the Flamens, Vestal Virgins, and Salii, being subordinate. Numa pretended that he met by night a nymph named Egeria, at a grotto under the Cœlian Hill, not far from the present site of the Baths of Caracalla, and that from time to time she gave him directions as to what rites would be acceptable to the gods. Another nymph, whom Numa commended to the special veneration of the Romans, was named Tacita, or the silent. This was appropriate for one of such quiet and unobtrusive manners as this good king possessed.

Romulus is said to have made the year consist of but ten months, the first being March, named from Mars, the god whom he delighted to honor; but Numa saw that his division was faulty, and so he added two months, making the first one January, from Janus, the god who loved civil and social unity, whose temple he had built; and the second February, or the month of purification, from the Latin word *februa*. If he had put in his extra months at

---

* Pontifex means bridge-builder (*pons*, a bridge, *facere*, to make), and the title is said to have been given to these magistrates because they built the wooden bridge over the Tiber, and kept it in repair, so that sacrifices might be made on both sides of the river. The building of this bridge is, however, ascribed to Ancus Martius at a later date, and so some think the name was originally *pompifex* (*pompa*, a solemn procession), and meant that the officers had charge of such celebrations.

some other part of the year, he might have allowed it still to begin in the spring, as it naturally does, and we should not be obliged to explain to every generation why the ninth, tenth, eleventh, and twelfth months are still called the seventh, eighth, ninth, and tenth.*

> The poets said in the peaceful days of Numa,
> Rust eats the pointed spear and double-edged sword.
> No more is heard the trumpet's brazen roar,
> Sweet sleep is banished from our eyes no more,

and that over the iron shields the spiders hung their threads, for it was a sort of golden age, when there was neither plot, nor envy, nor sedition in the state, for the love of virtue and the serenity of spirit of the king flowed down upon all the happy subjects. In due time, after a long reign and a peaceful and useful life, Numa died, not by disease or war, but by the natural decline of his faculties. The people mourned for him heartily and honored him with a costly burial.

After the death of this king an interregnum followed, during which the senate ruled again, but it was not long before the Sabines chose as king a Roman, Tullus Hostilius, grandson of that Hostus Hostilius who had won distinction in the war with the Sabines. The new sovereign thought that the nation was losing its noble prestige through the quietness with which it lived among its neighbors, and therefore he embraced every opportunity to stir

---

* We shall find that in the course of time this arrangement of the year proved very faulty in its turn, and that Julius Cæsar made another effort to reform it. (See page 247.)

up war with the surrounding peoples, and success followed his campaigns. The peasants between Rome and Alba* afforded him the first pretext, by plundering each other's lands. The Albans were ready to settle the difficulty in a peaceful manner, but Tullus, determined upon aggrandizement, refused all overtures. It was much like a civil war, for both nations were of Trojan origin, according to the traditions. The Albans pitched their tents within five miles of Rome, and built a trench about the city. The armies were drawn up ready for battle, when the Alban leader came out and made a speech, in which he said that as both Romans and Sabines were surrounded by strange nations who would like to see them weakened, as they would undoubtedly be by the war, he proposed that the question which should rule the other, ought to be decided in some less destructive way.

It happened that there were in the army of the Romans three brothers known as the Horatii, of the same age as three others in the Alban army called the Curiatii, and it was agreed that these six should fight in the place of the two armies. At the first clash of arms two of the Romans fell lifeless, though every one of the Curiatii was wounded. This caused the Sabines to exult, especially as they saw the remaining Roman apparently running away. The flight of Horatius was, however, merely feigned, in order to separate the opposing brothers, whom he met as they followed him, and killed in

*Alba became the chief of a league of thirty Latin cities, lying in the southern part of the great basin through which the Tiber finds its way to the sea, between Etruria and Campania.

MONUMENT OF THE HORATII AND THE CURIATII.

succession. As he struck his sword into the last of the Albans, he exclaimed: "Two have I offered to the shades of my brothers; the third will I offer to the cause of this war, that the Roman may rule over the Alban!" A triumph * followed; but it appears that a sister of Horatius, named Horatia, † was to have married one of the Curiatii, and when she met her victorious brother bearing as his plunder the military robe of her lover that she had wrought with her own hands, she tore her hair and uttered bitter exclamations. Horatius in his anger and impatience thrust her through with his sword, saying: "So perish every Roman woman who shall mourn an enemy?" For this act, the victorious young man was condemned to death, but he appealed to the people, and they mitigated his sentence in consequence of his services to the state.

Another war followed, with the Etruscans this time, and the Albans not behaving like true allies, their city was demolished and its inhabitants removed to Rome, where they were assigned to the Cœlian Hill. Some of the more noble among them were enrolled among the Patricians, and the others were added to the Plebs, who then became for the first time an organic part of the social body, though not

* A "triumph" was a solemn rejoicing after a victory, and included a *pompa*, or procession of the general and soldiers on foot with their plunder. Triumphs seem to have been celebrated in some style in the earliest days of Rome. In later times they increased very much in splendor and costliness.

† The Romans seem in one respect to have had little ingenuity in the matter of names, though generally they had too many of them, and formed that of a woman from the name of a man by simply changing the end of it from the masculine form to the feminine.

belonging to the Populus Romanus (or Roman People), so called. On another occasion Tullus made war upon the Sabines and conquered them, but finally he offended the gods, and in spite of the fact that he bethought himself of the good Numa and began to follow his example, Jupiter smote him with a thunder-bolt and destroyed him and his house.

Again an interregnum followed, and again a king was chosen, this time Ancus Marcius, a Sabine, grandson of the good Numa, a man who strove to emulate the virtues of his ancestor. It is to be noticed that the four kings of Rome thus far are of two classes, the warlike and peaceful alternating in the legends. The neighbors expected that Ancus would not be a forceful king, and some of them determined to take advantage of his supposed weakness. He set himself to repair the neglected religion, putting up tables in the forum on which were written the ceremonial law, so that all might know its demands, and seeking to lead the people to worship the gods in the right spirit. Ancus seems to have united with his religious character, however, a proper regard for the rights of the nation, and when the Latins who lived on the river Anio, made incursions into his domain, thinking that he would not notice it, in the ardor of his services at the temples and altars, he entered upon a vigorous and successful campaign, conquering several cities and removing their inhabitants, giving them homes on the Aventine Hill, thus increasing the lands that could be divided among the Romans and adding to the number of the Plebeians. Ancus founded a colony at Ostia at the mouth of the Tiber, and built a fortress on the Janiculum Hill, across the river, connecting it with the other regions by means of the first Roman bridge, called the *Pons Sublicius*, or in simple English, the wooden bridge. This is the one that the Romans wanted to cut down at a later period, as we shall see, and had great difficulty in destroying. Another relic of Ancus is seen in a chamber of the damp Mamertine prison under the Capitoline Hill, the first prison in the city, rendered necessary by the increase of crime. After a reign of twenty-four years, Ancus Martius died, and a new dynasty, of Etruscan origin, began to control the fortunes of the now rapidly growing nation.

III.

HOW CORINTH GAVE ROME A NEW DYNASTY.

THE city of Corinth, in Greece, was one of the most wealthy and enterprising on the Mediterranean in its day, and at about the time that Rome is said to have been founded, it entered upon a new period of commercial activity and foreign colonization. So many Greeks went to live on the islands around Italy, and on the shores of Italy itself, indeed, that that region was known as *Magna Græcia*, or Great Greece, just as in our day we speak of Great Britain, when we wish to include not England only, but also the whole circle of lands under British rule. At this time of commercial activity there came into power in Corinth a family noted for its wealth and force no less than for the luxury in which it lived, and the oppression, too, with which it ruled the people. One of the daughters of the sovereign married out of the family, because she was so ill-favored that no one in her circle was willing to have her as wife.

In due time the princess became the mother of a boy, of whom the oracle at Delphi prophesied that he should be a formidable opponent of the ruling dynasty. Whenever the oracle made such a prophecy about a child, it was customary for the ruler to try to make away with it, and that the ruler of Corinth did in this case. All efforts were unsuccessful, however, because his homely mother hid him in a chest when the spies came to the house. Now the Greek word for chest is *kupsele*, and therefore this boy was called Cypselus. He grew up to be a fine young man, and entered political life as champion of the people—the *demos*, as the Greeks would say, and was therefore a *democratic* politician.*

He opposed the aristocratic rulers, and at last succeeded in overturning their government and getting into the position of supreme ruler himself. He ruled thirty years in peace, and was so much loved by the Corinthians that he went about among them in safety without any body-guard.

When Cypselus came into power the citizens of Corinth who belonged to the aristocratic family were obliged to go elsewhere, somewhat as those princes called *émigrés* (emigrants) left France during the Revolution, in 1789. One of them, whose name was Demaratus, a wealthy and intelligent merchant, concluded to go westward, to Magna Græcia, into the part of the world from which his ships had brought him his revenues. Accordingly, accompanied by his family, a great retinue, and some artists and sculptors, he sailed away for Italy and settled at the Etruscan town of Tarquinii. He did not go more than five or six hundred miles from home, but his enterprise was

---

* A politician is a person versed in the science of government, from the Greek words *polis*, a city, *polites*, a citizen. Though a very honorable title, it has been debased in familiar usage until it has come to mean in turn a partisan, a dabbler in public affairs, and even an artful trickster.

as marked as that of our fathers was considered when, in the last generation, they removed from New York to Chicago, though the distance was not nearly so great. No wonder Demaratus thought that it would be a comfort to have with him some of the artists and sculptors whose genius had made his Corinthian home beautiful.

As he had come to Tarquinii to spend all his days, Demaratus married a lady of the place, and she became the mother of a son, Lucomo. When this young man grew up, he found that, though a native of the city, he was looked upon as a foreigner on his father's account, and that, though he belonged to a family of the highest rank and wealth through his mother's connections, he was excluded from political power and influence. He had inherited the love of authority that had possessed his father's ancestors, and as his father had migrated from home to gain peace, he felt no reluctance in leaving Tarquinii in the hope of gaining the power he thought his wealth and pedigree entitled him to. There was no more attractive field for his ambition than Rome presented, and Lucomo probably knew that that city had been from its very foundation an asylum for strangers. Thither, therefore, he decided to take himself.

We can imagine the removal, as the long procession of chariots and footmen slowly passed over the fifty miles that separated Tarquinii from Rome. Just above Civita Vecchia you may see on your modern map of Italy a town called Corneto, and a mile from that, perhaps, another named Turchina, which is all that remains of the old town in which Lucomo lived. Even now relics of the Tarquinians are found there, and there are many in the museums of Europe that illustrate the ancient civilization of the Etruscans, which was greater at this time than that of the Romans. On his journey Lucomo was himself seated in a chariot with his wife Tanaquil, whom he seems to have honored very highly, and the long train of followers stretched behind them. It represented all that great wealth directed by considerable cultivation could purchase, and must have formed an imposing sight. Rome was approached from the south side of the Tiber, by the way of the Janiculum Hill and over the wooden bridge.

When the emigrants reached the Janiculum, and saw the hills and the modest temples of Rome before them, an eagle, symbol of royalty, flew down, and gently stooping, took off Lucomo's cap. Then, after having flown around the chariot with loud screams, it replaced it, and was soon lost again in the blue heavens. It was as though it had been sent by the gods to encourage the strangers to expect good fortune in their new home. Tanaquil, who was well versed in the augury of her countrymen, embraced her husband; told him from what divinity the eagle had come, and from what auspicious quarter of the heavens; and said that it had performed its message about the highest part of the body, which was in itself prophetic of good.

Considerable impression must have been made upon the subjects of Ancus Martius as the distinguished stranger and his long suite entered the city over the bridge, and when Lucomo bought a fine house, and showed himself affable and courteous, he was received with a cordial welcome, and soon admitted to the rights of a Roman citizen. Seldom had the town received so acceptable an addition to its population. Lucomo soon changed his name to Lucius Tarquinius, and to this, in after years, when there were two of the same family name, the word Priscus, or Elder, was added. Tarquinius, as we may now call him, flattered the Romans by invitations to his hospitable mansion, where his entertainments added greatly to his popularity, and in time Ancus himself heard of his acts of kindness, and added his name to the list of the new citizen's intimate friends. Tarquinius was admitted by the king to private as well as public deliberations about matters of foreign and domestic importance, and doubtless his knowledge of other countries stood him in good stead on these occasions.

The stranger had taken the king and people by storm, and when Ancus died, he left his sons to the guardianship of Tarquinius, and the Populus Romanus chose him to be their king. Thus Rome came to have at the head of its affairs a man not a Roman nor a Sabine, but a citizen of Greek extraction, who was familiar with a much higher state of civilization than was known on the banks of the Tiber. The result is seen in the great strides in advance that the city took during his reign. The architectural grandeur of Rome dates its beginning from this time. Tarquinius laid out vast drains to draw away the water that stood in the Lacus Curtius, between the Capitoline and the Palatine hills, and these remain to this day, as any one who has visited Rome remembers—the mouth of the Cloaca Maxima (the great sewer) being one of the remarkable sights there. The king also drained other parts of the city; vowed to build, and perhaps began, the temple on the Capitoline; built a wall about the city, and erected the permanent buildings on the great forum. These works involved vast labor and expense, and must have been very burdensome to the people. Like other oppressive monarchs, Tarquinius planned games and festivities to amuse them. He enlarged the Circus Maximus, and imported boxers and horses from his native country to perform at games there, which were afterwards celebrated annually. Besides these victories of peace, this king conquered the people about him, and greatly added to the number of his subjects. He for the first time instituted the formal "triumph," as it was afterwards celebrated, riding into the city after a victory in a chariot drawn by four white horses, and wearing a robe bespangled with gold. He brought in also the augural science of his country, which had been only partially known before.

While Tarquinius was thus adding to the greatness of Rome, there appeared in the palace one of those marvels that the early historians delighted to relate, such as, indeed, mankind in all ages has been pleased with. A boy was asleep in the portico when a flame was seen encircling his little head, and the attendants were about to throw water upon it, when

MOUTH OF CLOACA MAXIMA, AT THE TIBER, AND THE SO-CALLED TEMPLE OF VESTA.

the queen interfered, forbidding the boy to be disturbed. She then brought the matter to the notice of her husband, saying: "Do you see this boy whom we are so meanly bringing up? He is destined to be a light in our adversity, and a help in our distress. Let us care for him, for he will become a great ornament to us and to the state." Tarquinius knew well the importance of his wife's advice, and educated the boy, whose name was Servius Tullius, in a way befitting a royal prince. In the course of time he married the king's daughter, and found himself in favor with the people as well as with his royal father-in-law.

For all the forty years of the prosperous reign of Tarquinius, the traditions would have us believe, the two sons of Ancus had been nursing their wrath and inwardly boiling over with indignation because they had been deprived of the kingship, and now, as they saw the popularity of young Servius, they determined to wrench the crown from him after destroying the king. They therefore sent two shepherds into his presence, who pretended to wish advice about a matter in dispute. While one engaged Tarquin's attention, the other struck him a fatal blow with his axe. The queen was, however, quick-witted enough to keep them from enjoying the fruit of their perfidy, for she assured the people from a window that the king was not killed but only stunned, and that for the present he desired them to obey the directions of Servius Tullius. She then called upon the young man to let the celestial flame with which the gods had surrounded his head in his youth arouse him to action. "The kingdom is yours!" she exclaimed; "if you have no plans of your own, then follow mine!" For several days the king's death was concealed, and Servius took his place on the throne, deciding some cases, and in regard to others pretending that he would consult Tarquinius (B.C. 578). Thus he made the senate and the people accustomed to seeing him at the head of affairs, and when the actual fact was allowed to transpire, Servius took possession of the kingdom with the consent of the senate, but without that of the people, which he did not ask. This was the first king who ascended the throne without the suffrages of the Populus Romanus. The sons of Ancus went into banishment, and the royal power, which had passed from the Romans to the Etruscans, now fell into the hands of a man of unknown citizenship, though he has been described as a native of Corniculum, one of the mountain towns to the northeast of Rome, which is never heard of excepting in connection with this reign.

IV.

THE RISE OF THE COMMONS.

WHATEVER may have been the origin of the new king, he was evidently not of the ruling class, the Populus Romanus, and for this reason his sympathies were naturally with the Plebeians, or, as they would now be called, the Commons. The long reign of Servius was marked by the victories of peace, though he was involved in wars with the surrounding nations, in which he was successful. These conquests seemed to fix the king more firmly upon the throne, but they did not render him much less desirous of obtaining the good-will of his subjects, and they never seemed to tempt him to exercise his power in a tyrannical manner. He thought that by marrying his two daughters to two sons of Tarquin, he might make his position on the throne more secure, and he accomplished this intention, but it failed to benefit him as he had expected.

Besides adding largely to the national territory, Servius brought the thirty cities of Latium into a great league with Rome, and built a temple on the Aventine consecrated to Diana (then in high renown at Ephesus), at which the Romans, Latins, and Sabines should worship together in token of their

THE SEVEN HILLS. 49

unity as one civil brotherhood, though it was understood that the Romans were chief in rank. On a brazen pillar in this edifice the terms of the treaty on which the league was based were written, and there they remained for centuries. The additions to Roman territory gave Servius an opportunity of strengthening his hold upon the commons, for he took advantage of it to cause a census to be taken under the direction of two Censors, on the basis of which he made new divisions of the people, and new laws by which the plebeians came into greater prominence than they had enjoyed before. The census showed that the city and suburbs contained eighty-three thousand inhabitants.

The increase of population led to the extension of the pomœrium, and Servius completed the city by including within a wall of stone all of the celebrated seven hills *—the Palatine, Aventine, Capitoline, Cœlian, Quirinal, Viminal, and Esquilian, — for, though new suburbs grew up beyond this wall, the legal limits of the city were not changed until the times of the empire.

The inhabitants within the walls were divided into four "regions," or districts—the Palatine, the Colline, the Esquiline, and the Suburran. The subjected districts outside, which were inhabited by plebeians, were divided into twenty-six other regions, thus forming thirty tribes containing both plebeians

---

* The "seven hills" were not always the same. In earlier times they had been : Palatinus, Cermalus, Velia, Fagutal, Oppius, Cispius, and Cœlius. Oppius and Cispius, were names of summits of the Esquiline ; Velia was a spur of the Palatine ; Cermalus and Fagutal, according to Niebuhr, were not hills at all.

and patricians. The census gave Servius a list of all the citizens and their property, and upon the basis of this information he separated the entire population into six classes, comprising one hundred and ninety-three subdivisions or " centuries," thus introducing a new principle, and placing wealth at the bottom of social distinctions, instead of birth. This naturally pleased the plebeians, but was not approved by the citizens of high pedigree, who thus lost some of their prestige. The newly formed centuries together constituted the *Comitia Centuriata* (gathering of the centuries), or National Assembly, which met for business on the Campus Martius, somewhat after the manner of a New England "Town Meeting." In these conclaves they elected certain magistrates, gave sanction to legislative acts, and decided upon war or peace. This Comitia formed the highest court of appeal known to Roman law.

Besides this general assembly of the entire Populus Romanus, Servius established a *Comitia* in each tribe, authorized to exercise jurisdiction in local affairs.

The first of the six general classes thus established comprised the Horsemen, *Equites*, Knights, or Cavalry, consisting of six patrician centuries of Equites established by Romulus, and twelve new ones formed from the principal plebeian families. Next in rank to them were eighty centuries composed of persons owning property (not deducting debts) to the amount of one hundred thousand ases (*æs*, copper, brass, bronze), and two centuries of persons not possessed of wealth, but simply *Fabrûm*, or workmen who manufactured things out of hard material, so important to the state were such considered at the time. One would not think it very difficult to get admission to this high class, when it is remembered that an *as* (originally a pound of copper in weight)* was worth but about a cent and a half, and that a hundred thousand such coins would amount to only about fifteen hundred dollars; though, of course, we should have to make allowance for the price of commodities if we wished to arrive at the exact value in the money of our time. The second, third, and fourth centuries were arranged on a descending grade of property qualification, and the fifth comprised those persons whose property was not worth less than twelve thousand five hundred ases, or about two hundred dollars. The sixth class included all whose possessions did not amount to even so little as this. These were called *Proletarii* or *Capite Censorum ; caput*, the Latin for head, being used in reference to these unimportant citizens for "person," as farmers use it nowadays when they enumerate animals as so many "head."

Though the new arrangement of Servius Tullius gave the plebeians power, it did not give them so much as might be supposed, because it was contrived that the richest class should have the greatest number of votes, and they with the Equites had so many that they were able to carry any measure upon which they agreed. The older men, too, had an advantage,

* The English word *ace* gets its meaning, "one," from the fact that in Latin *as* signified the unit either of weight or measure. Two and a half ases were equal to a sestertius, and ten ases (or four sesterces) equalled one denarius, worth about sixteen cents.

for every class was divided into Seniors and Juniors, each of which had an equal number of votes, though it is apparent that the seniors must have been always in the minority. Servius did not dare to abolish the old Comitia Curiata, and he felt obliged to enact that the votes of the new Comitia should be valid only after having received the sanction of the more ancient body. Thus it will be seen that there were three assemblies, with sovereignty well defined.

The armor of the different classes was also accurately ordered by the law. The first class was authorized to wear, for the defence of the body, brazen helmets, shields, and coats of mail, and to bear spears and swords, excepting the mechanics, who were to carry the necessary military engines and to serve without arms. The members of the second class, excepting that they had bucklers instead of shields and wore no coats of mail, were permitted to bear the same armor, and to carry the sword and spear. The third class had the same armor as the second, excepting that they could not wear greaves for the protection of their legs. The fourth had no arms excepting a spear and a long javelin. The fifth merely carried slings and stones for use in them. To this class belonged the trumpeters and horn-blowers.

These reforms were very important, and very reasonable, too, but though they gained for the king many friends, it was rather among the plebeians than among the more wealthy patricians, and from time to time hints were thrown out that the consent of the people had not been asked when Servius took

ROMAN SOLDIERS, COSTUMES, AND ARMOR

his seat upon the throne, and that without it his right to the power he wielded was not complete. There was a very solemn and striking ceremony on the Campus Martius after the census had been finished. It was called the Lustration or *Suovetaurilia*. The first name originated from the fact that the ceremony was a purification of the people by water, and the second because the sacrifice on the occasion consisted of a pig, a sheep, and an ox, the Latin names of which were *sus*, *ovis*, and *taurus*, these being run together in a single manufactured word. Words are not easily made to order, and this one shows how awkward they are when they do not grow naturally.

On the completion of the census (B.C. 566) Servius ordered the members of all the Centuries to assemble on the Campus Martius, which was enclosed in a bend of the Tiber outside of the walls that he built. They came in full armor, according to rank, and the sight must have been very grand and impressive. Three days were occupied in the celebration. Three times were the pig, the sheep, and the bull carried around the great multitude, and then, amid the flaunting of banners, the burning of incense, and the sounding of trumpets, the libation was poured forth, and the inoffensive beasts were sacrificed for the purification of the people. Once every five years the inhabitants were thus counted, and once in five years were they also purified, and in this way it came to pass that that period was known as a *lustrum*.

Uneasy lies the head that wears a crown, says the proverb, and it was true in the case of Servius, for he could never forget that the people had not voted in his favor. For this reason he divided among them the lands that he had taken from the enemies he had defeated, and then, supposing that he had obtained their good-will, he called upon them to vote whether they chose and ordered that he should be king. When the votes came to be counted, Servius found that he had been chosen with a unanimity that had not been manifested before in the selection of a sovereign. Whatever confidence he may have derived from this vote, his place was not secure, and his fatal enemy proved to be in his own household.

It happened that of the two husbands of the daughters of Servius, one was ambitious and unprincipled, and the other quiet and peaceable. The same was true of their wives, only the unprincipled wife found herself mated with the well-behaving husband. Now the wicked wife agreed with the wicked husband that they should murder their partners and then marry together, thus making a pair, both members of which should be ambitious and without principle. This was accomplished, and then the wicked wife, whose name was Tullia, told her husband, whose name was Lucius Tarquinius, that what she wanted was not a husband whom she might live with in quiet like a slave, but one who would remember of whose blood he was, who would consider that he was the rightful king; and that if *he* would not do it he had better go back to Tarquinii or Corinth and sink into his original race, thus shaming his father and Tanaquil, who had bestowed thrones upon her husband and her son-in-law. The taunts and instigations of Tullia led Lucius to solicit the younger patricians to support him in making an effort for the throne. When he thought he had obtained a sufficient number of confederates, he one day rushed into the forum at an appointed time, accompanied by a body of armed men, and, in the midst of a commotion that ensued, took his seat upon the throne and ordered the senate to attend " King Tarquinius." That august body convened very soon, some having been prepared beforehand for the summons, and then Tarquinius began a tirade against Servius, whom he stigmatized as " a slave and the son of a slave," who had favored the most degraded classes, and had, by instituting the census, made the fortunes of the better classes unnecessarily conspicuous, so as to excite the envy and base passions of the meaner citizens.

Servius came to the senate-house in the midst of the harangue, and called to Lucius to know by what audacity he had taken the royal seat, and summoned the senate during the life of the sovereign. Lucius replied in an insulting manner, and, taking advantage of the king's age, seized him by the middle, carried him out, and threw him down the steps to the bottom! Almost lifeless, Servius was slain by emissaries of Lucius as he was making his way to his home on the Esquiline Hill (B.C. 534) The royal retinue, in their fright, left the body where it fell, and there it was when Tullia, returning from having congratulated her husband, reached the place. Her driver, terrified at the sight, stopped, and would have avoided the king's corpse, though the narrowness of the street made it difficult; but the insane daughter ordered him to drive on, and stained and sprinkled herself with her father's blood, which seemed to cry out for vengeance upon such a cruel act! The vengeance came speedily, as we shall see.

V.

HOW A PROUD KING FELL.

THE new king was a tyrant. He was elected by no general consent of the people he governed; he allowed himself to be bound by no laws; he recognized no limit to his authority; and he surrounded himself with a body-guard for protection from the attacks of any who might wish to take the crown from him in the way that he had snatched it from his predecessor. As soon as possible after coming to the throne, he swept away all privilege and right that had been conceded to the commons, commanded that there should no longer be any of those assemblages on the occasions of festivals and sacrifices that had before tended to unite the people and to break the monotony of their lives; he put the poor at task-work, and mistrusted, banished, or murdered the rich. To strengthen the position of Rome as chief of the confederates cities, and his own position as the ruler of Rome, he gave his daughter to Octavius Mamilius of Tusculum to wife; and to beautify the capital he warred against other peoples, and with their spoil pushed forward the work on the great temple on the Capitoline Hill,* a wonderful and massy structure.

It is said that Amalthea, the mysterious sibyl of Cumæ, one day came to Tarquin with nine sealed prophetical books (which, she said, contained the destiny of the Romans and the mode to bring it about), that she offered to sell. The king refused, naturally unwilling to pay for things that he could not examine ; and thereupon the unreasonable being went away and destroyed three of the volumes that she had described as of inestimable value. Soon after she returned and offered the remaining six for the price that she had demanded for the nine. Once more, the tyrant declined the offer, and again the aged sibyl destroyed three, and demanded the original price for the remainder. The king's curiosity was now aroused, and he bought the three books, upon which the prophetess vanished. The volumes were placed under the new temple on the Capitoline, no one doubting that they actually contained precepts of the utmost importance. The wise-looking augurs came together, peered into the rolls, and told the king and the people that they were right, and age after age the books were appealed to for direction, though, as the people never were permitted even to peep into the sacred cell in which they were hidden, they never could be quite certain that the augurs who consulted them found any thing in them that they did not put there themselves.

* This hill is said to have received its name from the fact that as the men were preparing for the foundation of the temple, they came upon a human head, fresh and bleeding, from which it was augured that the spot was to become the head of the world. (*Caput*, a head.)

While Tarquinius was going on with his great works, while he was oppressing his own people and conquering his neighbors uninterruptedly, he was suddenly startled by a dire portent. A serpent crawled out from beneath the altar in his palace and coolly ate the flesh of the royal sacrifice. The meaning of this appalling omen could not be allowed to remain uncertain, and as no one in Italy was able to explain it, Tarquin sent to the oracle of Apollo at Delphi, to ask the signification. Delphi is a place situated in the midst of the most sublime scenery of Greece, just north of the Gulf of Corinth. Shut in on all sides by stupendous cliffs, among which flow the inspiring waters of the Castalian Spring, thousands of feet above which frowns the summit of Parnassus, on which Deucalion is said to have landed after the deluge, this romantic valley makes a deep impression on the mind of the visitor, and it is not strange that at an age when signs and wonders were looked for in every direction, it should have become the home of a sibyl.

The king's messengers to Delphi were his two sons and a nephew named Lucius Junius Brutus, a young man who had saved his life by taking advantage of the fact that a madman was esteemed sacred by the Romans, and assuming an appearance of stupidity * at a time when his tyrannical uncle had put his brother to death that he might appropriate his wealth. Upon hearing the question of the king, the oracle said that the portent foretold the fall of Tarquin. The sons then asked who should take his

* *Brutus* in Latin means irrational, dull, stupid, brutish, which senses our word " brute " preserves.

THE RAVINE OF DELPHI.

throne, and the reply was: "He who shall first kiss his mother." Brutus had propitiated the oracle by the present of a hollow stick filled with gold, and learned the symbolical meaning of this reply. The sons decided to allow their remaining brother Sextus to know the answer, and to determine by lot which of them should rule; but Brutus kept his own counsel, and on reaching home, fell upon mother earth, as by accident, and kissed the ground, thus observing the terms of the oracle.

The prophecy now hastened to its fulfilment. As the army lay before the town of Ardea, belonging to the Rutulians, south of Rome, a dispute arose among the sons of the king and their cousin Collatinus, as to which had the most virtuous wife. There being nothing to keep them in camp, the young men arose from their cups and rode to Rome, where they found the princesses at a banquet revelling amid flowers and wine. Lucretia, the wife of Collatinus, was found at Collatia among her maidens spinning, like the industrious wife described in the Proverbs. The evil passions of Sextus were aroused by the beauty of his cousin's wife, and he soon found an excuse to return to the home of Collatinus. He was hospitably entertained by Lucretia, who did not suspect the demon that he was, and one night he entered her apartment and with vile threats overcame her. In her terrible distress, Lucretia sent immediately for her father, Lucretius, and her husband, Collatinus. They came, each bringing a friend, Brutus being the companion of the outraged husband. To them, with bitter tears, Lucretia, clad in the garments of mourning and almost beside herself with sorrow, told the story of crime, and, saying that she could not survive dishonor, plunged a knife into her bosom and fell in the agony of shame and death!

At this juncture Brutus threw off the assumed stupidity that had veiled the strength of his spirit, and taking up the reeking knife, exclaimed: "By this blood most pure, I swear, and I call you, O gods, to witness my oath, that I shall pursue Lucius Tarquin the Proud, his wicked wife, and all the race, with fire and sword, nor shall I permit them or any other to reign in Rome!" So saying, the knife was handed to each of the others in turn, and they all took the same oath to revenge the innocent blood. The body of Lucretia was laid in the forum of Collatia, her home, and the populace, maddened by the sight, were easily persuaded to rise against the tyrant. A multitude was collected, and the march began to Rome, where a like excitement was stirred up; a gathering at the forum was addressed by Brutus, who recalled to memory not only the story of Lucretia's wrongs, but also the horrid murder of Servius, and the blood-thirstiness of Tullia. On the Campus Martius the citizens met and decreed that the dignity of king should be forever abolished and the Tarquins banished. Tullia fled, followed by the curses of men and women; Sextus found his way to Gabii, where he was slain; and the tyrant himself took refuge in Cære, a city of Etruria, the country of his father.

There is a tradition that it had been the intention of Servius to resign the kingly honor, and to institute in its stead the office of Consul, to be jointly held by two persons chosen annually. There seems to be some ground for this belief, because immediately after the banishment of the Tarquins, the republic was established with two consuls at its head.* The first to hold the highest office were Lucius Junius Brutus and Lucius Tarquinius Collatinus, husband of Lucretia.

Some time after Tarquin had fled to Cære, he found an asylum at Tarquinii, and from that city made an effort to stir up a conspiracy in his favor at Rome. He sent messengers ostensibly to plead for the restoration of his property, but really for the purpose of exciting treason. There were at Rome vicious persons who regretted that they were obliged to return to regular ways, and there were patricians who disliked to see the plebeians again enjoying their rights. Some of these were ready to take up the cause of the deposed tyrant. The conspirators met for consultation in one of the dark chambers of a Roman house, and their conference was overheard. They were brought before the consuls in the Comitium, and, to the dismay of Brutus, two of his own sons were found among the number. With the unswerving virtue of a Roman or a Spartan, he condemned them to death, and they were executed be-

---

* The custom of confiding the chief civil authority and the command of the army to two magistrates who were changed each year, was not given up as long as the republic endured, but towards its end, Cinna maintained himself in the office alone for almost a year, and Pompey was appointed sole consul to keep him from becoming dictator. The authority of consul was usurped by both Cinna and Marius. The consuls were elected by the comitia of the centuries. They could not appear in public without the protection of twelve lictors, who bore bundles of twigs (fasces) and walked in single file before their chiefs.

fore his eyes. The discovery of the plot of Tarquin put an end to his efforts to regain any foothold at Rome by peaceable methods, and he made the appeal to arms. These plots led to the banishment of the whole Tarquinian house, even the consul whose troubles had brought the result about being obliged to lay down his office and leave the city. Publius Valerius was appointed in his stead. For a time he was in office alone, and several times he was re-chosen. He was afterwards known as Poplicola, "the people's friend," on account of certain laws that he passed, limiting the power of the aristocrats and alleviating the condition of the plebeians.*

In pursuance of his new plans, Tarquin obtained the help of the people of Veii and Tarquinii and marched against Rome. He was met by an army under Brutus, and a bloody battle was fought near Arsia. Brutus was killed and the Etruscans were about to claim the victory, when, in the night, the voice of the god Silvanus was heard saying that the killed among the Etruscans outnumbered by one man those of the Romans. Upon this the Etruscans fled, knowing that ultimate victory would not be theirs. This is not the way that a modern army would have acted. Valerius returned to Rome in

* When Valerius was consul alone he began to build a house for himself on the Velian Hill, and a cry was raised that he intended to make himself king, upon which he stopped building. The people were ashamed of their conduct and granted him land to build on. One of his laws enacted that whoever should attempt to make himself king should be devoted to the gods, and that any one might kill him. When Valerius died he was mourned by the matrons for ten months. See Plutarch, *Poplicola*.

triumph, and the matrons mourned Brutus as the avenger of Lucretia, an entire year.

This is the time of heroes and of highly ornamented lays, and we are not surprised to find truth covered up beneath a mass of fulsome bombast. It is related that Tarquinius now obtained the help of Prince or Lars Porsena of Clusium in Etruria, and with a large army proceeded undisturbed quite up to the Janiculum Hill on his march to Rome. There he found himself separated from the object of his long struggle only by the wooden bridge. We may picture to ourselves the city stirred to its centre by the fearful prospect before it. The bridge that had been of so much use, that the pontifices had so carefully built and preserved, must be cut away, or all was lost. At this critical juncture, the brave Horatius Cocles, with one on either hand, kept the enemy at bay while willing arms swung the axes against the supports of the structure, and when it was just ready to fall uttered a prayer to Father Tiber, plunged into the muddy torrent, fully armed as he was, and swam to the opposite shore amid the plaudits of the rejoicing people, as related in the ballad of Lord Macaulay. Then it was, too, that the people determined to erect a bridge which could be more readily removed in case of necessity. Baffled in this attempt to enter Rome, the enemy laid siege to the city, and as it was unprepared, it soon suffered the distress of famine. Then another brave man arose, Caius Mucius by name, and offered to go to the camp of the invaders and kill the hated king. He was able to speak the Etruscan language, and felt that a little audacity was all that he needed to carry his mission out safely. Though he went boldly, he killed a secretary dressed in purple, instead of his master, and was caught and threatened with torture. Putting his right hand into the fire on the altar near by, he held it there until it was destroyed,* and said that suffering had no terrors for him, nor for three hundred of his companions who had all vowed to kill the king. The Roman writers say that, thereupon Porsena took hostages from them and made peace. It is true that peace was made, but Rome was forced to agree not to use iron except in cultivating the earth, and she lost ten of her thirty "regions," being all the territory that the kings had conquered on the west bank of the Tiber. †

Tarquin had been foiled in his attempts to regain his throne, but still he tried again, the last time having the aid of his son-in-law, Mamilius of Tusculum. It was a momentous juncture. The weakened Romans were to encounter the combined powers of the thirty Latin cities that had formerly been in league with them. They needed the guidance of one strong man; but they had decreed that there should never be a king again, and so they appointed a "dictator" with unlimited power, for a limited time. We shall find them resorting to this expedient on other occasions of sudden and great trouble. A fierce struggle followed at Lake Regillus, in which the Latins were turned to flight through the intervention of Castor and Pollux, who fought at the head of the Roman knights on foaming white steeds. There was no other quarter to which Tarquinius

* Mucius was after this called Scævola, the left-handed.
† See Niebuhr's *Lectures*, chapter xxiv.

could turn for help, and he therefore fled to Cumæ, where he died after a wretched old age. A temple was erected on the field of the battle of Lake Regillus in honor of Castor and Pollux, and thither annually on the fifteenth of July the Roman knights were wont to pass in solemn procession, in memory of the fact that the twins had fought at the head of their columns in the day of distress when fortune seemed to be about to desert the national cause. At this battle Caius Marcius, a stripling descended from Ancus Marcius, afterwards known as Coriolanus, received the oaken crown awarded to the man who should save the life of a Roman citizen, because he struck down one of the Latins, in the presence of the commander, just as he was about to kill a Roman soldier.

In the year 504 B.C., there was in the town of Regillum, a man of wealth and importance, who, at the time of the war with the Sabines, had advocated peace, and as his fellow-citizens were firmly opposed to him, left them, accompanied by a long train of followers (much as we suppose the first Tarquin left Tarquinii), and took up his abode in Rome. The name of this man was Atta Clausus, or perhaps Atta Claudius, but, however that may be, he was known at Rome as Appius Claudius. He was received into the ranks of the patricians, ample lands were assigned to him and his followers, and he became the ancestor of one of the most important Roman families, that of Claudius, noted through a long history for its hatred of the plebeians. His line lasted some five centuries, as we shall have occasion to observe.

VI.

THE ROMAN RUNNYMEDE.

THE establishment of the republic marked an era in the history of Rome. The people had decreed, as has been said, that for them there never should be a king, and the law was kept to the letter; though, if they meant that supreme authority should never be held among them by one man, it was violated many times. The story of Rome is unique in the history of the world, for it is not the record of the life of one great country, but of a city that grew to be strong and successfully established its authority over many countries. The most ancient and the most remote from the sea of the cities of Latium, Rome soon became the most influential, and began to combine in itself the traits of the peoples near it; but owing to the singular strength and rare impressiveness of the national character, these were assimilated, and the inhabitant of the capital remained distinctively a Roman in spite of his intimate association with men of different origin and training.

The citizen of Rome was practical, patriotic, and faithful to obligation; he loved to be governed by inflexible law; and it was a fundamental principle with him that the individual should be subordinate to the state. His kings were either organizers, like Numa and Ancus Marcius, or warriors, like Romulus and Tullus Hostilius; they either made laws, like Servius, or they enforced them with the despotism of Tarquinius Superbus. It is difficult for us to conceive of such a majestic power emanating from a territory so insignificant. We hardly realize that Latium did not comprise a territory quite fifty miles by one hundred in extent, and that it was but a hundred miles from the Mediterranean to the Adriatic. It was but a short walk from Rome to the territory of the Etruscans, and when Tarquin found an asylum at Cære, he did not separate himself by twenty miles from the scene of his tyranny. Ostia was scarcely more distant, and one might have ridden before the first meal of the day to Lavinium, or Alba, or Veii, or to Ardea, the ancient city of the Rutuli. It is important to keep these facts in mind as we read the story of the remarkable city.

All towns were built on hills in these early days, for safety in case of war, as well as because the valleys were insalubrious, but this is not a peculiarity of the Romans, for in New England in the late ages of our own ancestors they were obliged to follow the same custom. On the tops and slopes of seven hills, as they liked to remind themselves, the Romans built their city. They were not impressive elevations, though their sides were sharp and rocky, for the loftiest rose less than three hundred feet above the sea level. Their summits were crowned with groves of beech trees and oaks, and in the lower lands grew osiers and other smaller varieties.

The earlier occupations of the Roman people were war and agriculture, or the pasturage of flocks and herds. They raised grapes and made wines; they cultivated the oil olive and knew the use of its fruit. They found copper in their soil and made a pound (*as*) of it their unit of value, but it was so cheap that ten thousand ases were required to buy a war horse, though cattle and sheep were much lower. They yoked their oxen and called the path they occupied a *jugerum* (*jugum*, a cross-beam, or a yoke), and this in time came to be their familiar standard of square measure, containing about two thirds of an acre. Two of these were assigned to a citizen, and seven were the narrow limit to which only one's landed possessions were for a long time allowed to extend. In time commerce was added to the pursuits of the men, and with it came fortunes and improved dwellings and public buildings.

Laziness and luxury were frowned upon by the early Romans. Mistress and maid worked together in the affairs of the household, like Lucretia and other noble women of whom history tells, and the man did not hesitate to hold the plow, as the example of Cincinnatus will show us. Time was precious, and thrift and economy were necessary to success. The father was the autocrat in the household, and exercised his power with stern rigidity.

Art was backward and came from abroad; of literature there was none, long after Greece had passed its period of heroic poetry. The dwellings of the citizens were low and insignificant, though as time passed on they became more massive and important.

The vast public structures of the later kings were comparable to the task-work of the builders of the Egyptian pyramids, and they still strike us with astonishment and surprise.

The religion of these strong conquerors was narrow, severe, and dreary. The early fathers worshipped native deities only. They recognized gods everywhere—in the home, in the grove, and on the mountain. They erected their altars on the hills; they had their Lares and Penates to watch over their hearthstones, and their Vestal Virgins kept everlasting vigil near the never-dying fires in the temples. With the art of Greece that made itself felt through Etruria, came also the influence of the Grecian mythology, and Jupiter, Juno, and Minerva found a shrine on the top of the Capitoline, where the first statue of a deity was erected. The mysterious Sibylline Books are also a mark of the Grecian influence, coming from Cumæ, a colony of Magna Græcia.

During the period we have considered, the city passed through five distinct stages of political organization. The government at first, as we have seen, was an elective monarchy, the electors being a patriarchal aristocracy. After the invasion of the Sabines, there was a union with that people, the sovereignty being held by rulers chosen from each; but it was not long before Rome became the head of a federal state. The Tarquins established a monarchy, which rapidly degenerated into an offensive tyranny, which aroused rebellion and at last led to the republic. We have noted that in Greece in the year 510 B.C., the tyranny of the family of Pisistratus was likewise overturned.

During all these changes, the original aristocrats and their descendants firmly held their position as the Populus Romanus, the Roman People, insisting that every one else must belong to an inferior order, and, as no body of men is willing to be condemned to a hopelessly subordinate position in a state, there was a perpetual antagonism between the patricians and the plebeians, between the aristocracy and the commonalty. This led to a temporary change under Servius Tullius, when property took the place of pedigree in establishing a man's rank and influence; but, owing to the peculiar method of voting adopted, the power of the commons was not greatly increased. However, they had made their influence felt, and were encouraged. The overturning of the scheme by Tarquin favored a union of the two orders for the punishment of that tyrant, and they combined; but it was only for a time. When the danger had been removed, the tie was found broken and the antagonism rather increased, so that the subsequent history for five generations, though exceedingly interesting, is largely a record of the struggles of the commons for relief from the burdens laid upon them by the aristocrats.

The father passed down to his son the story of the oppression of the patricians, and the son told the same sad narrative to his offspring. The mother mourned with her daughter over the sufferings brought upon them by the rich, for whom their poor father and brothers were obliged to fight the battles while they were not allowed to share the spoil, nor to divide the lands gained by their own prowess. The struggle was not so much between patrician and plebeian as between the rich and the poor. It was intimately connected with the uses of money in those times. What could the rich Roman do with his accumulations? He might buy land or slaves, or he might become a lender; to a certain extent he could use his surplus in commerce; but of these its most remunerative employment was found in usury. As there were no laws regulating the rates of interest, they became exorbitant, and, as it was customary to compound it, debts rapidly grew beyond the possibility of payment. As the rich made the laws, they naturally exerted their ingenuity to frame them in such a way as to enable the lender to collect his dues with promptness, and with little regard for the feelings or interests of the debtor.

It is difficult, if not impossible, for us to form a proper conception of the magnitude of the wrongs involved in the system of money-lending at Rome during the period of the republic. The small farmers were ever needy, and came to their wealthy neighbors for accommodation loans. If these were not paid when due, the debtor was liable to be locked up in prison, to be sold into slavery, with his children, wife, and grandchildren; and the heartless law reads, that in case the estate should prove insufficient to satisfy all claims, the creditors were actually authorized to cut the body to pieces, that each Shylock might take the pound of flesh that he claimed.

At last the severity of the lenders overreached itself. It was in the year four hundred and ninety-five, B.C., that a poor, but brave debtor, one who had been at the very front in the wars, broke out of his prison, and while the wind flaunted his rags in the face of the populace, clanked his chains and told the story of his calamities so effectually in words of natural eloquence, that the commons were aroused to madness, and resolved at last to make a vigorous effort and seek redress for their wrongs in a way that could not be resisted. The form of this man stands out forever on the pages of Roman history, as he entered the forum with all the badges of his misery upon him.* His pale and emaciated body was but partially covered by his wretched tatters; his long hair played about his shoulders, and his glaring eyes and the grizzled beard hanging down before him added to his savage wildness. As he passed along, he uncovered the scars of near twoscore battles that remained upon his breast, and explained to enquirers that while he had been serving in the Sabine war, his house had been pillaged and burned by the enemy; that when he had returned to enjoy the sweets of the peace he had helped to win, he had found that his cattle had been driven off, and a tax imposed. To meet the debts that thronged upon him, and the interest by which they were aggravated, he had stripped himself of his ancestral farms. Finally, pestilence had overtaken him, and as he was not able to work, his creditor had placed him in a house of detention, the savage treatment in which was shown by the fresh stripes upon his bleeding back.

* See Livy, Book II., chapter xxiii.

At the moment a war was imminent, and the forum—the entire city, in fact—already excited, was filled with the uproar of the angry plebeians. Many confined for debt broke from their prison houses, and ran from all quarters into the crowds to claim protection. The majesty of the consuls was insufficient to preserve order, and while the discord was rapidly increasing, horsemen rushed into the gates announcing that an enemy was actually upon them, marching to besiege the city. The plebeians saw that their opportunity had arrived, and when proud Appius Claudius called upon them to enroll their names for the war, they refused the summons, saying that the patricians might fight their own battles; that for themselves it was better to perish together at home rather than to go to the field and die separated. Threatened with war beyond the gates, and with riot at home, the patricians were forced to promise to redress the civil grievances. It was ordered that no one could seize or sell the goods of a soldier while he was in camp, or arrest his children or grandchildren, and that no one should detain a citizen in prison or in chains, so as to hinder him from enlisting in the army. When this was known, the released prisoners volunteered in numbers, and entered upon the war with enthusiasm. The legions were victorious, and when peace was declared, the plebeians anxiously looked for the ratification of the promises made to them.

Their expectations were disappointed. They had, however, seen their power, and were determined to act upon their new knowledge. Without undue haste, they protected their homes on the Aventine, and retreated the next year to a mountain across the Anio, about three miles from the city, to a spot which afterwards held a place in the memories of the Romans similar to that which the green meadow on the Thames called Runnymede has held in British history since the June day when King John met his commons there, and gave them the great charter of their liberties.

The plebeians said calmly that they would no longer be imposed upon; that not one of them would thereafter enlist for a war until the public faith were made good. They reiterated the declaration that the lords might fight their own battles, so that the perils of conflict should lie where its advantages were. When the situation of affairs was thoroughly understood, Rome was on fire with anxiety, and the enforced suspense filled the citizens with fear lest an external enemy should take the opportunity for a successful onset upon the city. Meanwhile the poor secessionists fortified their camp, but carefully refrained from actual war. The people left in the city feared the senators, and the senators in turn dreaded the citizens lest they should do them violence. It was a time of panic and suspense. After consultation, good counsels prevailed in the senate, and it was resolved to send an embassy to the despised and down-trodden plebeians, who now seemed, however, to hold the balance of power, and to treat for peace, for there could be no security until the secessionists had returned to their homes.

The spokesman on the occasion was Menenius

Agrippa Lanatus, who was popular with the people and had a reputation for eloquence. In the course of his argument he related the famous apologue which Shakespeare has so admirably used in his first Roman play. He said:

"At a time when all the parts of the body did not, as now, agree together, but the several members had each its own scheme, its own language, the other parts, indignant that every thing was procured for the belly by their care, labor, and service, and that it, remaining quiet in the centre, did nothing but enjoy the pleasures afforded it, conspired that the hands should not convey food to the mouth, nor the mouth receive it when presented, nor the teeth chew it. They wished by these measures to subdue the belly by famine, but, to their dismay, they found that they themselves and the entire body were reduced to the last degree of emaciation. It then became apparent that the service of the belly was by no means a slothful one; that it did not so much receive nourishment as supply it, sending to all parts of the body that blood by which the entire system lived in vigor."

Lanatus then applied the fable to the body politic, showing that all the citizens must work in unity if its greatest welfare is to be attained. The address of this good man had its desired effect, and the people were at last willing to listen to a proposition for their return. It was settled that there should be a general release of all those who had been handed over to their creditors, and a cancelling of debts, and that two of the plebeians should be selected as their protectors, with power to veto objectionable laws, their persons being as inviolable at all times as were those of the sacred messengers of the gods. These demands, showing that the plebeians did not seek political power, were agreed to, the Valerian laws were reaffirmed, and a solemn treaty was concluded, each party swearing for itself and its posterity, with all the formality of representatives of foreign nations. The two leaders of the commons, Caius Licinius and Lucius Albinius, were elected the first Tribunes of the People, as the new officers were called, with two Ædiles to aid them.* They were not to leave the city during their term of office; their doors being open day and night, that all who needed their protection might have access to them. The hill upon which this treaty had been concluded was ever after known as the Sacred Mount; its top was enclosed and consecrated, an altar being built upon it, on which sacrifices were offered to Jupiter, the god of terror and deliverance, who had allowed the commons to return home in safety, though they had gone out in trepidation. Henceforth the commons were to be protected; they were better fitted to share the honors as well as the benefits of their country, and the threatened dissolution of the nation was averted.

Towards the end of the year, Lanatus, the successful intercessor, died, and it was found that his poverty was so great that none but the most ordinary funeral could be afforded. Thereupon the plebeians contributed enough to give him a splendid burial; but the sum was afterwards presented to his children, because the senate decreed that the funeral expenses should be defrayed by the state. (B.C. 494.)

* The duties of the ædiles were various, and at first they were simple assistants of the tribunes. *Ædes* means house or temple, and the ædiles seem to have derived their name from the fact that they had the care of the temple of Ceres, goddess of agriculture, a very important divinity in Rome as well as in Greece.

VII.

HOW THE HEROES FOUGHT FOR A HUNDRED YEARS.

THERE is a long story connected with the young stripling who, at the battle of Lake Regillus received the oaken crown for saving the life of a Roman citizen. The century after that event was filled with wars with the neighboring peoples, and in one of them this same Caius Marcius fought so bravely at the taking of the Latin town of Corioli that he was ever after known as Coriolanus (B.C. 493). He was a proud patrician, and on one occasion when he was candidate for the office of consul, behaved with so much unnecessary haughtiness toward the plebeians that they refused him their votes.* After a while a famine came to Rome,—famines often came there,—and though in a former emergency of the kind Coriolanus had himself obtained corn and beef for the people, he was now so irritated by his defeat that when a contribution of grain arrived from Syracuse, in Sicily (B.C. 491), he actually advocated that it should not be distributed among the people unless they would consent to give

* The whole interesting story is found in Plutarch's Lives, and in Shakespeare's play which bears the hero's name.

up their tribunes which had been assured to them by the laws of the Sacred Mount! This enraged the plebeians very much, and they caused Coriolanus to be summoned for trial before the comitia of the tribes, which body, in spite of his acknowledged services to the state, condemned him to exile. When he heard this sentence, Coriolanus angrily determined to cast in his lot with his old enemies the Volscians, and raised an army for them with which he marched victoriously towards Rome. As he went, he destroyed the property of the plebeians, but preserved that of the patricians. The people were in the direst state of anxious fear, and some of the senators were sent out to plead with the dreaded warrior for the safety of the city. These venerable ambassadors were repelled with scorn. Again, the sacred priests and augurs were deputed to make the petition, this time in the name of the gods of the people; but, alas, they too entreated in vain. Then it was remembered that the stern man had always reverenced his mother, and she with an array of matrons, accompanied by the little ones of Coriolanus, went out to add their efforts to those which had failed. As they appeared, Coriolanus exclaimed, as Shakespeare put it:

> "I melt, and am not
> Of stronger earth than others.—My mother bows;
> As if Olympus to a molehill should
> In supplication nod; and my young boy
> Hath an aspect of intercession, which,
> Great Nature cries: 'Deny not.' Let the Volsces
> Plow Rome and harrow Italy; I'll never
> Be such a gosling to obey instinct; but stand,
> As if a man were author of himself,
> And knew no other kin!"

The strong man is finally melted, however, by the soft influences of the women, and as he yields, says to them:

> "Ladies, you deserve
> To have a temple built you; all the swords
> In Italy, and her confederate arms,
> Could not have made this peace!"

A temple was accordingly built in memory of this event, and in honor of Feminine Fortune, at the request of the women of Rome, for the senate had decreed that any wish they might express should be gratified. As for Coriolanus, he is said to have lived long in banishment, bewailing his misfortune, and saying that exile bore heavily on an old man. The entire story, heroic and tragic as it is related to us, is not substantiated, and we do not really know whether if true it should be assigned to the year 488 B.C., or to a date a score of years later.

During all the century we are now considering, the plebeians were slowly gaining ground in their attempts to improve their political condition, though they did not fail to meet rebuffs, and though they were many times unjustly treated by their proud opponents. These efforts at home were complicated, too, by the fact that nearly all the time there was war with one or another of the adjoining nations. Treaties were made at this period with some of the neighboring peoples, by a good friend of the plebeians, Spurius Cassius, who was consul in the year 486, and these to a certain extent repaired the losses that had followed the war with Porsena after the fall of the Tarquins. Cassius tried to strengthen the state internally, too, by dividing certain lands among the people, and by requiring rents to be paid for other tracts, and setting the receipts aside to pay the commons when they should be called out as soldiers. This is known as the first of the many Agrarian Laws (*ager*, a meadow, a field) that are recorded in Roman history, though something of the same nature is said to have existed in the days of Servius Tullius.

There were public and private lands in Roman territory, just as there are in the territory of the United States, and in those days, just as in our own, there were " squatters," as they have been called in our history, who settled upon public lands without right, and without paying any thing to the government for the privileges they enjoyed. Laws regulating the use and ownership of the public lands were passed from time to time until Julius Cæsar (B.C. 59) enacted the last. They had for their object the relief of poverty and the stopping of the clamors of the poor, the settling of remote portions of territory, the rewarding of soldiers, or the extension of the popularity of some general or other leader. The plan was not efficient in developing the country, because those to whom the land was allotted were often not at all adapted to pursue agriculture successfully, and because the evils of poverty are not to be met in that way.

It was a sign of the power of the people that this proposition of Cassius should have been successful; but it irritated the patricians exceedingly, because they had derived large wealth from the improper use of the public lands. The following year consuls came into power who were more in sympathy with the patricians, and they accused Cassius of laying plans to be made king. His popularity was undermined, and his reputation blasted. Finally he was declared guilty of treason by his enemies, and condemned to be scourged and beheaded, while his house was razed to the ground. For seven years after this one of the consuls was always a member of the powerful family of the Fabii, which had been influential in thus overthrowing Cassius. The Fabians had opposed the laws dividing the lands, and they now refused to carry them out. The result was that the commons, deprived of their rights, again went to the extreme of refusing to fight for the state; and when on one occasion they were brought face to face with an enemy, they refused to conquer when they had victory in their hands. A little later they went one step further, and attempted to stop entirely the raising of an army. One of the patrician family just mentioned, Marcus Fabius, proved too noble willingly to permit such strife between the classes to interfere with the progress of the state, and determined to conciliate the commons. He succeeded, and led them to battle, and, though his army won victory, was himself killed in the combat (B.C. 481). The other members of the family took up the cause, cared kindly for the wounded, and thus still further ingratiated themselves with the army. The next year (B.C. 480) another Fabian was consul, and he too determined to stand up for the laws of Spurius Cassius. He was treated with scorn by his fellow patricians, and finding that he could not carry out his principles and live at peace in Rome, determined to exile himself. Going out with his followers, he established a camp on the side of the river Cremera, a few miles above Rome, and alone carried on a war against the fortified city of Veii. The unequal strife was continued for two years; but then the brave family was completely cut off. There was not a member left, excepting one who seems to have refused to renounce the former opinions of the family, and had remained at Rome * (B.C. 477). He became the ancestor of the Fabii of after-history.

The support thus received from the aristocratic Fabii encouraged the commons, and the sacrifice of the family exasperated them. They felt anew that it was possible for them to exert some power in the state, and they promptly accused one of the consuls, Titus Menenius, of treason, because he had allowed his army to lie inactive near Cremera while the Fabii were cut off before him. Menenius was found guilty, and died of vexation and shame. The aristocrats now attempted to frighten the commons by treachery and assassination, and succeeded, until one, Volero Publilius, arose and took their part. He boldly proposed a law by which the tribunes of the people, instead of being chosen by the comitia of the centuries, in which, as we have seen, the aristocrats had the advantage, should be chosen by the comitia of the tribes, in which there was no such inferiority of

* The Fabii were cut off on the Cremera on the 16th of July, a day afterwards marked by a terrible battle on the Allia, in which the Gauls defeated the Romans.

the commons. Though violently opposed by the patricians, this law was passed, in the year 471 B.C. Other measures were, however, still necessary to give the plebeians a satisfactory position in the state.

In the year 458, the ancient tribe of the Æquians came down upon Rome, and taking up a position upon Mount Algidus, just beyond Alba Longa, repulsed an army sent against them, and surrounded its camp. We can imagine the clattering of the hoofs on the hard stones of the Via Latina as five anxious messengers, who had managed to escape before it was too late, hurried to Rome to carry the disheartening news. All eyes immediately turned in one direction for help. There lived just across the Tiber a member of an old aristocratic family, one Lucius Quintius, better known as Cincinnatus, because that name had been added to his others to show that he wore his hair long and in curls. Lucius was promptly appointed Dictator—that is, he was offered supreme authority over all the state,—and messengers were sent to ask him to accept the direction of affairs. He was found at work on his little farm, which comprised only four jugera, either digging or plowing, and after he had sent for his toga, or outer garment, which he had thrown off for convenience in working, and had put it on, he listened to the message, and accepted the responsibility. The next morning he appeared on the forum by daylight, like an early-rising farmer, and issued orders that no one should attend to private business, but that all men of proper age should meet him on the field of Mars by sunset with food sufficient for five days. At the appointed hour the army was ready, and, so rapidly did it march, that before midnight the camp of the enemy was reached. The Æquians, not expecting such promptness, were astonished to hear a great shout, and to find themselves shut up between two Roman armies, both of which advanced and successfully hemmed them in. They were thus forced to surrender, and Cincinnatus obliged them to pass under the yoke, in token of subjugation. (*Sub*, under, *jugum*, a yoke.) The yoke in this case was made of two spears fastened upright in the ground with a third across them at the top. In the short space of twenty-four hours, Lucius Quintius Cincinnatus raised an army, defeated an enemy, and laid down his authority as dictator! It was decreed that he should enter the city in triumph. He rode in his chariot through the streets, the rejoicing inhabitants spreading tables in front of their houses, laden with meat and drink for the soldiers. The defeated chiefs walked before the victor, and after them followed the standards that had been won, while still farther behind were the soldiers, bearing the rich spoils. It was customary in those days for a conqueror to take every thing from the poor people whom he had vanquished,—homes, lands, cattle, wealth of every sort,—and then even to carry the men, women, and children away into slavery themselves. Thus a subjugated country became a desolation, unless the conquerors sent settlers to occupy the vacant homes and cultivate the neglected farms. Bad and frightful as war is now, it is not conducted on such terrible principles as were followed in early times.

Though from time to time concessions were made to the commons, they continued to feel that they were deprived of many of their just political rights, and the antagonism remained lively between them and the patricians. The distresses that they suffered were real, and endured even for two centuries after the time assigned to Coriolanus. We have now, indeed, arrived at a period of their sore trial, though it was preceded by some events that seemed to promise them good. In the year 454, Lucius Icilius, one of the tribunes of the people, managed to have the whole of the Aventine Hill given up to them, and as it was, after the Capitoline, the strongest of all the seven, their political importance was of course increased. It was but a few years later (B.C. 451) when, according to tradition, after long and violent debates it was decided that a commission should be sent to Athens, or to some colony of the Greeks, to learn what they could from the principles of government adopted by that ancient and wise people, which was then at the very height of its prosperity and fame. After this commission had made its report (in the year B.C. 450), all the important magistrates, including the consuls, tribunes, and ædiles, were replaced by ten patricians, known as Decemvirs (*decem*, ten, *vir*, a man), appointed to prepare a new code of laws.

The chief of this body was an Appius Claudius, son of the haughty patrician of the same name, and equally as haughty as he ever was. The laws of Rome before this time had been in a mixed condition, partly written and partly unwritten and traditional; but now all were to be reduced to order, and incorporated with those two laws that could not be touched—that giving the Aventine to the plebeians, and the sacred law settled on the Roman Runnymede after the first secession to the Sacred Mount. After a few months the ten men produced ten laws, which were written out and set up in public places for the people to read and criticise. Suggestions for alterations might be made, and if the ten men approved them, they made them a part of their report, after which all was submitted to the senate and the curiæ, and finally approved. The whole code of laws was then engraved on ten tables of enduring brass and put up in the comitium, where all might see them and have no excuse for not obeying them.

We do not know exactly what all these laws were, but enough has come down to us to make it clear that they were drawn up with great fairness, because they met the expectations of the people; and this shows, of course, that the political power of the plebeians was now considerable, because ten patricians would not have made the laws fair, unless there had been a strong influence exerted over them, obliging them to be careful in their action. The ten had acted so well, indeed, that it was thought safe and advisable to continue the government in the same form for another year. This proved a mistake, for Appius managed to gain so much influence that he was the only one of the original ten who was reelected, and he was able also to cause nine others to be chosen with him who were weak men, whom he felt sure that he could control. When the new decemvirs came into power, they soon added two new laws to the original ten, and the whole are now known, therefore, as the "Twelve Tables." The additional laws proved so distasteful to the people that they were much irritated, and seemed ready to revolt against the government on the slightest provocation. The decemvirs became exceedingly ostentatious and haughty, too, in their bearing, as well as tyrannical in their acts, so that the city was all excitement and opposition to the government that a few weeks before had been liked so well. Nothing was needed to bring about an outbreak except a good excuse, and that was not long waited for. Nations do not often have to wait long for a cause for fighting, if they want to find one.

A war broke out with the Sabines and the Æquians at the same time, and armies were sent against them both, commanded by friends of the plebeians. Lucius Sicinius Dentatus, one of the bravest, was sent out at the head of one army with some traitors, who, under orders from the decemvirs, murdered him in a lonely place. The other commander was Lucius Virginius, who will be known as long as literature lasts as father of the beautiful but unfortunate Virginia. While Virginius was fighting the city's war against the Æquians, the tyrant Appius was plotting to snatch from him his beloved daughter, who was affianced to the tribune Lucius Icilius, the same who had caused the Aventine to be assigned to the plebeians. At first wicked Appius endeavored to entice the maiden from her noble

THE TRAGEDY OF VIRGINIA.   91

lover, but without success; and he therefore determined to take her by an act of tyranny, under color of law. He caused one of his minions to claim her as his slave, intending to get her into his hands before her father could hear of the danger and return from the army. The attempt was not successful, for trusty friends carried the news quickly, and Virginius reached Rome in time to hear the cruel sentence by which the tyrant thought to gratify his evil intention. Before Virginia could be taken from the forum, Virginius drew her aside, suddenly snatched a sharp knife from a butcher's stall, and plunged it in her bosom, crying out: "This is the only way, my child, to keep thee free!" Then, turning to Appius, he held the bloody knife on high and cried: "On thy head be the curse of this blood." Vainly did Appius call upon the crowd to arrest the infuriated father; the people stood aside to allow him to pass, as though he had been something holy, and he rushed onward toward his portion of the army, which was soon joined by the troops that Dentatus had commanded. Meantime, Icilius held up the body of his loved one before the people in the forum, and bade them gaze on the work of their decemvir. A tumult was quickly stirred up, in the midst of which Appius fled to his house, and the senate, hastily summoned, cast about for means to stop the wild indignation of the exasperated populace; for the people were then, as they are now, always powerful in the strength of outraged feeling or righteous indignation.

All was vain. The two armies returned to the

Aventine united, and from the other parts of the city the plebeians flocked to them. This was the second secession, and, like the first, it was successful. The decemvirs were compelled to resign, their places being filled by two consuls; Appius was thrown into prison, to await judgment, and took his life there; and ten tribunes of the people were chosen to look out for the interests of the commons, Virginius and Icilius being two of the number. Thus, for the first time since the days of Publius Valerius, the control of government was in the hands of men who wished to carry it on for the good of the country, rather than in the interest of a party. Thus good came out of evil.

Among the laws of the Twelve Tables, the particular one which had at this time excited the plebeians was a statute prohibiting marriages between members of their order and the patricians. There had been such marriages, and this made the opposition to the law all the more bitter, though no one was powerful enough to cause it to be abolished. There now arose a tribune of the people who possessed force and persistence, Caius Canuleius by name, and he urged the repeal of this law. For the third time the plebeians seceded, this time going over the Tiber to the Janiculum Hill, where it would have been possible for them to begin a new city, if they had not been propitiated. Canuleius argued with vigor against the consuls who stood up for the law, and at last he succeeded. In the year 445 the restriction was removed, and plebeian girls were at liberty to become the wives of patrician men, with the assurance that their children should enjoy the rank of their fathers. This right of intermarriage led in time to the entrance of plebeians upon the highest magistracies of the city, and it was, therefore, of great political importance.

It was agreed in 444 B.C. that the supreme authority should be centred in two magistrates, called Military Tribunes, who should have the power of consuls, and might be chosen from the two orders. The following year, however (443 B.C.), the patricians were allowed to choose from their own order two officers known as Censors, who were always considered to outrank all others, excepting the dictator, when there was one of those extraordinary magistrates. The censors wore rich robes of scarlet, and had almost kingly dignity. They made the register of the citizens at the time of the census,* administered the public finances, and chose the members of the senate, besides exercising many other important duties connected with public and private life. The term of office of the censors at first was a lustrum or five years, but ten years later it was limited to eighteen months. In 421, the plebeians made further progress, for the office of quæstor (paymaster) was opened to them, and they thus became eligible to the senate. A score of years passed, however, before any plebeian was actually chosen to the office of military tribune even, owing to the great influence of the patricians in the comitia centuriata.

All the time that these events were occurring,

* After the expulsion of the Tarquins, the consuls took the census, and this was the first appointment of special officers for the purpose.

Rome was carrying on intermittent wars with the surrounding nations, and by her own efforts, as well as by the help of her allies, was adding to her warlike prestige. Nothing in all the story of war exceeds in interest the poetical narrative that relates to the siege and fall of the Etruscan city of Veii, with which, since the days of Romulus, Rome had so many times been involved in war.

Year after year the army besieged the strong place, and there seemed no hope that its walls would fall. It was allied with Fidenæ, another city halfway between it and Rome, which was taken by means of a mine in the year 426. A peace with Veii ensued, after which the incessant war began again, and fortune sometimes favored one side and sometimes the other. The siege of the city can be fittingly compared to that of Troy. Seven years had passed without result, when of a sudden, in the midst of an autumn drought, the waters of the Alban Lake, away off to the other side of Rome, began to rise. Higher and still higher they rose without any apparent cause, until the fields and houses were covered, and then they found a passage where the hills were lowest, and poured down in a great torrent upon the plains below. Unable to understand this portent, for such it was considered, the Romans called upon the oracle at Delphi for counsel, and were told that not until the waters should find their way into the lowlands by a new channel, should not rush so impetuously to the sea, but should water the country, could Veii be taken. It is hardly necessary to say that no one but an oracle or a poet could see the connection between the draining of a lake fifteen miles from Rome on one side, and the capture of a fortress ten miles away on the other. However, the lake was drained. With surprising skill, a tunnel was built directly through the rocky hills, and the waters allowed to flow over the fields below. The traveller may still see this ancient structure performing its old office. It is cut for a mile and a half, mainly through solid rock, four feet wide and from seven to ten in height. The lake is a thousand feet above the sea-level, and of very great depth.

Marcus Furius Camillus is the hero who now comes to the rescue. He was chosen dictator in order that he might push the war with the utmost vigor. The people of Veii sent messengers to him to sue for peace, but their appeal was in vain. Steadily the siege went on. We must not picture to ourselves the army of Camillus using the various engines of war that the Romans became acquainted with in later times through intercourse with the Greeks, but trusting more to their strong arms and their simple means of undermining the walls or breaking down the gates. Their bows and slings and ladders were weak instruments against strong stone walls, and the siege was a long and wearisome labor. It proved so long in this case, indeed, that the soldiers, unable to make visits to their homes to plant and reap their crops, were for the first time paid for their services.

As the unsuccessful ambassadors from Veii turned away from the senate-house, one of them uttered a fearful prophecy, saying that though the unmerciful Romans feared neither the wrath of the gods nor the vengeance of men, they should one day be rewarded for their hardness by the loss of their own country.

Summer and winter the Roman army camped before the doomed city, but it did not fall. At last, to ensure success, Camillus began a mine or tunnel under the city, which he completed to a spot just beneath the altar in the temple of Juno. When but a single stone remained to be taken away, he uttered a fervent prayer to the goddess, and made a vow to Apollo consecrating a tenth part of the spoil of the city to him. He then ordered an assault upon the walls, and at the moment when the king was making an offering on the altar of Juno, and the augur was telling him that victory in the contest was to fall to him who should burn the entrails then ready, the Romans burst from their tunnel, finished the sacrifice, and rushing to the gates, let their own army in. The city was sacked, and as Camillus looked on, he exclaimed: "What man's fortune was ever so great as mine?" A magnificent triumph was celebrated in Rome. Day after day the temples were crowded, and Camillus, hailed as a public benefactor, rode to the capitol in a chariot drawn by four white horses. The territory of the conquered city was divided among the patricians, but Camillus won their hatred after a time by calling upon them to give up a tenth part of their rich booty to found a temple to Apollo, in pursuance of his vow, which he claimed to have forgotten meanwhile. It was not long before he was accused of unfairness in distributing the spoils, some of which he was said to have retained himself, and when he saw that the people were so incensed at him that condemnation was inevitable, he went into banishment. As he went away, he added a malediction to the prophecy of the ambassador from Veii, and said that the republic might soon have cause to regret his loss. He was, as he had expected, condemned, a fine of one hundred and fifty thousand ases being laid upon him.

Thus was the territory of Rome greatly increased, after a hundred years of war and intrigue, and thus did the warrior to whom the city owed the most, and whom it had professed to honor, go from it with a malediction on his lips. Let us see how the ill omens were fulfilled.

VIII.

A BLAST FROM BEYOND THE NORTH-WIND.

WHEN the Greeks shivered in the cold north-wind, they thought that Boreas, one of their divinities who dwelt beyond the high mountains, had loosened the blast from a mysterious cave. The North was to them an unknown region. Far beyond the hills they thought there dwelt a nation known as Hyperboreans, or people beyond the region of Boreas, who lived in an atmosphere of feathers, enjoying Arcadian happiness, and stretching their peaceful lives out to a thousand years. That which is unknown is frightful to the ignorant or the superstitious, and so it was that the North was a land in which all that was alarming might be conjured up. The inhabitants of the Northern lands were called Gauls by the Romans. They lived in villages with no walls about them, and had no household furniture; they slept in straw, or leaves, or grass, and their business in life was either agriculture or war. They were hardy, tall, and rough in appearance; their hair was shaggy and light in color compared with that of the Italians, and their fierce appearance struck the dwellers under sunnier climes with dread.

These warlike people had come from the plains of

Asia, and in Central and Northern Europe had increased to such an extent that they could at length find scarcely enough pasturage for their flocks. The mountains were full of them, and it was not strange that some looked down from their summits into the rich plains of Italy, and then went thither; and, tempted by the crops, so much more abundant than they had ever known, and by the wine, which gave them a new sensation, at last made their homes there. It was a part of their life to be on the move, and by degrees they slipped farther and farther into the pleasant land. They flocked from the Hercynian forests, away off in Bohemia or Hungary, and swarmed over the Alps; they followed the river Po in its course, and they came into the region of the Apennines too.* It was they who had weakened the Etruscans and made it possible for the Romans to capture Veii. Afterwards they came before the city of Clusium (B.C. 391), and the people in distress begged for aid from Rome. No help was given, but ambassadors were sent to warn the invaders courteously not to attack the friends of the Roman people who had done them no harm. Such a request might have had an effect upon a nation that knew the Romans better, but the fierce Northerners who knew nothing of courtesy replied that if the Clusians would peaceably give up a portion of their lands, no harm should befall them; but that otherwise they should be attacked, and that in the presence of the

* No one knows exactly when the Gauls first entered Northern Italy. Some think that it was as long back as the time of the Tarquins, while others put it only ten or twenty years before the battle of the Allia—410-400 B.C.

Romans, who might thus take home an account of how the Gauls excelled all other mortals in bravery. Upon being asked by what right they proposed to take a part of the Clusian territory, Brennus, the leader of the barbarians, replied that all things belonged to the brave, and that their right lay in their trusty swords.

In the battle that ensued, the Roman ambassadors fought with the Clusians, and one of them killed a Gaul of great size and stature. This was made the basis for an onset upon Rome itself. Then the Romans must have remembered how just before the hero of Veii had gone into banishment, a good and respectable man reported to the military tribunes that one night as he was going along the street near the temple of Vesta, he heard a voice saying plainly to him: "Marcus Cædicius, the Gauls are coming!" Probably they remembered, too, how lightly they esteemed the information, and how even the tribunes made sport of it. Now the Northern scourge was actually rushing down upon them, and Camillus was gone! In great rage the invaders pushed on towards the city, alarming all who came in their way by their numbers, their fierceness, and the violence with which they swept away all opposition. There was little need of fear, however, for the rough men took nothing from the fields, and, as they passed the cities, cried out that they were on their way to Rome, and that they considered the inhabitants of all cities but Rome friends who should receive no harm.

The Romans had a proverb to the effect that whom the gods wish to destroy they first make mad, and, according to their historian Livy, it was true in this case, for when the city was thus menaced by a new enemy, rushing in the intoxication of victory, and impelled by the fury of wrath and the thirst for vengeance, they did not take any but the most ordinary precautions to protect themselves; leaving to the usual officers the direction of affairs, and not bestirring themselves as much as they did when threatened by the comparatively inferior forces of the neighboring states. They even neglected the prescribed religious customs and the simplest precautions of war. When they sent out their army they did not select a fit place for a camp, nor build ramparts behind which they might retreat, and they drew up the soldiers in such a way that the line was unusually weak in the parts it presented to the on-rushing enemy.

Under such unpropitious circumstances the impetuous Gauls were met on the banks of the river Allia, ten miles from Rome, on the very day on which the Fabii had been destroyed by the Etruscans the century before (July 16, 390). The result was that terror took possession of the soldiers, and the Gauls achieved an easy victory, so easy, indeed, that it left them in a state of stupefied surprise. A part of the Romans fled to the deserted stronghold of Veii, and others to their own city, but many were overtaken by the enemy and killed, or were swept away by the current of the Tiber.*

* That this was a terrible defeat is proved by the fact that the sixteenth of July was afterward held unlucky (*ater*, black), and no business was transacted on it. Ovid mentions it as " the day to which calamitous Allia gives a name in the calendar," and on which " tearful Allia was stained with the blood of the Latian wounds."

There was dire alarm in the city. The young and vigorous members of the senate, with their wives and children and other citizens, found refuge in the capitol, which they fortified; but the aged senators took their seats in the forum and solemnly awaited the coming of Brennus and his hosts. The barbarians found, of course, no difficulty in taking and burning the city, and for days they sacked and pillaged the houses. The venerable senators were immediately murdered, and the invaders put the capitol in a state of siege.

Then the curses of the ambassador of Veii and of Camillus found their fulfilment; and then also did the thoughts of the Romans turn to their once admired commander, who, they were now sure, could help them. The refugees at Veii, too, turned in their thoughts to Camillus, and messengers were sent to him at Ardea, where he was in exile, asking him to come to the assistance of his distressed countrymen. Camillus was too proud to accept a command to which he was not called by the senate, while he was under condemnation for an offence of which he did not feel guilty. The senate was shut up in the capitol, and hard to get at, but an ambitious youth offered to climb the precipitous hill, in spite of the besieging barbarians, and obtain the requisite order. The daring man crossed the Tiber, and scaled the hill by the help of shrubs and projecting stones. After obtaining for Camillus the appointment of dictator, he successfully returned to Veii, and then the banished leader accepted the supreme office for the second time.

The sharp watchers among the Gauls had, however, noticed in the broken shrubs and loosened stones the marks of the daring act of the messenger who had climbed the hill, and determined to take the hint and enter the capitol in that way themselves. In the dead of night, but by the bright light of the moon we may suppose, since the battle of Allia was fought at the full of the moon, the daring barbarians began slowly and with great difficulty to climb the rocky hill. They actually reached its summit, and, to their surprise, were not noisy enough to awaken the guards; but, alas for them, the sacred geese of the capitol, kept for use in the worship of Juno, were confined near the spot where the ascent had been made. Alarmed by the unusual occurrence, the geese uttered their natural noises and awakened Marcus Manlius, who quickly buckled on his armor and rushed to the edge of the cliff. He was just in time to meet the first Gaul as he came up, and to push him over on the others who were painfully following him. Down he fell backwards, striking his companions and sending them one after another to the foot of the precipice in promiscuous ruin. In the morning the captain of the watch was in turn cast down upon the heads of the enemies, to whom his neglect had given such an advantage.

Now there remained nothing for the Gauls to do but sit down and wait, to see if they could st.rve the Romans confined in the capitol. Months passed, and, indeed, they almost accomplished their object, but while they were listlessly waiting, the hot Roman autumn was having its natural effect upon them, accustomed as they were to an active life in those Northern woods where the cool winds of the mountains fanned them and the leafy shades screened their heads from the heat of the sun. The miasma of the low lands crept up into their camps, and the ashes of the ruins that they had made blew into their faces and affected their health. They might almost as well have been shut up on the hill. The result was that both Gaul and Roman felt at last that peace would be a boon no matter at how high a price purchased, and it was agreed by Brennus that if the Romans would weigh him out a thousand pounds of rich gold, he would take himself and his horde back to the more comfortable woods. The scales were prepared and the gold was brought out, but the Romans found that their enemies were cheating in the weight. When asked what it meant, Brennus pulled off his heavy sword, threw it into the balances and said: "What does it mean, but woe to the vanquished!" "*Væ victis!*"

It was very bad for the Romans, but the story goes on to tell us that at that very moment, the great Camillus was knocking at the gates, that he entered at the right instant with his army, took the gold out of the scales, threw the weights, and the scales themselves, indeed, to the Gauls, and told Brennus that it was the custom of the Romans to pay their debts in iron, not in gold. The Gauls immediately called their men together and hastened from the city, establishing a camp eight miles away on the road to Gabii, where Camillus overtook them the next day and defeated them with such great

THE CAPITOL RESTORED.

slaughter that they were able to do no further damage.

It seems a pity to spoil so good a story, but it is like many others that have grown up in the way that reminds one of the game of "scandal" that the children play. The Roman historians always wished to glorify their nation, and they took every opportunity to make the stories appear well for the old heroes. It seems that at this time some Gauls were really cut off by the people of Cære, or some neighboring place, and, to improve the story, it was at first said that they were the very ones that had taken Rome. Then, another writer added, that the gold given as a ransom for the city was retaken with the captives; and, as another improvement, it was said that Camillus was the one who accomplished the feat, but that it was a long time afterwards, when the Gauls were besieging another city. The last step in adding to the story was taken when some one, thinking that it could be improved still more, and the national pride satisfied, brought Camillus into the city at the very moment that the gold was in the scales, so that he could keep it from being delivered at all, and then proceed to cut off all the enemy, so that not a man should be left to take the terrible tale back over the northern mountains! The story is not all false, for there are good evidences that Rome was burned, but the heroic embellishments are doubtless the imaginative and patriotic additions of historians who thought more of national pride than historic accuracy.

Camillus now proceeded to rebuild the city, and

came to be honored as the second founder of Rome. The suffering people rushed out of the capitol weeping for very joy; the inhabitants who had gone elsewhere came back; the priests brought the holy things from their hiding-places; the city was purified; a temple was speedily erected to Rumor or Voice on the spot where Cædicius had heard the voice announcing the coming barbarians; and there was a diligent digging among the ashes to find the sites of the other temples and streets. It was a tedious and almost hopeless task to rebuild the broken-down city, and the people began to look with longing to the strongly-built houses and temples still standing at Veii, wondering why they might not go thither in a body and live in comfort, instead of digging among ashes to rebuild a city simply to give Camillus, of whom they quickly began to be jealous, the honor that had been an attribute of Romulus only. Then the senate appealed to the memories of the olden time; the stories of the sacred places, and especially of the head that was found on the Capitoline Hill, were retold, and by dint of entreaty and expostulation the distressed inhabitants were led to go to work to patch up the ruins. They brought stones from Veii, and to the poor the authorities granted bricks, and gradually a new, but ill-built, city grew up among the ruins, with crooked streets and lanes, and with buildings, public and private, huddled together just as happened to be the most convenient for the immediate occasion.

Camillus lived twenty-five years longer, and was repeatedly called to the head of affairs, as the city found itself in danger from the Volscians, Æquians, Etruscans and other envious enemies. Six times was he made one of the tribunes, and five times did he hold the office of dictator. When the Gauls came again, in the year 367, Camillus was called upon to help his countrymen for the last time, and though he was some fourscore years of age, he did not hesitate, nor did victory desert him. The Gauls were defeated with great slaughter, and it was a long time before they again ventured to trouble the Romans. The second founder of Rome, after his long life of warfare, died of a plague that carried away many of the prominent citizens in the year 365. His victories had not all been of the same warlike sort, however. "Peace hath her victories no less renowned than war," and Camillus gained his share of them.

Marcus Manlius, the preserver of the capitol, was less fortunate, for when he saw that the plebeians were suffering because the laws concerning debtors were too severe, and came forward as patron of the poor, he received no recognition, and languished in private life, while Camillus was a favorite. He therefore turned to the plebeians, and devoted his large fortune to relieving suffering debtors. The patricians looking upon him as a deserter from their party, brought up charges against him, and though he showed the marks of distinction that he had won in battles for the country, and gained temporary respite from their emnity, they did not relent until his condemnation had been secured. He was hurled from the fatal Tarpeian Rock, and his house was razed to the ground in the year 384.

Eight years after the death of Manlius (B.C. 376), two tribunes of the plebeians, one of whom was Caius Licinius Stolo, proposed some new laws to protect poor debtors, whose grievances had been greatly increased by the havoc of the Gauls, and after nine more years of tedious discussion and effort, they were enacted (B.C. 367), and are known as the Licinian Laws, or rather, Rogations, for a law before it was finally passed was known as a rogation, and these were long discussed before they were agreed to. (*Rogare*, to ask, that is, to ask the opinion of one.) So great was the feeling aroused by this discussion, that Camillus was called upon to interfere, and he succeeded in pacifying the city ; Lucius Sextius was chosen as the first plebeian consul, and Camillus, having thus a third time saved the state, dedicated a temple to Concord. As a plebeian had been made consul, the disturbing struggles between the two orders could not last much longer, and we find that the plebeians gradually gained ground, until at last the political distinction between them and the patricians was wiped out for generations. The laws that finally effected this were those of Publilius, in 339, and of Hortensius, the dictator, in 286.

The period of the death of Camillus is to be remembered on account of several facts connected with a plague that visited Rome in the year 365. The people, in their despair, for the third time in the history of the city, performed a peculiar sacrifice called the *Lectisternium* (*lectus*, a couch, *sternere*, to spread), to implore the favor of offended deities. They placed images of the gods upon cushions or couches and offered them viands, as if the images could really eat them. Naturally this did not effect any abatement of the ravaging disease, and under orders of the priests, stage plays were instituted as a means of appeasing the wrath of heaven. The first Roman play-writer, Plautus, did not live till a hundred years after this time, and these performances were trivial imitations of Etruscan acting, which thus came to Rome at second-hand from Greece; but, as the Romans did not particularly delight in intellectual efforts at that time, buffoonery sufficed instead of the wit which gave so much pleasure to the cultivated attendants at the theatre of Athens. Livy says that these plays neither relieved the minds nor the bodies of the Romans; and, in fact, when on one occasion the performances were interrupted by the overflowing waters of the Tiber which burst into the circus, the people turned from the theatre in terror, feeling that their efforts to soothe the gods had been despised. It was at this time that the earth is said to have been opened in the forum by an earthquake, and that Curtius cast himself into it as a sacrifice; but, as we have read of the occurrence before we shall not stop to consider it again. The young hero was called Mettus Curtius in the former instance, but now the name given to him is Marcus Curtius.

IX.

HOW THE REPUBLIC OVERCAME ITS NEIGHBORS.

WE have now reached the time when Rome had brought under her sway all the country towards Naples as far as the river Liris, and, gaining strength, she is about to add materially to her territory and to lay the foundation for still more extensive conquests. During the century that we are next to consider, she conquered her immediate neighbors, and was first noticed by that powerful city which was soon to become her determined antagonist, Carthage. It was the time when the great Macedonian conqueror, Alexander, finished his war in Persia, and the mention of his name leads Livy to pause in his narrative, and, reflecting that the age was remarkable above others for its conquerors, to enquire what would have been the consequences if Alexander had been minded to turn his legions against Rome, after having become master of the Eastern world. Alexander died, however, before he had an opportunity to get back from the East; but, as the old historian says, it is entertaining and relaxing to the mind to digress from weightier considerations and to embellish historical study with variety, and he decides that if the great Eastern conqueror had marched against Rome, he would have been defeated. While Livy was probably influenced in this decision by that desire to magnify the prowess of his country which is plainly seen throughout his work, we may agree with him without fear of being far from correct, especially when we remember that Alexander achieved his great success against peoples that had not reached the stage of military science that Rome had by this time attained. "The aspect of Italy," Livy says, "would have appeared to him quite different from that of India, which he traversed in the guise of a reveller at the head of a crew of drunkards * * * Never were we worsted by an enemy's cavalry, never by their infantry, never in open fight, never on equal ground," but our army "has defeated and will defeat a thousand armies more formidable than those of Alexander and the Macedonians, provided that the same love of peace and solicitude about domestic harmony in which we now live continue permanent." This is what patriotism says for Rome, and we can hardly say less, when we remember that when she came into conflict with great Carthage, led by diplomatic and scientific Hannibal, she proved the victor. We are, however, more interested now in what the Roman arms actually accomplished than in enquiries, however interesting, about what they might have done. They subjugated the world, and that is enough for us.

One of the most favored and celebrated families in the history of Rome for a thousand years was that called Valerian, and at the time to which our thoughts are now directed, one of the members comes into prominence as the most illustrious general of the era. Marcus Valerius Corvus was born at about the time when the rogations of Licinius Stolo became laws, and in early life distinguished himself as a soldier in an assault made on the Romans by the Gauls, who seem not to have all been swept away for a long time. It was in the year 349. The dreaded enemy rushed upon Rome, and the citizens took up arms in a mass. One soldier, Titus Manlius, met a gigantic Gaul on a bridge over the Anio, and after slaying him, carried off a massy chain that he bore on his neck. *Torquatus* in Latin means "provided with a chain," and this word was added to the name of Manlius ever after. It was at the same time that Marcus Valerius encountered another huge Gaul in single combat, and overcame him, though he was aided by a raven which settled on his helmet, and in the contest picked at the eyes of the barbarian. *Corvus* is the Latin word for raven, and it was added to the other names of Valerius. A golden crown and ten oxen were presented to him, and the people chose him consul.

Corvus was no less powerful than popular. He competed with the other soldiers in their games of the camp, and listened to their jokes like a companion without taking offence. He thus established a bond between the two orders. Six times he served as consul, and twice as dictator. Never was such a man more needed than was he now. At an unknown period there had come down from the snowy tops of the Apennines a strong people, known afterwards as Samnites, who now began to press upon the inhabitants of the region called Campania, in the midst of which is the volcano Vesuvius.* There, too, were Cumæ and Capua, of which we have had occasion to speak, and Herculaneum and Pompeii; there was Naples on its beautiful bay, and there was Palæopolis, the " old city," not far distant (*Nea*, new, *polis*, city; *palaios*, old, *polis*, city). This was a part of Magna Græcia, which included many rich cities in the southern portion of the peninsula, among which were Tarentum, and there had been the earliest of the Greek colonies, Sybaris, the abode of wealth and luxury, until its destruction at the time of the fall of the Tarquins.

The Campanians invoked the help of Rome against their sturdy foes, and a struggle for the mastery of Italy began, which lasted for more than half a century, though there were three wars, separated by intervals of peace. The first struggle lasted from 343 to 341, and is important for its first battle, which was fought at the foot of Mount Gaurus, three miles from Cumæ. It is memorable because Valerius Corvus, who lived until the Samnites had been finally subdued, was victorious, and the historian Niebuhr tells us that though we find it but little spoken of, it is one of the most noteworthy in all the history

* Among the strange customs of the olden times in Italy was one called *ver sacrum* (sacred spring). In time of distress a vow would be made to sacrifice every creature born in April and May to propitiate an offended deity. In many cases man and beast were thus offered; but in time humanity revolted against the sacrifice of children, and they were considered sacred, but allowed to grow up, and at the age of twenty were sent blindfolded out into the world beyond the frontier to found a colony wherever the gods might lead them. The Mamertines in Sicily sprang from such emigrants, and it is supposed that the Samnites had a similar origin.

of the world, because it indicated that Rome was to achieve the final success, and thus take its first step towards universal sovereignty. After this victory the Carthaginians, with whom Rome was to have a desperate war afterwards, sent congratulations, accompanied by a golden crown for the shrine of Jupiter in the capitol. It is said that at the time of the expulsion of the Tarquins, the Romans and Carthaginians had entered into a treaty of friendship, which had been renewed five years before the war with the Samnites, but we are not certain of it.

The results of the burning of Rome by the Gauls had not all ceased to be felt, and many of the plebeians were still suffering under the burden of debts that they could not pay. A portion of the army, composed, as we know, of plebeians, was left to winter at Capua. There it saw the luxurious extravagance of the citizens, and felt its own burdens more than ever by contrast. A mutiny ensued, and though it was quelled, more concessions were made to the plebeians, and their debts were generally abolished. Meantime the Latins saw evidence that the power of Rome was growing more rapidly than their own, and they, therefore, determined to go to war to obtain the equality that they thought the terms of the treaty between the nations authorized them to expect. The Samnites were now the allies of Rome, and fought with her. The armies met under the shadow of Mount Vesuvius. In a vision, so the story runs, it had been foretold to the Romans that the leader of one army and the soldiers of the other were forfeited to the gods; and when, during the battle, the plebeian consul, Marcus Decius Mus, who had been a hero in the previous war, saw that his line was falling back, he uttered a solemn prayer and threw himself into the thickest of the fight. By thus giving up his life, as the partial historians like to tell us that many Romans have done at various epochs, he ensured victory on this occasion, and subsequently the conquest of the world, to his countrymen. Other battles and other victories followed, and the people of Latium became dependent upon Rome. The last engagement was at Antium, an ancient city on a promontory below Ostia, which, having a little navy, had interfered with the Roman commerce. The prows of the vessels of Antium were set up in the Roman forum as an ornament to the *suggestum*, or stage from which orators addressed the people. This was called the *rostra* afterward. (*Rostra*, beaks of birds or ships.)

Thus the city kept on adding to its dependents, and increasing its power. In 329, the Volscians were overcome and their long warfare with Rome ended. Two years later, the Romans declared war against Palæopolis and Neapolis, and after taking the Old City, made a league with the New. One war thus led to another, and as the Samnites, getting jealous of the increasing power of their ally, had aided these two cities, Rome declared war the second time against them, in 326. It proved the most important of the three Samnite wars, lasting upward of twenty years. The aim of each of the combatants seems to have been to gain as many allies as possible, and to lessen the adherents of the enemy. For this reason the war was peculiar, the armies of Rome being often found in Apulia, and those of the enemy being ever ready to overrun Campania.

Success at first followed the Samnite banners, and this was notably the case at the battle of Caudine Forks, fought in a pass on the road from Capua to Beneventum (then Maleventum), in the year 321, when the Romans were entrapped and all obliged to pass under the yoke. Such a success is apt to influence allies, and this tended to strengthen the Samnites. It was not until seven years had passed that the Romans were able to make decided gains, and though their cause appeared quite hopeful, the very success brought new troubles, because it led the Etruscans to take part with the Samnites and to create a diversion on the north. This outbreak is said to have been quelled by Fabius Maximus Rullus, (a general whose personal prowess is vaunted in the highest terms by the historians of Rome,) who defeated the Etruscans at Lake Vadimonis, B.C. 310. Success followed in the south, also, and in the year 304, Bovianum, in the heart of Samnium, which had been before taken by them, fell into the hands of the Romans and closed the war, leaving Rome the most powerful nation in Central Italy.

Unable to overcome its northern neighbor, Samnium now turned to attack Lucania, the country to the south, which reached as far as the Tarentine Gulf, just under the great heel of Italy. Magna Græcia was then in a state of decadence, and Lucania was an ally of Rome, which took its part against Samnium, not as loving Samnium less, but as loving power more. The struggle became very general. The Etruscans had begun a new war with Rome, but were about to treat for peace, when the Samnites induced them to break off the negotiations, and they attacked Rome at once on the north and the south. The undaunted Romans struck out with one arm against the Etruscans and their allies the Gauls on the north, and with the other hurled defiance at the Samnites on the south. The war was decided by a battle fought in 295, on the ridge of the Apennines, near the town of Sentinum in Umbria, where the allies had all managed to unite their forces. On this occasion it is related that Publius Decius Mus, son of that hero who had sacrificed himself at Mount Vesuvius, followed his father's example, devoted himself and the opposing army to the infernal gods, and thus enabled the Romans to achieve a splendid victory.

The Samnites continued the desperate struggle five years longer, but in the year 290 they became subject to Rome; their leader, the hero of the battle of the Caudine Forks, having been taken two years previously and perfidiously put to death in Rome as the triumphal car of the victor ascended the Capitoline Hill. This is considered one of the darkest blots on the Roman name, and Dr. Arnold forcibly says that it shows that in their dealings with foreigners, the Romans "had neither magnanimity, nor humanity, nor justice."

The Etruscans and the Gauls did not yet cease their wars on the north, and in 283 they encountered the Roman army at the little pond, between the Ciminian Hills and the Tiber, known as Lake Vadimonis, on the spot where the Etrurian power had been broken thirty years before by Fabius Maximus, and were defeated with great slaughter. The constant wars had made the rich richer than before, while at the same time the poor were growing poorer, and after the third Samnite war we are ready to believe that debts were again pressing with heavy force upon many of the citizens. Popular tumults arose, and the usual remedy, an agrarian law, was proposed. There was a new secession of the people to the Janiculum, followed by the enactment of the Hortensian laws, celebrated in the history of jurisprudence because they deprived the senate of its veto and declared that the voice of the people assembled in their tribes was supreme law. Debts were abolished or greatly reduced, and seven jugera of land were allotted to every citizen. We see from this that the commotions of our own days, made by socialists, communists, and nihilists, as they are called, are only repetitions of such agitations as those which took place so many centuries ago.

In the midst of a storm in the especially boisterous winter season of the year 280, the waves of the Mediterranean washed upon the shores of Southern Italy a brave man more dead than alive, who was to take the lead in the last struggle against the supremacy of Rome among its neighbors. The winds and the waves had no respect for his crown. They knew not that he ruled over a strong people whose extensive mountainous land was known as the " continent," and that he had left it with thousands of archers and slingers and footmen and knights; and that he had also huge elephants trained to war, beasts then unknown in Italian warfare, which he expected would strike horror into the cavalry of the country he had been cast upon.

As we study history, we find that at almost every epoch it centres about the personality of some strong man who has either power to control, or sympathetic attractiveness that holds to him those who are around him. It was so in this case. Pyrrhus, King of Epirus, was born seven years after the great Alexander died, and was at this time thirty-seven years of age. Claiming descent from Pyhrrus, son of Achilles, and being a son of Æacides, he was in the direct line the Kings of Epirus. He was also cousin of an Alexander, who, in the year 332, had crossed over from Epirus to help the Tarentines against the Lucanians, had formed an alliance with the Romans, and had finally been killed by a Lucanian on the banks of the Acheron, in 326. After a variety of vicissitudes, Pyrrhus had ascended the throne of his father at the age of twenty-three, and, taking Alexander the Great as his model, had soon become popular and powerful. Aiming at the conquest of the whole of Greece, he attacked the king of Macedonia and overcame him. After resting a while upon his laurels, he found a life of inactivity unbearable, and accepted a request, sent him in 281, to follow in the footsteps of his cousin Alexander, and go to the help of the people of Tarentum against the Romans, with whom they were then at war. This is the reason why he was voyaging in haste to Italy, and it was this ambition that led to his shipwreck on a winter's night.

Pyrrhus had a counsellor named Cineas, who asked him how he would use his victory if he should be so fortunate as to overcome the Romans, who were reputed great warriors and conquerors of many peoples. The Romans overcome, replied the king, no city, Greek nor barbarian, would dare to oppose me, and I should be master of all Italy. Well, Italy conquered, what next? Sicily next would hold out its arms to receive me, Pyrrhus replied. And, what next? These would be but forerunners of greater victories. There are Libya and Carthage, said the king. Then? Then, continued Pyrrhus, I should be able to master all Greece. And then? continued Cineas. Then I would live at ease, eat and drink all day, and enjoy pleasant conversation. And what hinders you from taking now the ease that you are planning to take after such hazards and so much blood-shedding? Here the conversation closed, for Pyrrhus could not answer this question.

Once on the Italian shore the invading king marched to Tarentum, and found it a city of people given up to pleasures, who had no thought of fighting themselves, but expected that he would do that work for them while they enjoyed their theatres, their baths, and their festivities. They soon found, however, that they had a master instead of a servant. Pyrrhus shut up the theatres and was inflexible in demanding the services of the young and strong in the army. His preparations were made as promptly as possible, but Rome was ahead of him, and her army was superior, excepting that the Grecians brought elephants with them. The first battle was fought on the banks of the river Liris, and the elephants gave victory to the invader, but the valor of the Romans was such that Pyrrhus is said to have boasted that if he had such soldiers he could conquer the world, and to have confessed that another such victory would send him back to Epirus alone. It is not to be wondered at, therefore, that he sent Cineas to Rome to plead for peace. The Romans were on the point of entering into negotiations, when aged and blind Appius Claudius, hearing of it, caused himself to be carried to the forum, where he delivered an impassioned protest against the proposed action. So effectual was he that the people became eager for war, and sent word to Pyrrhus that they would only treat with him when he should withdraw his forces from Italy. Pyrrhus then marched rapidly towards Rome, but when he had almost reached the city, after devastating the country through which he had passed, he learned that the Romans had made peace with the Etruscans, with whom they had been fighting, and that thus another army was free to act against him. He therefore retreated to winter quarters at Tarentum. The next year the two forces met on the edge of the plains of Apulia, at Asculum, but the battle resulted in no gain to Pyrrhus, who was again obliged to retire for the winter to Tarentum. (B.C. 279.)

In the last battle the brunt of the fighting had fallen to the share of the Epirots, and Pyrrhus was not anxious to sacrifice his comparatively few re-

THE CAREER OF PYRRHUS CLOSED. 123

maining troops for the benefit of the Tarentines. Therefore, after arranging a truce with Rome, he accepted an invitation from the Greeks of Sicily to go to their help against the Carthaginians. For two years he fought, at first with success; but afterwards he met repulses, so that being again asked to assist his former allies in Italy, he returned, in 276, and for two years led the remnants of his troops and the mercenaries that he had attracted to his standard against the Romans. His Italian career closed in the year 274, when he encountered his enemy in the neighborhood of Maleventum, and was defeated, the Romans having learned how to meet the formerly dreaded elephants. The name of this place was then changed to Beneventum. Two years later still, in 272, Tarentum fell under the sway of Rome, which soon had overcome every nation on the peninsula south of a line marked by the Rubicon on the east and the Macra on the west,—the boundaries of Gallia Cisalpina. (*Cis*, on this side, *alpina*, alpine.)

Not only had Rome thus gained power and prestige at home, but she had begun to come in contact with more distant peoples. Carthage had offered to assist her after the battle of Asculum, sending a large fleet of ships to Ostia in earnest of her good faith. Now, when the news of the permanent repulse of the proud king of Epirus was spread abroad, great Ptolemy Philadelphus, the Egyptian patron of art, literature, and science, sent an embassy empowered to conclude a treaty of amity with the republic. The proposition was accepted with earnestness, and ambassadors of the highest rank were sent to

Alexandria, where they were treated with extraordinary consideration, and allowed to see all the splendor of the Egyptian capital.

Rome had now reached a position of wealth and physical prosperity; the rich had gained much land, and the poor had been permitted to share the general progress; commerce, agriculture, and, to some extent, manufactures had advanced. Rome kept a firm hold upon all of the territory she had won, connecting them with the capital by good roads, but making no arrangements for free communication between the chief cities of the conquered regions. The celebrated military roads, of which we now can see the wonderful remains, date from a later period, with the exception of the Appian Way, which was begun in 312, and, after the conquest of Italy was completed to Brundusium, through Capua, Tres Taberna, and Beneventum. Other than this there were a number of earth roads leading from Rome in various directions. One of the most ancient of these was that over which Pyrrhus marched as far as Præneste, known as the Via Latina, which ran over the Tusculum Hills, and the Alban Mountain. The Via Ostiensis ran down the left bank of the Tiber; the Via Saleria ran up the river to Tibur, and was afterward continued, as the Via Valeria, over the Apennines to the Adriatic.

The population of Italy (at this time less than three million)was divided into three general classes: first, the *Roman Citizens*, comprising the members of the thirty-three tribes, stretching from Veii to the river Liris, the citizens in the Roman colonies, and in certain municipal towns; the *Latin Name*, including the inhabitants of the colonies generally, and some of the most flourishing towns of Italy; and the *Allies*, or all other inhabitants of the peninsula who

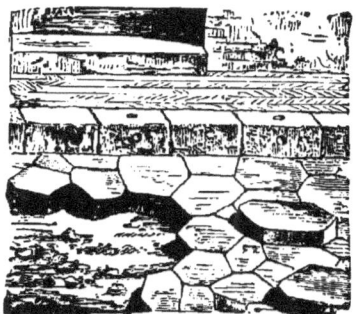

ROMAN STREET PAVEMENT.

were dependent upon Rome, but liked to think that they were not subjects. The Romans had been made rich and prosperous by war, and were ready to plunge into any new struggle promising additional power and wealth.

X.

AN AFRICAN SIROCCO.

ALL the time that the events that we have been giving our attention to were occurring—that is to say, ever since the foundation of Rome, another city had been growing up on the opposite side of the Mediterranean Sea, in which a different kind of civilization had been developed. Carthage, of which we have already heard, was founded by citizens of Phœnicia. The early inhabitants were from Tyre, that old city of which we read in the Bible, which in the earliest times was famous for its rich commerce. How long the people of Phœnicia had lived in their narrow land under the shadow of great Libanus, we cannot tell, though Herodotus, when writing his history, went there to find out, and reported that at that time Tyre had existed twenty-three hundred years, which would make its foundation forty-five hundred years ago, and more. However that may be, the purple of Tyre and the glass of Sidon, another and still older Phœnician city, were celebrated long before Rome was heard of. It was from this ancient land that the people of Carthage had come. It has been usual for emigrants to call their cities in a new land "new," (as Nova Scotia, New York, New England, New Town, or Newburg,) and that is the way in which Carthage was named, for the word means, in the old language of the Phœnicians, simply new city, just as Naples was merely the Greek for new city, as we have already seen.

Through six centuries, the people of Carthage had been permitted by the mother-city to attend diligently to their commerce, their agriculture, and to

A PHŒNICIAN VESSEL (TRIREME).

the building up of colonies along the southern coast of the Mediterranean, and the advantages of their position soon gave them the greatest importance among the colonies of the Phœnicians. There was Utica, near by, which had existed for near three centuries longer than Carthage, but its situation was not so favorable, and it fell behind. Tunes, now called Tunis, was but ten or fifteen miles away, but it also was of less importance. The commerce of Carthage opened the way for foreign conquest, and so, besides having a sort of sovereignty over all the peoples on the northern coast of Africa, she established colonies on Sardinia, Corsica, Sicily, and other Mediterranean islands, and history does not go back far enough to tell us at how early a date she had obtained peaceable possessions in Spain, from the mines of which she derived a not inconsiderable share of her riches.

Perhaps it may be thought strange that Carthage and Rome had not come into conflict before the time of which we are writing, for the distance between the island of Sicily and the African coast is so small that but a few hours would have been occupied in sailing across. It may be accounted for by the facts that the Carthaginians attended to their own business, and the Romans did not engage to any extent in maritime enterprises. On several occasions, however, Carthage had sent her compliments across to Rome, though Rome does not appear to have reciprocated them to any great degree; and four formal treaties between the cities are reported, B.C. 509, 348, 306, and 279.

It is said that when Pyrrhus, King of Epirus, was about to leave Sicily, he exclaimed: " What a grand arena* this would be for Rome and Carthage to contend upon!" It did not require the wisdom of an

---

* *Arena* in Latin meant "sand," and as the cental portions of the amphitheatres were strewn with sand to absorb the blood of the fighting gladiators and beasts, an arena came to mean, as at present, any open, public place for an exhibition. To the ancients, however, it brought to mind the desperate combats to which the thousands of spectators were wont to pay wrapt attention, and it was a much more vivid word than it now is.

oracle to suggest that such a contest would come at some time, for the rich island lay just between the two cities, apparently ready to be grasped by the more enterprising or the stronger. As Carthage saw the gradual extension of Roman authority over Southern Italy, she realized that erelong the strong arm would reach out too far in the direction of the African continent. She was, accordingly, on her guard, as she needed to be.

At about the time of the beginning of the war with Pyrrhus, a band of soldiers from Campania, which had been brought to Sicily, took possession of the town of Messana, a place on the eastern end of the island not far from the celebrated rocks Scylla and Charybdis, opposite Rhegium. Calling themselves Mamertines, after Mars, one form of whose name was Mamers, these interlopers began to extend their power over the island. In their contests with Hiero, King of Syracuse, they found themselves in need of help. In the emergency there was a fatal division of counsel, one party wishing to call upon Rome and the other thinking best to ask Carthage, which already held the whole of the western half of the island and the northern coast, and had for centuries been aiming at complete possession of the remainder. Owing to this want of united purpose it came about that both cities were appealed to, and it very naturally happened that the fortress of the Mamertines was occupied by a garrison from Carthage before Rome was able to send its army.

The Roman senate had hesitated to send help to the Mamertines because they were people whom they had driven out of Rhegium, as robbers, six years before, with the aid of the same Hiero, of Syracuse, who was now besieging them. However, the people of Rome, not troubled with the honest scruples of the senate, were, under the direction of the consuls, inflamed by the hope of conquest and of the riches that they expected would follow success, and a war which lasted twenty-three years was the result of their reckless greed (B.C. 264).

The result was really decided during the first two years, for the Romans persuaded the Mamertines to expel the Carthaginians from Messana, and then, though besieged by them and by Hiero, drove them both off, and in the year 263 took many Sicilian towns and even advanced to Syracuse. Then Hiero concluded a peace with Rome to which he was faithful to the time of his death, fifty years afterward. The Sicilian city next to Syracuse in importance was Agrigentum, and this the Romans took the next year, thus turning the tables and making themselves instead of the Carthaginians masters of most of the important island, with the exception of Panormus and Mount Eryx, near Drepanum (B.C. 262).

The Carthaginians, being a commercial people, were well supplied with large ships, and the Romans now saw that they, too, must have a navy. Possessing no models on which to build ships of war larger than those with three banks of oars,* they took advantage

---

* The ancient war vessels were moved by both sails and oars; but the oars were the great dependence in a fight. At first there was but one bank of oars; but soon there were two rows of oarsmen, seated one above the other, the uppermost having long oars. After awhile three banks were arranged, then four, now five, and later more, the

of the fact that a Carthaginian vessel of five banks
(a *quinquireme*) was wrecked on their shores, and in
the remarkably short space of time of less than two
months built and launched one hundred and thirty
vessels of that size! They were clumsy, however,
and the crews that manned them were poorly trained,
but, nevertheless, the bold Romans ventured, under
command of Caius Duilius, to attack the enemy off

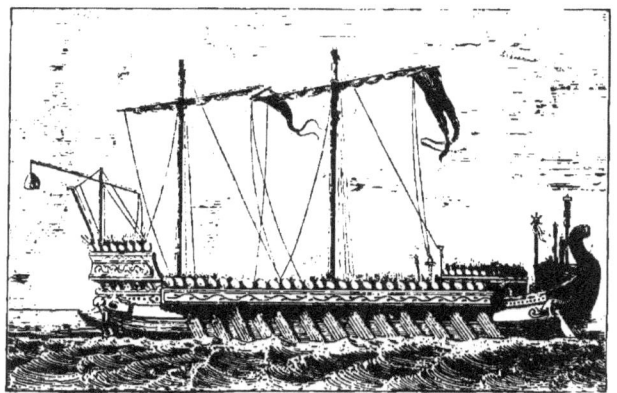

A ROMAN WAR VESSEL.

the Sicilian town of Mylæ, and the Carthaginians
were overwhelmed, what remained of their fleet being forced to seek safety in flight. The naval prestige

uppermost oars being of immense length, and requiring several men
to operate each. We do not now know exactly how so many ranges of
rowers were accommodated, nor how such unwieldly oars were managed. The Athenians tried various kinds of ships, but concluded that
light and active vessels were better than awkward quinquiremes.

of Carthage was destroyed. There was a grand celebration of the victory at Rome, and a column adorned with the ornamental prows of ships was set up in the forum.

For a few years the war was pursued with but little effect; but in the ninth year, when the favorite Marcus Atilius Regulus was consul, it was determined to carry it on with more vigor, to invade Africa with an overwhelming force, and, if possible, close the struggle. Regulus sailed from Economus, not far from Agrigentum, with three hundred and thirty vessels and one hundred thousand men, but his progress was soon interrupted by the Carthaginian fleet, commanded by Hamilcar. After one of the greatest sea-fights of all time, in which the Carthaginians lost nearly a hundred ships and many men, the Romans gained the victory, and found nothing to hinder their progress to the African shore. The enemy hastened with the remainder of their fleet to protect Carthage, and the conflict was transferred to Africa. Regulus prosecuted the war with vigor, and, owing to the incompetence of the generals opposed to him, was successful to an extraordinary degree. Both he and the senate became intoxicated to such an extent, that when the Carthaginians made overtures for peace, only intolerable terms were offered them. This resulted in prolonging the war, for the Carthaginians called to their aid Xanthippus, a Spartan general, who showed them the weakness of their officers, and, finally, when his army had been well drilled, offered battle to Regulus on level ground, where the dreaded African elephants were of service, instead of among the mountains. The Roman army was almost annihilated, and Regulus himself was taken prisoner (B.C. 255).

The Romans saw that to retain a footing in Africa they must first have control of the sea. Though the fleet that brought back the remains of the army of Regulus was destroyed, another of two hundred and twenty ships was made ready in three months, only, however, to meet a similar fate off Cape Palinurus on the coast of Lucania. The Romans, at Panormus (now Palermo), were, in the year 250, attacked by the Carthaginians, over whom they gained a victory which decided the struggle, though it was continued nine years longer, owing to the rich resources of the Carthaginians. After this defeat an embassy was sent to Rome to ask terms of peace. Regulus, who had then been five years a captive, accompanied it, and, it is said, urged the senate not to make terms. He then returned to Carthage and suffered a terrible death. The character given him in the old histories and his horrible fate made Regulus the favorite of orators for ages.

The Romans now determined to push the war vigorously, and began the siege of Lilybæum (now Marsala), which was the only place besides Drepanum, fifteen miles distant, yet remaining to the enemy on the island of Sicily (B.C. 250). It was not until the end of the war that the Carthaginians could be forced from these two strongholds. Six years before that time (B.C. 247), there came to the head of Carthaginian affairs a man of real greatness, Hamilcar Barca, whose last name is said to mean lightning; but even he was not strong enough to overcome the difficulties caused by the faults of others, and in 241 he counselled peace, which was accordingly concluded, though Carthage was obliged to pay an enormous indemnity, and to give up her claim to Sicily, which became a part of the Roman dominion (the first "province" so-called), governed by an officer annually sent from Rome. Hamilcar had at first established himself on Mount Erete, overhanging Panormus, whence he made constant descents upon the enemy, ravaging the coast as far as Mount Ætna. Suddenly he quitted this place and occupied Mount Eryx, another height, overlooking Drepanum, where he supported himself two years longer, and the Romans despaired of dislodging him.

In their extremity, they twice resorted to the navy, and at last, with a fleet of two hundred ships, defeated the Carthaginians off the Ægusæ Islands, to the west of Sicily, and as the resources of Hamilcar were then cut off, it was only a question of time when the armies at Eryx, Drepanum, and Lilybæum would be reduced by famine. It was in view of this fact that the settlement was effected.

A period of peace followed this long war, during which at one time, in the year 235, the gates of the temple of Janus, which were always open during war and had not been shut since the days of Numa, were closed, but it was only for a short space. After this war, the Carthaginians became involved with their own troops, who arose in mutiny because they could not get their pay, and Rome took advantage of this to rob them of the islands of Sardinia and Corsica, and at the same time to demand a large addition to the indemnity fund that had been agreed upon at the peace (B.C. 227). Such arbitrary treatment of a conquered foe could not fail to beget and keep alive the deepest feelings of resentment, of which, in after years, Rome reaped the bitter fruits.

The Adriatic Sea was at that time infested with pirates from Illyria, the country north of Epirus, just over the sea to the east of Italy, and as Roman towns suffered from their inroads, an embassy was sent to make complaint. One of these peaceful messengers was murdered by direction of the queen of the country, Teuta, by name, and of course war was declared, which ended in the overthrow of the treacherous queen. Her successor, however, when he thought that the Romans were too much occupied with other matters to oppose him successfully, renewed the piratical incursions (B.C. 219), and in spite of the other wars this brought out a sufficient force from Rome. The Illyrian sovereign was forced to fly, and all his domain came under the Roman power.

Meantime the Romans had begun to think of the extensive tracts to the north acquired from the Gauls, and in 232 B.C., a law was passed dividing them among the poorer people and the veterans, in the expectation of attracting inhabitants to that part of Italy. The barbarians were alarmed by the prospect of the approach of Roman civilization, and in 225, united to make a new attack upon their old enemies. When it was rumored at Rome that the Gauls were preparing to make a stand and probably intended to invade the territory of their southern neighbors, the terrible days of the Allia were vividly brought to mind and the greatest consternation reigned. The Sibylline or other sacred books were carefully searched for counsel in the emergency, and in obedience to instructions therein found, two Gauls and two Greeks (a man and a woman of each nation) were buried alive in the Forum Boarium,* and the public excitement somewhat allayed in that horrible way. A large army was immediately raised, and sent to meet the Gauls at Ariminum on the Adriatic, but they avoided it by taking a route further to the west. They were met by a reserve force, however, which suffered a great defeat, probably near Clusium. Afterwards the main army effected a junction with another body coming from Pisa, and as the Gauls were attacked on both sides at once, they were annihilated. This battle occurred near Telamon, in Etruria, not far from the mouth of the Umbria. The victory was followed up, and after three years, the whole of the valley of the Po, between the Alps and the Apennines, was made a permanent addition to Roman territory. Powerful colonies were planted at Placentia and Cremona to secure it.

No greater generals come before us in the grand story of Rome than those who are now to appear.

---

* The Forum Boarium, though one of the largest and most celebrated public places in the city, was not a regular market surrounded with walls, but an irregular space bounded by the Tiber on the west, and the Palatine Hill and the Circus Maximus on the east. The Cloaca Maxima ran beneath it, and it was rich in temples and monuments. On it the first gladiatorial exhibition occurred, B.C. 264, and there too, other burials of living persons had been made, in spite of the long-ago abolishment of such rites by Numa.

One was born while the first Punic war was still raging, and the other in the year 235, when the gates of the temple of Janus were, for the first time in

HANNIBAL.

centuries, closed in token that Rome was at peace with the world. Hannibal, the elder of the two was son of Hamilcar Barca, and inherited his father's hatred of Rome, to which, indeed, he had been bound by a solemn oath, willingly sworn upon the altar at the dictation of his father.

When Livy began his story of the second war between Rome and Carthage, he said that he was about to relate the most memorable of all wars that ever were waged; and though we may not express ourselves in such general terms, it is safe to say that no struggle recorded in the annals of antiquity, or of the middle age, surpasses it in importance or in historical interest. The war was to decide whether the conqueror of the world was to be self-centred Rome; or whether it should be a nation of traders, commanded by a powerful general who dictated to them their policy,—a nation not adapted to unite the different peoples in bonds of sympathy,—one whose success would, in the words of Dr. Arnold, "have stopped the progress of the world."

Hannibal stands out among the famed generals of history as one of the very greatest. We must remember that we have no records of his own countrymen to show how he was estimated among them; but we know that though he was poorly supported by the powers at home, he was able to keep together an army of great size, by the force of his own personality, and to wage a disastrous war against the strongest people of his age, far from his base of supplies, in the midst of the enemy's country. It has well been said that the greatest masters of the art of war, from Scipio to Napoleon, have concurred in homage to his genius.

The other hero, and the successful one, in the great struggle, was Publius Cornelius Scipio, who was born in that year when the temple of Janus was closed, of a family that for a series of generations had been noted in Roman history, and was to continue illustrious for generations to come.

Another among the many men of note who came into prominence during the second war with Carthage was Quintus Fabius Maximus, a descendant of that Rullus who in the Sabine wars brought the names Fabius and Maximus into prominence. His life is given by Plutarch under the name Fabius, and he is remembered as the originator of the policy of delay in war, as our dictionaries tell us, because his plan was to worry his enemy, rather than risk a pitched battle with him. On this account the Romans called him *Cunctator*, which meant delayer, or one who is slow though safe, not rash. He was called also *Ovicula*, or the lamb, on account of his mild temper, and *Verrucosus*, because he had a wart on his upper lip (*Verruca*, a wart).

The second Punic war was not so much a struggle between Carthage and Rome, as a war entered into by Hannibal and carried on by him against the Roman republic in spite of the opposition of his own people; and this fact makes the strength of his character appear in the strongest light. Just at the close of the first war, the Carthaginians had established in Spain a city which took the name of New Carthage—that is, New New City,—and had extended their dominion over much of that country, as well as over most of the territory on the south shore of the Mediterranean Sea. Hannibal laid seige to the independent city of Saguntum, on the northeast of

New Carthage, and, after several months of desperate resistance, took it, thus throwing down the gauntlet to Rome and completing the dominion of Carthage in that region (B.C. 218). Rome sent ambassadors to Carthage, to ask reparation and the surrender of Hannibal: but "War!" was the only response, and for seventeen years a struggle of the most determined sort was carried on by Hannibal and the Roman armies.

After wintering at New Carthage, Hannibal started for Italy with a great army. He crossed the Pyrenees, went up the valley of the Rhone, and then up the valley of the Isère, and most probably crossed the Alps by the Little St. Bernard pass. It was an enterprise of the greatest magnitude to take an army of this size through a hostile country, over high mountains, in an inclement season; but no difficulty daunted this general. In five months he found himself in the valley of the Duria (modern Dora Baltea), in Northern Italy, with a force of twenty thousand foot and six thousand cavalry (the remains of the army of ninety-four thousand that had left New Carthage), with which he expected to conquer a country that counted its soldiers by the hundred thousand. The father of the great Scipio met Hannibal in the plains west of the Ticinus, and was routed, retreating to the west bank of the Trebia, where the Romans, with a larger force, were again defeated, though the December cold caused the invading army great suffering and killed all the elephants but one. The success of the Carthaginians led the Gauls to flock to their standard, and Hanni-

TERENCE, THE LAST ROMAN COMIC POET.

bal found himself able to push forward with increasing vigor.

Taking the route toward the capital, he met the Romans at Lake Trasimenus, and totally routed them, killing the commander, Caius Flaminius, who had come from Arretium to oppose him. The defeat was accounted for by the Romans by the fact that Flaminius, always careless about his religious observances, had broken camp at Ariminum, whence he had come to Arretium, though the signs had been against him, and had also previously neglected the usual solemnities upon his election as consul before going to Ariminum. The policy of Hannibal was to make friends of the allies of Rome, in order to attract them to his support, and after his successes he carefully tended the wounded and sent the others away, often with presents. He hoped to undermine Rome by taking away her allies, and after this great success he did not march to the capital, though he was distant less than a hundred miles from it, because he expected to see tokens that his policy was a success.

The dismay that fell upon Rome when it was known that her armies had twice been routed, can better be imagined than described. The senate came together, and for two days carefully considered the critical state of affairs. They decided that it was necessary to appoint a dictator, and Fabius Maximus was chosen. Hannibal in the meantime continued to avoid Rome, and to march through the regions on the Adriatic, hoping to arouse the inhabitants to his support. In vain were his efforts. Even the Gauls seemed now to have forgotten him, and Carthage itself did not send him aid. Fabius strove to keep to the high lands, where it was impossible for Hannibal to attack him, while he harassed him or tried to shut him up in some defile.

In the spring of the year 216, both parties were prepared for a more terrible struggle than had yet been seen. The Romans put their forces under one Varro, a business man, who was considered the champion of popular liberty. The armies met on the field of Cannæ, on the banks of the river Aufidus which enters the Adriatic, and there the practical man was defeated with tremendous slaughter, though he was able himself to escape toward the mountains to Venusia, and again to return to Canusium. There he served the state so well that his defeat was almost forgotten, and he was actually thanked by the senate for his skill in protecting the remnant of the wasted army.

The people now felt that the end of the republic had come, but still they would not listen to Hannibal when he sent messengers to ask terms of peace. They were probably surprised when, instead of marching upon their capital, the Carthaginian remained in comparative inactivity, in pursuance of his former policy. He was not entirely disappointed this time, in expecting that his brilliant victory would lead some of the surrounding nations to declare in his favor, for finally the rich city of Capua, which considered itself equal to Rome, opened to him its gates, and he promised to make it the capital of Italy (B.C. 216). With Capua went the most of Southern

Italy, and Hannibal thought that the war would soon end after such victories, but he was mistaken.

Two other sources of help gave him hope, but at last failed him. Philip V., one of the ablest monarchs of Macedon, who had made a treaty with Hannibal after the battle of Cannæ, tried to create a diversion in his favor on the other side of the Adriatic, but his schemes were not energetically pressed, and failed. Again, a new king of Syracuse, who had followed Hiero, offered direct assistance, but he, too, was overcome, and his strong and wealthy city taken with terrible carnage, though the scientific skill of the famous Archimedes long enabled its ruler to baffle the Roman generals (B.C. 212). The Romans overran the Spanish peninsula, too, and though they were for a time brought to a stand, in the year 210 the state of affairs changed. A young man of promise, who had, however, never been tried in positions of great trust, was sent out. It was the great Scipio, who has been already mentioned. He captured New Carthage, made himself master of Spain, and was ready by the year 207 to take the last step, as he thought it would be, by carrying the war into Africa, and thus obliging Hannibal to withdraw from Italy.

At home, the aged Fabius was meantime the trusted leader in public counsels, and by his careful generalship Campania had been regained. Capua, too, had been recaptured, though that enterprise had been undertaken in spite of his cautious advice. Hannibal was thus obliged to withdraw to Lower Italy, after he had threatened Rome by marching boldly up to its very gates. The Samnites and

Lucanians submitted, and Tarentum fell into the hands of Fabius, whose active career then closed. He had opposed the more aggressive measures of Scipio which were to lead to success, but we can hardly think that the old commander was led to do this

PUBLIUS CORNELIUS SCIPIO AFRICANUS.

because, seeing that victory was to be the result, he envied the younger soldier who was to achieve the final laurels, though Plutarch mentions that sinister motive. The career of Fabius, which had opened at the battle of Cannæ, and had been successful ever since, culminated in his triumph after the fall of Tarentum, which occurred in B.C. 209.

Now the Carthaginian army in Spain, under command of Hasdrubal, made an effort to go to the help of Hannibal, and, taking the same route by the Little St. Bernard pass, arrived in Italy (B.C. 208) almost before the enemy was aware of its intention. Hannibal, on his part, began to march northward from his southern position, and after gaining some unimportant victories, arrived at Canusium, where he stopped to wait for his brother. The Romans, however, managed to intercept the dispatches of Hasdrubal, and marched against him, in the spring of 207, after he had wasted much time in unsuccessfully besieging Placentia. The two armies met on the banks of the river Metaurus. The Carthaginians were defeated with terrible slaughter, and the Romans felt that the calamity of Cannæ was avenged. Hasdrubal's head was sent to his brother, who exclaimed at the sight: "I recognize the doom of Carthage!"

For four years Hannibal kept his army among the mountains of Southern Italy, feeling that his effort at conquering Rome had failed. Meantime Scipio was making arrangements to carry out his favorite project, though in face of much opposition from Fabius and from the senate, which followed his lead. The people were, however, with Scipio, and though he was not able to make such complete preparations as he wished, by the year 204 he had made ready to set out from Lilybæum for Africa. At Utica he was joined by his allies, and, in 203, defeated the

Carthaginians and caused them to look anxiously across the sea toward their absent general for help. Pretending to desire peace, they took advantage of the time gained by negotiations to send for Hannibal, who reached Africa before the year closed, after an absence of fifteen years, and took up his position at Hadruméntum, where he looked over the field and sadly determined to ask for terms of peace. Scipio was desirous of the glory of closing the long struggle, and refused to make terms, thus forcing Hannibal to continue the war. The Romans went about ravaging the country until, at last, a pitched battle was brought about at a place near Zama, in which, though Hannibal managed his army with his usual skill, he was overcome and utterly routed. He now again advised peace, and accepted less favorable terms than had been before offered. Henceforth Carthage was to pay an annual war-contribution to Rome, and was not to enter upon war with any nation in Africa, or anywhere else, without the consent of her conquerors. Scipio returned to Rome in the year 201, and enjoyed a magnificent triumph, the name Africanus being at the same time added to his patronymic. Other honors were offered him, but the most extraordinary of them he declined to accept.

Hannibal, though overcome, stands forth as the greatest general. At the age of forty-five he now found himself defeated in the proud plans of his youth; but, with manly strength, he refused to be cast down, and set about work for the improvement of his depressed city. It was not long before he aroused the opposition which has often come to public benefactors, and was obliged to flee from Carthage. From that time, he was a wanderer on the earth. Ever true to his hatred of Rome, however, he continued to plot for her downfall even in his exile. He went to Tyre and then to Ephesus, and tried to lead the Syrian monarch Antiochus to make successful inroads upon his old enemy. Obliged to flee in turn from Ephesus, he sought an asylum at the court of Prusias, King of Bithynia. At last, seeing that he was in danger of being delivered up to the Romans, in despair he took his own life at Libyssa, in the year 182 or 181. Thus ignominiously ended the career of the man who stood once at the head of the commanders of the world, and whose memory is still honored for the magnificence of his ambition in daring to attack and expecting to conquer the most powerful nation of his time.

XI.

THE NEW PUSHES THE OLD—WARS AND CONQUESTS.

THERE were days of tumult in Rome in the year 195, which illustrate the temper of the times, and show how the city and the people had changed, and were changing, under the influence of two opposite forces. A vivid picture of the scenes around the Capitol at the time has been preserved. Men were hastening to the meeting of the magistrates from every direction. The streets were crowded, and not with men chiefly, for something which interested the matrons seemed to be uppermost, and women were thronging in the same direction, in spite of custom, which would have kept them at home; in spite even of the commands of many of their husbands, who were opposed to their frequenting public assemblies. Not only on one day did the women pour out into all the avenues leading to the forum, but once and again they thrust themselves into the presence of the law-makers. Nor were they content to stand or sit in quiet while their husbands and brothers argued and made eloquent speeches; they actually solicited the votes of the stronger sex in behalf of a motion that was evidently very important in their minds.

Of old time, the Romans had thought that women

should keep at home, and that in the transaction of private business even they should be under the direction of their parents, brothers, or husbands. What had wrought so great a change that on these days the Roman matrons not only ventured into the forum, but actually engaged in public business, and that, as has been said, in many instances, in opposition to those parents, brothers, and husbands who were in those old times their natural directors? We shall find the reason by going back to the days when the cost of the Punic wars bore heavily upon the state. It was then that a law was passed that no woman should wear any garment of divers colors, nor own more gold than a half-ounce in weight, nor ride through the streets of a city in a carriage drawn by horses, nor in any place nearer than a mile to a town, except for the purpose of engaging in a public religious solemnity. The spirited matrons of Rome were ever ready to bear their share of the public burdens, and though some thought this oppressive, but few murmurs escaped them as they read the Oppian law, as it was called, when it was passed, for the days were dark, and the shadow of the defeat at Cannæ was bowing down all hearts, and their brothers and parents and husbands were trembling, strong men that they were, at the threatening situation of the state. Now, however, the condition of affairs had changed. The conquests of the past few years had brought large wealth into the city, and was it to be expected that women should not wish to adorn themselves, as of yore, with gold and garments of richness?

A ROMAN MATRON.

When now the repeal of the law was to be discussed, the excitement became so intense that people forgot that Spain was in a state of insurrection, and that war threatened on every side. Women thronged to the city from towns and villages, and even dared, as has been said, to approach the consuls and other magistrates to solicit their votes. Marcus Porcius Cato, a young man of about forty years, who had been brought up on a farm, and looked with the greatest respect upon the virtue of the olden times, before Grecian influences had crept in to soften and refine the hard Roman character, represented the party of conservatism. Now, thought he, is an opportunity for me to stand against the corrupting influence of Magna Græcia. He therefore rose and made a long speech in opposition to the petition of the matrons. He thought they had become thus contumacious, he said, because the men had not individually exercised their rightful authority over their own wives. "The privileges of men are now spurned, trodden under foot," he exclaimed, "and we, who have shown that we are unable to stand against the women separately, are now utterly powerless against them as a body. Their behavior is outrageous. I was filled with painful emotions of shame as I just now made my way into the forum through the midst of a body of women. Will you consent to give the reins to their intractable nature and their uncontrolled passions? The moment they had arrived at equality with you, they will have become your superiors. What motive that common decency will allow is pretended for this female insurrection? Why, that they may shine in gold and purple; that they may ride through our city in chariots triumphing over abrogated law; that there may be no bounds to waste and luxury! So soon as the law shall cease to limit the expenses of the wife, the husband will be powerless to set bounds to them." As the uttermost measure of the abasement to which the women had descended, Cato declared with indignation that they had solicited votes, and he concluded by saying that though he called upon the gods to prosper whatever action should be agreed upon, he thought that on no account should the Oppian law be set aside.

When Cato had finished, one of the plebeian tribunes, Lucius Valerius, replied to him sarcastically, saying that in spite of the mild disposition of the speaker who had just concluded, he had uttered some severe things against the matrons, though he had not argued very efficiently against the measure they supported. He referred his hearers to a book of Cato's,* called *Origines*, or "Antiquities," in which it was made clear that in the old times women had appeared in public, and with good effect too. "Who rushed into the forum in the days of Romulus, and stopped the fight with the Sabines?" he asked. "Who went out and turned back the army of the great Coriolanus? Who brought their gold and jewels into the forum when the Gauls demanded a great ransom for the city? Who went out to the sea-shore during the late war to receive the Idæan

* Livy is authority for this statement, but it has been doubted if Cato's book had been written at the time.

mother (Cybele) when new gods were invited hither to relieve our distresses? Who poured out their riches to supply a depleted treasury during that same war, now so fresh in memory? Was it not the Roman matrons? Masters do not disdain to listen to the prayers of their slaves, and we are asked, forsooth, to shut our ears to the petitions of our wives!

"I have shown that women have now done no new thing. I will go on and prove that they ask no unreasonable thing. It is true that good laws should not be rashly repealed; but we must not forget that Rome existed for centuries without this one, and that Roman matrons established their high character, about which Cato is so solicitous, during that period, the return of which he now seems to think would be subversive of every thing good. This law served well in a time of trial; but that has passed, and we are enjoying the return of plenty. Shall our matrons be the only ones who may not feel the improvement that has followed a successful war? Shall our children, and we ourselves, wear purple, and shall it be interdicted to our wives? Elegances of appearance and ornaments and dress are the women's badges of distinction; in them they delight and glory, and our ancestors called them the women's world. Still, they desire to be under control of those who are bound to them by the bonds of love, not by stern law, in these matters. The consul just now used invidious terms, calling this a female 'secession,' as though our matrons were about to seize the Sacred Mount or the Aventine, as the

ROMAN HEAD-DRESSES.

plebeians did of yore; but their feeble nature is incapable of such a thing. They must necessarily submit to what you think proper, and the greater your power the more moderation should you use in exercising it." Thus, day after day, the men spoke and the women poured out to protest, until even stern and inflexible Cato gave way, and women were declared free from the restrictions of the Oppian law.

Cato and Scipio represented the two forces that were at this time working in society, the one opposing the entrance of the Grecian influence, and the other encouraging the refinement in manners and modes of living that came with it, even encouraging ostentation and the lavish use of money for pleasures. When Scipio was making his arrangements to go to Africa, he was governor of Sicily, and lived in luxury. Cato, then but thirty years old, had been sent to Sicily to investigate his proceedings, and act as a check upon him; but Scipio seems to have been little influenced by the young reformer, telling him that he would render accounts of his *actions*, not of the money he spent. Upon this Cato returned to Rome, and denounced Scipio's prodigality, his love of Greek literature and art, his magnificence, and his persistence in wasting in the gymnasium or in the pursuit of literature time which should have been used in training his troops. Joining Fabius, he urged that an investigating committee be sent to look into the matter, but it returned simply astonished at the efficient condition of the army, and orders were given for prompt advance upon Carthage.

GLADIATORS AT A FUNERAL.

The influences coming from Greece at this time were not all the best, for that land was in its period of decadence, and Cato did well in trying to protect his countrymen from evil. While literature in Greece had reached its highest and had become corrupt, there had been none in Rome during the five centuries of its history. All this time, too, there had been but one public holiday and a single circus; but during the interval between the first and second Punic wars a demagogue had instituted a second circus and a new festival, called the plebeian games. Other festivals followed, and in time their cost became exceedingly great, and their influence very bad. Fights of gladiators were introduced just at the outbreak of the first Punic war, on the occasion of the funeral of D. Junius Brutus, and were given afterward on such occasions, because it was believed that the manes, the spirits of the departed, loved blood. Persons began to leave money for this purpose in their wills, and by degrees a fondness for the frightful sport increased, for the Romans had no leaning towards the ideal, and delighted only in those pursuits which appealed to their coarse, strong, and, in its way, pious nature. Humor and comedy with them became burlesque, sometimes repulsive in its grotesqueness. Dramatic art grew up during this period. We have seen that dramatic exhibitions were introduced in the year 363, from Etruria, at a time of pestilence, but they were mere pantomimes. Now plays began to be written. Trustworthy history begins at the time of the Punic wars, and the annals of Fabius Pictor commence with the year 216, after the battle of Cannæ.

Rome itself was changed by the increased wealth of these times. The streets were made wider; temples were multiplied; and aqueducts were built to bring water from distant sources; the same Appius who constructed the great road which now bears his name, having built the first, which, however, disappeared long ago. Another, forty-three miles in length, was paid for out of the spoils of the war with Pyrrhus, and portions of it still remain. With the increase of wealth and luxury came also improvement in language and in its use, and in the year 254, studies in law were formally begun in a school established for the purpose.

ACTORS' MASKS.

The Romans had conquered Italy and Carthage, and the next step was to make them masters of the East. Philip V., King of Macedon, was, as we have seen, one of the most eminent of monarchs of that country. His treaty with Hannibal after the battle of Cannæ, involved him in war with the Romans, which continued, with intermissions, until Scipio was about to go over into Africa. Then the Romans were glad to make peace, though no considerable results followed the struggle, and it had indeed been pursued with little vigor for much of the time. By the year 200, Philip had been able to establish himself in Greece, and the Romans were somewhat rested from the war with Carthage. The peace of 205 had been considered but a cessation of hostilities, and both people were therefore ready for a new war. There were pretexts enough. Philip had made an alliance with Antiochus the Great, of Syria, against Ptolemy Epiphanes, of Egypt, who applied to Rome for assistance; and he had sent aid to soldiers to help Hannibal, who had fought at the battle of Zama. Besides this he had attempted to establish his supremacy in the Ægean Sea at the expense of the people of Rhodes, allies of Rome, who were assisted by Attalus, King of Pergamus, likewise in league with Rome.

The senate proposed that war should be declared against Philip, but the people longed for rest after their previous struggles, and were only persuaded to consent by being told that if Philip, then at the pitch of his greatness, were not checked, he would follow the example of Hannibal, as he had been urged to follow that of Pyrrhus. No great progress was made in the war until the command of the Roman army in Greece was taken by a young man of high family and noble nature, well acquainted with Greek culture, in the year 197. Flamininus, for this was the name of the new commander, met the army of Philip that year on a certain morning when, after a rain, thick clouds darkened the plain on which they were. The armies were separated by low hills known as the Dog-heads (Cynocephalæ), and when at last the sun burst out it showed the Romans and Macedonians struggling on the uneven ground with varying success. The Macedonians were finally defeated, with the loss of eight thousand slain and five thousand prisoners. In 196 peace was obtained by Philip, who agreed to withdraw from Greece, to give up his fleet, and to pay a thousand talents for the expenses of the war.

At the Isthmian games, the following summer, Flamininus caused a trumpet to command silence, and a crier to proclaim that the Roman senate and he, the proconsular general, having vanquished Philip, restored to the Grecians their lands, laws, and liberties, remitting all impositions upon them and withdrawing all garrisons. So astonished were the people at the good news that they could scarcely believe it, and asked that it might be repeated. This the crier did, and a shout rose from the people (who all stood up) that was heard from Corinth to the sea, and there was no further thought of the entertainment that usually engrossed so much attention. Plutarch says gravely that the disruption of the air was so great that crows accidentally flying over the race-course at the moment fell down dead into it! Night only caused the people to leave the circus, and then they went home to carouse together. So grateful were they that they freed the Romans who had been captured by Hannibal and had been sold to them, and when Flamininus returned to Rome with a reputation second only, in the popular esteem, to Scipio Africanus, these freed slaves followed in the procession on the occasion of his triumph, which was one of the most magnificent, and lasted three days.

Scarcely had Flamininus left Greece before the Ætolians, who claimed that the victory at Cynocephalæ was chiefly due to their prowess, made a combination against the Romans, and engaged Antiochus to take their part. This monarch had occupied Asia Minor previously, and would have passed into Greece but for Flamininus. This was while Hannibal was at the court of Antiochus. The Romans declared war, and sent an army into Thessaly, which overcame the Syrians at the celebrated pass of Thermopylæ, on the spot where Leonidas and his brave three hundred had been slaughtered by the Persians two hundred and eighty-nine years before (B.C. 191). Lucius Cornelius Scipio, brother of Africanus, closed the war by defeating Antiochus at Magnesia, in Asia Minor, at the foot of Mount Sipylus (B.C. 190). The Syrian monarch is said to have lost fifty-three thousand men, while but four hundred of the Romans fell. Antiochus resigned to the Romans all of Asia west of the Taurus mountains, agreed to pay them fifteen thousand talents, and to surrender Hannibal. The great Carthaginian, however, escaped to the court of Prusias, King of Bithynia, where, as we have already seen, he took his own life. Scipio carried immense booty to Rome, where he celebrated a splendid triumph, and, in imitation of his brother Africanus, added the name Asiaticus to his others.

The succeeding year, the Ætolians were severely punished, their land was ravaged, and they were required to accept peace upon humiliating terms. Never again were they to make war without the consent of Rome, whose supremacy they acknowledged, and to which they paid an indemnity of five hundred talents. At this time the most famous hero of later

Grecian history comes before us indirectly, just as the greatness of his country was sinking from sight forever. Philopœmen, who was born at Megalopolis in Arcadia (not far from the spot from which old Evander started for Italy), during the first Punic war, just before Hamilcar appeared upon the scene, raised himself to fame, first by improving the armor and drill of the Achæan soldiers, when he became chief of the ancient league, and then by his prowess at the battle of Mantinea, in the year 207, when Sparta was defeated. He revived the ancient league, which had been dormant during the Macedonian supremacy; but in 188, he took fierce revenge upon Sparta, for which he was called to account by the Romans; and five years later, in 183, he fell into the hands of the Messenians, who had broken from the league, and was put to death by poison. It was in the same year that both Hannibal and Scipio, the two other great soldiers of the day died.*

Philip V. of Macedon followed these warriors to the grave five years later, after having begun to prepare to renew the war with Rome. His son Perseus continued these preparations, but war did not actually break out until 171, and then it was continued for three years without decisive result. In 168 the Romans met the army of Perseus at Pydna, in Macedonia, north of Mount Olympus, on the 22d June,† and utterly defeated it. Perseus was

* See the Student's Merivale, ch. xxv., for remarks about these three warriors.

† This date is proved by an eclipse of the sun which occurred at the time. It had been foretold by a scientific Roman so that the army should not see in it a bad omen.

afterward taken prisoner and died at Alba. From the battle of Pydna the great historian Polybius, who was a native of Megalopolis, dates the complete establishment of the universal empire of Rome, since after that no civilized state ever confronted her on an equal footing, and all the struggles in which she engaged were rebellions or wars with "barbarians" outside of the influence of Greek or Roman civilization, and since all the world recognized the senate as the tribunal of last resort in differences between nations; the acquisition of Roman language and manners being henceforth among the necessary accomplishments of princes. Rome had never before seen so grand a triumph as that celebrated by Æmilius Paulus, the conqueror of Macedonia, after his return. Plutarch gives an elaborate account of it.

In pursuance of its policy of conquest a thousand of the noblest citizens of Achæa were sent to Italy to meet charges preferred against them. Among them was the historian Polybius, who became well acquainted with Scipio Æmilianus, son by adoption of a son of the conqueror of Hannibal. For seventeen years these exiles were detained, their numbers constantly decreasing, until at last even the severe Cato was led to intercede for them and they were returned to their homes. Exasperated by their treatment they were ready for any desperate enterprise against their conquerors, but Polybius endeavored to restrain them. The historian went to Carthage, however, and while he was away disputes were stirred up which gave Rome an excuse for interfering. Corinth was taken with circumstances of barbarous cruelty, and plundered of its priceless works of art, the rough and ignorant Roman commander sending them to Italy, after making the contractors agree to replace any that might be lost with others of equal value! With Corinth fell the liberties of Greece; a Roman province took the place of the state that for six centuries had been the home of art and eloquence, the intellectual sovereign of antiquity; but though overcome and despoiled she became the guide and teacher of her conqueror.

When Carthage had regained some of its lost riches and population, Rome again became jealous of her former rival, and Cato gave voice to the feeling that she ought to be destroyed. One day in the senate he drew from his toga a bunch of early figs, and, throwing them on the floor, exclaimed: "Those figs were gathered but three days ago in Carthage; so close is our enemy to our walls!" After that, whenever he expressed himself on this subject, or any other, in the senate, he closed with the words "*Delenda est Carthago*,"—"Carthage ought to be destroyed!" Internal struggles gave Rome at last an opportunity to interfere, and in 149 a third Punic war was begun, which closed in 146 with the utter destruction of Carthage. The city was taken by assault, the inhabitants fighting with desperation from street to street. Scipio Æmilianus, who commanded in this war, was now called also Africanus, like his ancestor by adoption.

For years the tranquillity of Spain, which lasted from 179 to 153, had been disturbed by wars, and it was not until Scipio was sent thither that peace was restored. That warrior first put his forces into an effective condition, and then laid seige to the city of Numantia, situated on an elevation and well fortified. The citizens defended themselves with the greatest bravery, and showed wonderful endurance, but were at last obliged to surrender, and the town was levelled to the ground, most of the inhabitants being sold as slaves.

The great increase in slaves, and the devastation caused by long and exhaustive wars, had brought about in Sicily a servile insurrection, before the Numantians had been conquered. It is said that the number of those combined against their Roman masters reached the sum of two hundred thousand. In 132, the strongholds of the insurgents were captured by a consular army, and peace restored. The barbarism of Roman slavery had nowhere reached such extremes as in Sicily. Freedmen who had cultivated the fields were there replaced by slaves, who were ill-fed and poorly cared for. Some worked in chains, and all were treated with indescribable brutality. They finally became bandits in despair, and efforts at repression of their disorders led to the open and fearful war. The same year that this war ended, the last king of Pergamos died, leaving his kingdom and treasures to the Roman people, as he had no children, and Pergamos became the "province" of Asia. Besides this, Rome had the provinces of Sicily, Sardinia and Corsica, Spain, Gallia Cisalpina, Macedonia, Illyricum, Southern Greece (Achæa), and Africa, to which was soon to be added the southern portion of Gaul over the Alps, between those mountains and the Pyrenees called *Provincia Gallia* (Provence).

XII.

A FUTILE EFFORT AT REFORM.

ONE day when the conqueror of Carthage, Scipio Africanus, was feasting with other senators at the Capitol, the veteran patrician was asked by the friends about him to give his daughter Cornelia to a young man of the plebeian family of Sempronia, Tiberius Gracchus by name. This young man was then about twenty-five years old; he had travelled and fought in different parts of the world, and had obtained a high reputation for manliness. Just at this time he had put Africanus under obligations to him by defending him from attacks in public life, and the old commander readily agreed to the request of his friends. When he returned to his home and told his wife that he had given away their daughter, she upbraided him for his rashness; but when she heard the name of the fortunate man, she said that Gracchus was the only person worthy of the gift. The mother's opinion proved to be correct. The young people lived together in happiness, and Cornelia became the mother of three children, who carried down the good traits of their parents. One of these was a daughter named, like her mother, Cornelia, who became the wife of Scipio Africanus the younger, and the others were her two brothers, Tiberius and Caius, who are known as *the* Gracchi. Tiberius Gracchus lived to be over fifty years old, and won still greater laurels in war and peace at home and in foreign lands. Cicero says that he did a great service to the state by gathering together on the Esquiline the freedmen who had spread themselves throughout the tribes, and restricting their franchise (B.C. 169). Thus, Cicero thought, he succeeded for a time in checking the ruin of the republic.*

There was sad need of some movement to correct abuses that had grown up in Rome, and the men destined to stand forth as reformers were the two Gracchi, sons of Cornelia and Tiberius. Their father did not live to complete their education, but their mother, though courted by great men, and by at least one king, refused to marry again, and gave up her time to educating her sons, whom she proudly called her "jewels" when the Roman matrons, relieved from the restrictions of the Oppian law, boastfully showed her the rich ornaments of gold and precious stones that they adorned themselves with. The brothers had eminent Greeks to give them instruction, and grew up wise, able and eloquent, though each exhibited his wisdom and ability in a different way.

Tiberius, who was nine years older than his brother, came first into public life. He went to Africa with his brother-in-law, when the younger Africanus completed the destruction of Carthage, and afterward he took part in the wars in Spain. It

---

* The freedmen had been confined to the four city tribes in 220 B.C.

is said that, as he went through Etruria on his way to Spain, he noticed that the fields were cultivated by foreign slaves, working in clanking chains, instead of by freemen; and that because the rich had taken possession of great ranges of territory, the poor Romans had not even a clod to call their own, though they had fought the battles by which the land had been made secure. The sight of so much distress in a fertile country lying waste affected Tiberius very deeply, and when he returned to Rome, he bethought himself that it was in opposition to law that the rich controlled such vast estates. He remembered that the Licinian Rogation, which became a law more than two hundred years before this time, forbade any man having such large tracts in his possession, and thought that so beneficent a law should continue to be respected. He told the people of Rome that the wild beasts had their dens and caves, while the men who had fought and exposed their lives for Italy enjoyed in it nothing more than light and air, and were obliged to wander about with their wives and little ones, their commanders mocking them by calling upon them to fight " for their tombs and the temples of their gods,"—things that they never possessed nor could hope to have any interest in. "Not one among many, many Romans," said he, "has a family altar or an ancestral tomb. They have fought to maintain the luxury of the great, and they are called in bitter irony the 'masters of the world,' while they do not possess a clod of earth that they may call their own!"

It was a noble patriotism that filled the heart of Tiberius, but it was not easy to carry out a reform like the one he contemplated. It may not have appeared difficult to re-enact the old law, but we must remember that, during two centuries of its neglect, generations of men had peaceably possessed the great estates, of which its enforcement would deprive them all at once. Was it to be supposed that they would quietly permit this to be done? Was it just to deprive men of possessions that they had received from their parents and grandparents without protest on the part of the nation? Cornelia urged Tiberius to do some great work for the state, telling him that she was called the "daughter of Scipio," while she wished to be known as the "mother of the Gracchi." The war in Sicily emphasized the troubles that Tiberius wished to put an end to, and in the midst of it he was elected one of the tribunes, the people hoping something from him, and putting up placards all over the city calling upon him to take their part.

The people seemed to feel sure that Gracchus was intending to do something for them, and they eagerly came together and voted for him, and when he was elected, they crowded into the city from all the regions about to vote in favor of the re-establishment of the Licinian laws, with some alterations. They were successful, much to the disgust of the aristocrats,* who hated Gracchus, and thenceforth

---

* Aristocrat is a word of Greek origin, and means one of a governing body composed of the best men (*aristos*, best) in the state. The aristocrats came to be called also *optimātēs*, from *optimus*, the corresponding Latin word for best.

plotted to overthrow him and his power. For a while, the lands that had been wrongfully occupied by the rich were taken by a commission and returned to the government.

When Attalus, the erratic king of Pergamus, left his estates to Rome, Gracchus had an opportunity to perform an act of justice, by refunding to the rich the outlays they had made on the lands of which they had been deprived. This would have been politic as well as just, but Gracchus did not see his opportunity. He proposed, on the other hand, to divide the new wealth among the plebeians, to enable them to buy implements and cattle for the estates they had acquired.

It was easy at that excited time to make false accusations against public men, and to cause the populace to act upon them, and, accordingly, the aristocrats now stirred up the people to believe that Gracchus was aspiring to the power of king, which, they were reminded, had been forever abolished ages before. No opportunity was given him to explain his intentions. A great mob was raised and a street fight precipitated, in the midst of which three hundred persons were killed with sticks and stones and pieces of benches. Among them was Gracchus himself, who thus died a martyr to his patriotic plans for the Roman republic.*

* The course of Gracchus was not understood at the time by all good citizens ; and even for ages after he was considered a designing demagogue. It was not until the great Niebuhr, to whom we owe so much in Roman history, explained fully the nature of the agrarian laws which Gracchus passed, that the world accepted him for the hero and honest patriot that he was.

Caius Gracchus was in Spain at the time of his brother's murder, and Scipio, his brother-in-law, was there also. So little did Scipio understand Tiberius, that when he heard of his death he quoted the words of Minerva to Mercury, which he remembered to have read in his Homer, "So perish he who doth the same again!" The next year brother and brother-in-law returned from Spain, but Caius did not seem to care to enter political life, and as he lived in quiet for some years, it was thought that he disapproved his brother's laws. Little did the public dream of what was to come.

Meantime Scipio became the acknowledged leader of the optimates, and in order to keep the obnoxious law from being enforced, proposed to take it out of the hands of the commission and give it to the senate. His proposition was vigorously opposed in the forum, and when he retired to his home to prepare a speech to be delivered on the subject, a number of friends thought it necessary to accompany him as protectors. The next morning the city was startled by the news that he was dead. His speech was never even composed. No effort was made to discover his murderer, though one Caius Papirius Carbo, a tribune, leader of the opposing party, was generally thought to have been the guilty one.

The eloquence of young Gracchus proved greater than that of any other citizen, and by it he ingratiated himself with the people to such an extent, that in the year 123 B.C. they elected him one of their tribunes. Though the aristocrats managed to have his name placed fourth on the list, his force and eloquence made him really first in all public labors, and he proceeded to use his influence to further his brother's favorite projects. He was impetuous in his oratory. As he spoke, he walked from side to side of the rostra, and pulled his toga from his shoulder as he became warm in his delivery. His powerful voice filled the forum, and stirred the hearts of his hearers, who felt that his persuasive words came from an honest heart.

The optimates were of course offended by the acts of the new tribune, who abridged the power of the senate, and in all ways showed an intention of working for the people. He was exceedingly active in works of public benefit, building roads and bridges, erecting mile-stones along the principal routes, extending to the Italians the right to vote, and alleviating the distressing poverty of the lower orders by directing that grain should be sold to them at low rates.

A ROMAN MILE-STONE.

The laws under which he accomplished these beneficent changes are known, from the family to which the Gracchi belonged, as the Sempronian Laws. In carrying out the necessary legislation and in executing the laws, Caius labored himself with great assiduity, and his activity afforded his enemies the opportunity to say falsely that he made some private gain from them.

The optimates soon saw that the labors of Gracchus had drawn the people close to him, and they determined to weaken his influence by indirect means, rather than venture to make any immediate display of opposition. They according adopted the sagacious policy of making it appear that they wished to do more for the people than their own champion proposed. They allowed a rich and eloquent demagogue, Marcus Livius Drusus, to act for them, and he deceived the people by proposing measures that appeared more democratic than those of Gracchus, whose power over the people was thus somewhat undermined. The next step was then taken. In the midst of an election a tumult was excited, and Gracchus was obliged to flee, over the wooden bridge, to the Grove of the Furies. Death was his only deliverance. The optimates tried to make it out that he had been an infamous man, but the common people afterward loved both the brothers and esteemed them as great benefactors who had died for them.

The fall of the Gracchi left the people without a leader, and the optimates easily kept possession of the government, though they did not yet feel disposed to proceed at once to carry out their own wishes fully, for fear that they might sting the *populares* beyond endurance. They stopped the assignments of lands, however, allowing those who had occupied large tracts to keep them, and thus the desolation and retrogression which had so deeply moved Gracchus continued and increased even more rapidly than it had in his time. The state fell into a condition of corruption in every department, and office was looked upon simply as a means of acquiring wealth, not as something to be held as a trust for the good of the governed. The nation suffered also from servile insurrections; the seas were overrun with pirates; the rich plunged into vice; the poor were pushed down to deeper depths of poverty; judicial decisions were sold for money; the inhabitants of the provinces were looked upon by the nobles as fit subjects for plunder, and the governors obtained their positions by purchase; everywhere ruin stared the commonwealth in the face, though there seems to have been no one with perceptions clear enough to perceive the trend of affairs.

In this degenerate time there arose two men of the most diverse traits and descent, whose lives, running parallel for many years, furnish at once instructive studies and involve graphic pictures of public affairs. The elder of them was with Scipio when Numantia fell into his hands, and with Jugurtha, a Numidian prince, won distinction by his valor on that occasion. Caius Marius was the name of this man, and he belonged to the commons. He was twenty-three years of age, and had risen from the low condition of a peasant to one of prominence in public affairs. Fifteen years after the fall of Numantia we find him a tribune of the people, standing for purity in the elections, against the opposition of the optimates. Rough, haughty, and undaunted, he carried his measures and waited for the gathering storm to furnish him more enlarged opportunties for the exercise of his strength and ambition.

The opponent and final conqueror of this commoner was but four years of age when Numantia fell, and came into public life later than Marius. Lucius Cornelius Sulla was an optimate of illustrious ancestry and hereditary wealth, a student of the literature and art of Greece and his native land, and he united in his person all the vices as well as accomplishments that Cato had been accustomed to denounce with the utmost vigor.

Marius and Sulla, the plebeian and the optimate, the man without education of the schools, and the master of classic culture, were brought together in Africa in the year 107. Numidia had long been an ally of Rome, but upon the death of one of its kings, Jugurtha, who had gained confidence in himself during the Numantian campaign, attempted to gain control of the government. Rome interfered, but so accessible were public men to bribes, that Jugurtha obtained from the senate a decree dividing the country between him and the rightful claimant of the throne. Not contented with this, he attempted to conquer his rival and obtain the undivided sway. This action aroused the Roman people, who were less corrupt than their senate, and they forced their rulers to interfere. War was declared, but the first commander was corrupted by African gold, and the struggle was intermitted. Jugurtha was called to Rome, with promise of safety, to testify against the officer who had been bribed, and remained there awhile, until he grew bold enough to assassinate one of his enemies, when he was ordered to leave Italy. As he left, he is said to have exclaimed * : " A city

---

* "*Urbem venalem, et mature perituram, si emptorem invenerit.*"— Sallust's " Jugurtha," chapter 35.

IN A ROMAN STUDY.

for sale, ready to fall into the hands of the first bidder!" These memorable words, whether really uttered by the Numidian or not, well characterize the state of affairs at this corrupt period.

One general and another were sent to oppose Jugurtha, but he proved too much for them, either corrupting them by bribes or overcoming them by skill of arms. The spirit of the Roman people was at last fully aroused, and an investigation was made, which resulted in convicting some of the optimates, one of them being Opimius, the consul, who had been cruelly opposed to Caius Gracchus. A general of integrity was chosen to go to Africa. He was Cæcilius Metellus, member of a family which had come into prominence during the first Punic war. Marius was with him, and when Jugurtha saw that men of this high character were opposed to him, he began to despair. While the struggle progressed, Marius remembered that a witch whom he had had with him in a former war had prophesied that the gods would help him in advancing himself, and resolved to go to Rome to try to gain the consulship. Metellus at first opposed this scheme, but was finally persuaded to allow Marius to leave. Though but few days elapsed before the election, after Marius announced himself as a candidate, he was chosen consul, and then he began to exult over the optimates who had so long striven to keep him down. He vaunted his lowly birth, declared that his election was a victory over the pusillanimity and license of the rich, and boldly compared his warlike prowess with the effeminacy of the nobility, whom he determined to persecute as vigorously as they had pursued him.

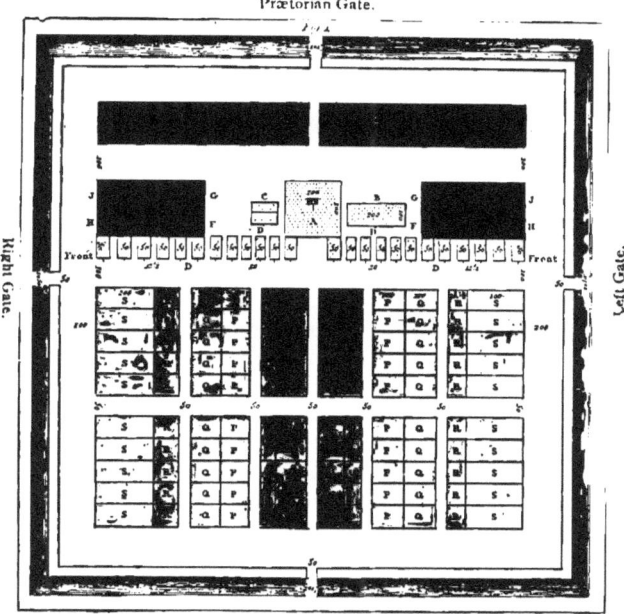

PLAN OF A ROMAN CAMP IN THE TIME OF THE REPUBLIC, FOR 16,800 INFANTRY AND 1,800 HORSE. (ABOUT 2,000 FEET SQUARE.)

A. Consul's tent, in the Prætorium.
B. Paymaster's headquarters.
C. Tents of the lieutenant-generals.
D. Tents of the tribunes.
F. Veteran cavalry.
G. Bodyguard cavalry.
H. Veteran infantry.
J. Bodyguard infantry.
K. Reserve cavalry.
L. Reserve infantry.
M. Legion cavalry.
O. Triarii (Third line).
Q. Hastati (Spearmen).
R. Allied cavalry.
S. Allied infantry.

Marius brought the Numidian War to a close by obtaining possession of Jugurtha in the year 106, but as his subordinate, Sulla, was the instrument in actually taking the king, the enemies of Marius claimed for the young aristocrat the credit of the capture, and Sulla irritated his senior still more by constantly wearing a ring on which he had caused to be engraved a representation of the surrender. Marius did not immediately return to Rome, but remained to complete the subjugation of Numidia, Sulla the meantime making every effort to ingratiate himself with the soldiers, sharing every labor, and sitting with them about the camp-fires as they softened the asperities of a hard life by telling tales of past experience, and making prophesies of the future.

Sulla was not a prepossessing person. His blue eyes were keen and glaring; but they were rendered forbidding and even terrible at times by the bad complexion of his face, which was covered with red blotches that told the story of his debaucheries. "Sulla is a mulberry sprinkled over with meal," is the expression that a Greek jester is said to have used in describing his frightful face.

It was the first of January, 104, when Marius entered Rome in triumph, accompanied by evidences of his victories, the greatest of which was the pitiful Numidian king himself, who followed in the grand procession, and was afterwards ruthlessly dropped into the horrible Tulliarium, or Mamertine prison, to perish by starvation in the watery chill. He is said to have exclaimed as he touched the water at the bottom of the prison, "Hercules! how cold are thy baths!"

During the absence of Marius in Africa, there had come over Rome the shadow of a greater peril than had been known since the days when Hannibal's advance had made the strongest hearts quail. The tumultuous multitudes who inhabited the unexplored regions of Central Europe, the Celts and Germans,* had gathered a mass comprising, it is said, more than three hundred thousand men capable of fighting, besides hosts of women and children, and were marching with irresistible force towards the Roman domains. Nine years before (B.C. 113), these barbarians had defeated a Roman army in Noricum, north of Illyricum, and after that they had roamed at will through Switzerland, adding to their numbers, and ravaging every region, until at last they had poured over into the plains of Gaul. Year after year passed, and army after army of the Romans was cut to pieces by these terrible barbarians.

As Marius entered the city he was looked upon as the only one who could stem the impetuous human torrent that threatened to overwhelm the republic, for, in the face of the supreme danger, as is usual in such cases, every party jealousy was forgotten. The proud commoner accepted the command with alacrity, setting out for distant Gaul immediately, and taking Sulla as one of his subordinates. After two years of inconsequent strategy, he overcame the barbarians at a spot twelve miles distant from *Aquæ Sextiæ* (the Springs of Sextius, the modern Aix, in

* The Cimbri, who formed a portion of this invading body, had their original home in the modern peninsula of Jutland, whence came also early invaders of Britain, and they were probably a Celtic people.

Provence), (B.C. 102). He collected the richest of the spoil to grace a triumph that he expected to celebrate, and was about to offer the remainder to the gods, when, just as he stood amid the encircling troops in a purple robe, ready to touch the torch to the pile, horsemen dashed into the space, announcing that the Romans had for the fifth time elected him consul! The village of Pourrières (*Campi Putridi*) now marks the spot, and the rustics of the vicinity still celebrate a yearly festival, at which they burn a vast heap of brushwood on the summit of one of their hills, as they shout *Victoire! victoire!* in memory of Marius.

During this period Sulla gained renown by his valorous deeds, but the jealousy that had begun in Africa increased, and in 103 or 102, he left Marius and joined himself to his colleague Lutatius Catulus, who was endeavoring to stem another torrent of barbarians, this time pouring down toward Rome from the valley of the Po. When Marius reached home after his victories in Gaul, he was offered a triumph, but refused to celebrate it until he had marched to the help of Catulus, who, he found, was then retreating before the invaders in a panic. After the arrival of Marius the flight was stopped, and the barbarians totally destroyed at a battle fought near Vercellæ. Though much credit for this wonderful victory was awarded to both Catulus and Sulla, the whole honor was at Rome given to Marius, who celebrated a triumph, was called the third founder of the city (as Camillus had been the second), and enjoyed the distinction of having his name joined with those of the gods when offerings and libations were made. The jealousy of Sulla was all this time growing from its small beginnings.

While Marius and Sulla were fighting the barbarians there had been a second insurrection among the slave population of Italy, and it was not distant Sicily only that was troubled at this time, for though the uprising spread to that island, many towns of Campania were afflicted, and at last the contagion had affected thousands of the slaves, who arose and struck for freedom. The outbreak in Campania was repressed in 103, but it was not until 99 that quiet was restored on the island, and then it was by the destruction of many thousands of lives. Large numbers of the captives were taken to Rome to fight in the arena with wild beasts, but they disappointed their sanguinary masters by killing each other instead in the amphitheatre. The condition of the slaves after this was worse than before. They were deprived of all arms, and even the spear with which the herdsmen were wont to protect themselves from wild beasts was taken away.

At this time the power of the optimates was rather decreasing, and signs of promise for the people appeared. In the year 103, a law had been passed which took from the senate the right to select the chief pontiffs, and it had been given to the populares.* An agrarian law was proposed in the follow-

---

* This important law was passed through the tribune Cneius Domitius Ahenobarbus, in order to effect his own election as pontiff in the place of his father, and is known as the Domitian law. The people elected him afterward out of gratitude. The chief pontiff was an influential factor in politics, as he pronounced the verdict of the Sibylline

ing year, a speaker on the subject asserting that in the entire republic there were not two thousand landholders, so rapidly had the rich been able to concentrate in themselves the ownership of the land. The powers of the senate were still further restricted in the year 100, by a law intended to punish magistrates who had improperly received money, and to take from the senators the right to try such offences.* At the same time the right of citizenship was offered to all Italians who should succeed in convicting a magistrate of peculation or extortion. Thus it seemed as though the reforms aimed at by the Gracchi might be brought about if only the man for the occasion were to present himself. Marius presented himself, but we shall find that he mistook his means, and only cast the nation down into deeper depths of misery. His star was at its highest when he celebrated his triumph, and it would have been better for his fame had he died at that time.

<small>books on public questions, and gave or withheld the divine approval from public acts, besides appointing the rites and sacrifices.

* The exact date of this law is uncertain. It was directed against Quintus Servilius Cæpio, who, when the barbarians were threatening Italy, commanded in Gaul, and enriched himself by the wealth of Tolosa, which he took (B.C. 106), thus giving rise to the proverb "He has gold of Toulouse"—ill-gotten gains (*aurum Tolosanum habet*). He was also held responsible for a terrible defeat at Arausio (Orange), where eighty thousand Romans and forty thousand camp-followers perished, October 6, B.C. 105. The day became another black one in the Roman calendar.</small>

XIII.

SOCIAL AND CIVIL WARS.

MARIUS was brave and strong and able to cope with any in the rush of war, but he knew little of the arts of peace and the science of government. Sulla, his enemy, was at Rome, living in quiet, but the same fiery, ambition that animated Marius, and the same jealousy of all who seemed to be growing in popularity, burned in his bosom and were ready to burst out at any time. The very first attempts of Marius at government ended in shame, and he retired from the city in the year 99. He had supported two rogations, called the Appuleian laws, from the demagogue who moved them, Lucius Appuleius Saturninus, and they were carried by violence and treachery. They enacted that the lands acquired from the barbarians should be divided among both the Italians and the citizens of Rome, thus affording relief to all Italy; and that corn should be sold to Romans by the state at a nominal price.

When Marius retired, the authority of the senate was restored, but the state was in a deplorable condition, for the violence and bloodshed that had been familiar for the half century since the triumph over Greece and Carthage, were bearing their legitimate fruits. Not only was the separation between the rich and poor constantly growing greater, but the effect of the luxury and license of the wealthy was debauching the public conscience, and faith was everywhere falling away. Impostors and foreign priests had full sway.

Opposed to Saturninus was a noble of the most exalted type of character, Marcus Livius Drusus, son of the Drusus who had opposed the Gracchi. A genuine aristocrat, possessed of a colossal fortune, strict in his morals and trustworthy in every position, he was a man of acknowledged weight in the national councils. In the year 91, he was elected tribune, and endeavored to bring about reform. He obtained the adherence of the people by laws for distributing corn at low prices, and by holding out to the allies hopes of the franchise. The allies had long looked for this, and as their condition had been growing worse year by year, their impatience increased, until at last they were no longer willing to brook delay. The Romans (whose party cry was "Rome for the Romans") ever opposed this measure, and now they stirred up opposition to the conservative Drusus, who paid the penalty of his life to his efforts at civil reform and the alleviation of oppression. Though he tried to please all parties, the senate first rendered his laws nugatory, and their partisans not satisfied with his civil defeat, afterwards caused him to be assassinated.* It was then

---

* Velleius Paterculus, the historian, relates that as Drusus was dying, he looked upon the crowd of citizens who were lamenting his fortune, and said, in conscious innocence: "My relations and friends, will the commonwealth ever again have a citizen like me?" He

enacted that all who favored the allies should be considered guilty of treason to the state. Many prominent citizens were condemned under this law, and the allies naturally became convinced that there was no hope for them except in revolution.

Rome was in consequence menaced by those who had before been her helpers, and the danger was one of the greatest that she had ever encountered. The Italians were prepared for the contest, but the Romans were not. It was determined by the allies that Rome should be destroyed, and a new capital erected at Corfinum, which was to be known as Italica. On both sides it was a struggle for existence.

The Marsians were the most prominent among the allies in one division, and the Samnites were at the head of another.* The whole of Central Italy became involved in the desperate struggle. The Etruscans and Umbrians took the part of Rome, being offered the suffrage for their allegiance. At the end of the first campaign this was offered also to those of the other antagonistic allies who would lay down their arms, and by this means discord was thrown into the camp of the enemy. The campaign of 89 was favorable to the Romans, who, led by

adds, as illustrating the purity of his intentions, that when Drusus was building a house on the Palatine, his architect offered to make it so that no observer could see into it, but he said : " Rather, build my house so that whatever I do may be seen by all."

* The Marsians were an ancient people of Central Italy, inhabiting a mountainous district, and had won distinction among the allies for their skill and courage in war. " The Marsic cohorts " was an almost proverbial expression for the bravest troops in the time of Horace and Virgil.

Sulla, drove the enemy out of Campania, and captured the town of Bovianum. The following year the war was closed, but Rome and Italy had lost more than a quarter of a million of their citizens, while the allies had nominally obtained the concessions that they had fought for.

Ten new tribes were formed in which the new citizens were enrolled, thus keeping them in a body by themselves; and it was natural that there should be much discontent among them on account of the manner in which their privileges had been awarded. The franchise could only be obtained by a visit to Rome, which was difficult for the inhabitants of distant regions, and there was besides no place in the city large enough to contain all the citizens, if they had been able to come. The new citizens found, too, that there was still a difference between themselves and those who had before enjoyed the suffrage, something like that which existed between the freedmen and the men who had never been enslaved.

Marius and Sulla, the ever-vigilant rivals, had both been engaged in the Marsic war, but they came out of it in far differing frames of mind. The young aristocrat boasted that fortune had permitted him to strike the last decisive blow; and the old plebeian, now seventy years of age, found his heart swelling with indignation because he received only new mortifications in return for his new services to the state, in whose behalf he had this time fought with reluctance. A spirit of dire vengeance was agitating his heart, the results of which we are soon to observe.

The troubles of the state now seemed to accumulate with terrible rapidity. Two wars broke out immediately upon the close of that which we have just considered, one at home and the other in Asia. The one was the strife of faction, and the other an effort to repel attacks upon allies of the republic. Mithridates the Great, King of Pontus, the sixth of his name, was remarkable for his physical and mental development, no less than for his great ambition and boundless activity. Under his rule his kingdom had reached its greatest power. This monarch had attempted to add to his dominion Cappadocia, the country adjoining Pontus on the south, by placing his nephew on the throne, but Sulla, who was then in Cilicia, prevented it. Mithridates next interfered in the government of Bithynia, to the southwest, expecting that the oppressive rule of the Roman governors would lead the inhabitants to be friendly to him, while the troubles of the Romans at home would make it difficult for them to interfere. The close of the Marsian struggle, however, left Rome free to engage the Eastern conqueror, and war was determined upon.

The success of Sulla in the East made it plain that he was the one to lead the army, but Marius was still ambitious to gain new laurels, and in order to prove that he was not too old to endure the hardships of a campaign, he went daily to the Campus Martius and exercised with the young men. His efforts proved vain, and he determined to take more positive measures. He procured the enactment of a law distributing the new citizens, who far outnumbered the old ones, among the tribes, knowing that they would vote in his favor. It was not without much opposition that this law was enacted, but Marius was then appointed, instead of Sulla, to lead the army against Pontus. Sulla meantime hastened to the army and obtained actual command of the soldiers, who loved him, caused the tribunes of Marius to be murdered, and left the old commander without support. Marius in turn raised another army by offering freedom to slaves, and with it attempted to resist Sulla, but in vain. He was obliged to fly, and a price was placed upon his head. He sailed for Africa, but was thrown back upon the shores of Italy, was cast into prison, and ordered to execution; but the slave commissioned to carry out the judgment was frightened by the flashing eyes of the aged warrior and refused to perform the act, as he heard a voice from the darkness of the cell haughtily asking: "Fellow, darest thou kill Caius Marius?" The magistrates, struck with pity and remorse, as they reflected that Marius was the preserver of Italy, let him go to meet his fate on other shores, and at last he found his way to Africa.

The departure of both Marius and Sulla from Rome left it exposed to a new danger. As soon as Sulla had left for Pontus, Lucius Cornelius Cinna, one of the consuls, began to form a popular party, composed largely of the newly made citizens, for the purpose of overpowering the senate and recalling Marius. A frightful conflict ensued on a day of voting, and thousands were butchered in the struggle. Cinna was driven from the city, but received the support of a vast number of Italians, which enabled him to march again upon Rome.

Meantime Marius returned from Africa, captured Ostia and other places, and joined Cinna. Then, by cutting off its supplies, he caused the city to yield. Marius and Cinna entered the gates, and again the streets ran blood; for every one who had given Marius cause to hate or fear him was hunted to the death without mercy, and with no respect to rank, talent, or former friendship. Cinna and Marius named themselves consuls for the year 86 without the form of election,* but the firm constitution of the old hero was completely undermined by his sufferings and fatigues, and he succumbed to an attack of pleurisy after a few days, during which, as Plutarch tells us, he was terrified by dreams and by the anticipated return of Sulla. The people rejoiced that they were freed from the cruelty of his ruthless tyranny, little knowing what new horrors the grim future had in store for them.

We return now to Sulla. When he had driven Marius from Rome, he was obliged to hasten away to carry on the war in Asia, though he marched first against Athens, which had become the head-quarters of the allies of Mithridates in Greece. The siege of this city was long and obstinate, and it was not until March 1, 86, that it was overcome, when Sulla gave it up to rapine and pillage. He then advanced into Bœotia, and success continued to follow his arms until the year 84, when he crossed the Hellespont to carry the war into Asia. Mithridates had put to

* See note on page 64.

death all Roman citizens and allies, wherever found, with all the reckless ferocity of an Asiatic tyrant, but had met many losses and was now anxious to have peace. Sulla settled the terms at a personal interview at Dardanus, in the Troad. Enormous sums (estimated at more than $100,000,000) were exacted from the rich cities, and a single settled government was restored to Greece, Macedonia, and Asia Minor. The soldiers were compensated for their fatigues by a luxurious winter in Asia, and, in the spring of 83, they were transferred, in 1,600 vessels, from Ephesus to the Piræus, and thence to Brundusium. Sulla carried with him from Athens the valuable library of Apellicon of Teos, which contained the works of Aristotle and his disciple, Theophrastus, then not in general circulation, for he did not forget his interest in literature even in war. Thus it was that the rich thoughts of the great philosopher came to the knowledge of the Roman students.*

Sulla sent a letter to the senate, announcing the close of the war and his intention to return, in the course of which he took occasion to recount his services to the republic, from the time of the war with Jugurtha to the conquest of Mithridates, and announced that he should take vengeance upon his enemies and upon those of the commonwealth. The senate was alarmed, and proposed to treat with him for peace, but Cinna hastened to oppose the

---

* Aristoteles, sometimes called the Stagirite, because he was born in Stagira, in Macedonia, lived at Athens in the fourth century before our era. Theophrastus was his friend and disciple, both at Stagira and Athens.

arrogant conqueror with force. He was, however, assassinated by his own soldiers.

On the sixth of July, after the arrival of Sulla at Brundusium (B.C. 83), Rome was thrown into a state of consternation by the burning of the capitol and the destruction of the temple of Jupiter Capitolinus, with the Sibylline oracles, those valuable books which had directed the counsels of the nation for ages, and the close of a historic era approached.* Sulla easily marched in triumph through lower Italy on his way to Rome, for his opponents were not well organized, but it was not until months had passed that the fierce struggle was decided. He was besieging Præneste, when the Samnites, after finding that they could not relieve it, marched directly upon Rome. Sulla followed them, and a bloody battle was fought at the Colline gate, on the northern side of the city. It was a fight for the very existence of Rome, for Pontius Telesinus, commander of the Samnites, declared that he intended to raze the city to the ground. Fifty thousand are said to have fallen on each side, and most of the leaders of the party of Marius perished or were afterward put to death. All the Samnites (8,000) who were taken were collected by Sulla in the Campus Martius and ruthlessly butchered.

If the former scenes had been terrible, much more so were those that now followed. Sulla was made dictator, an officer that had been unknown for a

* Ambassadors were afterwards sent to various places in Greece, Asia, and Italy, to make a fresh collection, and when the temple was rebuilt it was put in the place occupied by the lost books.

century and a quarter, and proceeded to show his adhesion to the optimates by attempting to blot out the popular party. He announced that he would give a better government to Rome, but he found it necessary to kill all whom he pretended to think her enemies. It was Marius who had brought on the era of carnage by attempting to deprive Sulla of his command in the war against Mithridates, and accordingly the body of the great plebeian was torn from its tomb and cast into the Anio. A list was drawn up of those whose possessions were to be confiscated, and who were themselves to be executed in vengeance. On this the names of the family of Marius came first. Fresh lists were constantly posted in the forum. Each of these was called a *tabula proscriptionis*, a list of proscription, and it presents the first instance of a proscription in Roman history.* Sulla placed on these lists not only the names of enemies of the state, but his personal opponents, those whose property he coveted, and those who were enemies of friends whom he desired to please. No man was safe, for his name might appear at any time on the terrible lists, and then he would be an outlaw, whom any one might kill with impunity. Especially were the rich and prominent liable to find themselves in this position. Many thousands of unfortunate citizens perished before Sulla was content to put a stop to the horrors. He

---

* A proscription had formerly been an offering for sale of any thing by advertisement ; but Sulla gave it a new meaning,—the sale of the property of those unfortunates who were put to death by his orders. The victims were said to be proscribed. The meaning given by Sulla still lives in the English word.

then celebrated with exceeding magnificence the postponed triumph on account of his victory over Mithridates, and received from a trembling people the title *Felix*, the lucky.

It has been said that after having killed the men with his sword, Sulla made it his work to kill the party that opposed him, by laws. He wished to have in Rome the silence and the autocracy of a camp. He put some three hundred new members into the senate, and gave that body the power to veto legislative enactments, while at the same time he restricted the authority of the tribunes of the people and of the *comitia tributa*, the general convention of the tribes. On the other hand, he reduced debts by one fourth, to conciliate the masses, and paid his soldiers for their services in the civil strife with vast amounts of booty and great numbers of slaves. The *pomœrium* was extended to embrace all Italy, and, as is supposed, the northern boundary of Roman territory was extended to the Rubicon. New courts were established and the judicial system was reorganized; the censors were practically shelved, but sumptuary laws were passed to prevent extravagance and luxury. All of the laws of Sulla were submitted to the people for formal approval; but as no one was hardy enough to differ from the dictator, it mattered little what the people thought.

By the beginning of the year 79, Sulla considered that his reforms were complete, and bethought himself of retiring to see at a little distance the effect of his regulations. He felt that no danger could overtake him, for he had settled his old veterans (called Cornelians), to the number of more than a hundred thousand, in colonies scattered throughout Italy, on the estates and in the cities that he had confiscated, and thought that they would prove his supporters in any event. He boldly summoned the people and, announcing his purpose, offered to render an account of his official conduct. He gave the crowd a *congiarium*, as it was called—that is, he glutted them with the costliest meats and the richest wines, and so great was his profusion that vast quantities that the gorged multitude were unable to eat were cast into the Tiber. He then discharged his armed attendants, dismissed his lictors, descended from the rostra, and retired on foot to his house, accompanied only by his friends, passing through the midst of the populace which he had given every reason to desire to wreak vengeance upon him. It was audacity of the supremest sort. Sulla afterwards withdrew to his estate at Puteoli, where he spent the brief remainder of his life in the most remarkable alternation of nocturnal orgies and cultured enjoyment, sharing his time with male and female debauchees and learned students of Greek literature, and concluding the memoirs of his life and times, in which, through twenty-two books, he recorded the story of his deeds, colored doubtless to a great extent by his own magnificent self-love. In the last words of his "Memoirs" he characterized himself, with a certain degree of truth from his own point of view, as "fortunate and all-powerful to his last hour."

The senate voted Sulla a gorgeous funeral, in spite of opposition on the part of the consul Lepidus, and his body was carried to the Campus Martius, preceded by the magistrates, the senate, the equites, the vestal virgins, and the veterans. There it was burned, that no future tyrant could treat it as that of Marius had been, though up to that time the Cornelian gens, to which Sulla belonged, had always buried their dead.

Thus lived and thus died the man who, though he relieved Rome of the last of her invaders, infused into her system a malady from which she was to suffer in the future; for the pampered veterans whom he had distributed throughout Italy in scenes of peace, all unwonted to such a life, were to be the ones on which another oppressor was to depend in his efforts to subvert the government.

XIV.

THE MASTER SPIRITS OF THIS AGE.

ROME was now ruled by an oligarchy,—that is, the control of public affairs fell into the hands of a few persons. There was an evident tendency, however, towards the union of all the functions of governmental authority in the person of a single man, whenever one should be found of sufficient strength to grasp them. The younger Gracchus had exercised almost supreme control, and Marius, Cinna, and Sulla had followed him; but their power had perished with them, leaving no relics in the fundamental principles of the government, except as it marked stages in the general progress. Now other strong men arise who pursue the same course, and lead directly up to the concentration of supreme authority in the hands of one man, and he not a consul, nor a tribune, nor a dictator, but an emperor, a titled personage never before known in Rome. With this culmination the life of the populus Romanus was destined to end.

A dramatist endeavoring to depict public life at Rome during the period following the death of Sulla, would find himself embarrassed by the multitude of men of note crowding upon his attention.

One of the eldest of these was Quintus Sertorius, a soldier of chivalric bravery, who had come into prominence during the Marian wars in Gaul. He had at that time won distinction by boldly entering the camp of the Teutones disguised as a spy, and bringing away valuable information, before the battle at Aix. When Sulla was fighting Mithridates, Sertorius was on the side of Cinna, and had to flee from the city with him. When the battle was fought at the Colline gate, Sertorius served with his old comrade Marius, whom he did not admire, and with Cinna, but we do not know that he shared the guilt of the massecre that followed. Certainly he punished the slaves that surrounded Marius for their cruel excesses. When Sulla returned, Sertorius escaped to Spain, where he raised an army, and achieved so much popularity that the Romans at home grew very jealous of him.* He did not intentionally go to live in Spain, but having heard that there were certain islands out in the Atlantic celebrated since the days of Plato as the abode of the blest; where gentle breezes brought soft dews to enrich the fertile soil; where delicate fruits grew to feed the inhabi-

---

* Sertorius is almost the only one among the statesmen of antiquity who seems to have recognized the modern truth, that education is a valuable aid in making a government firm. He established a school in Spain in which boys of high rank, dressed in the garb of Romans, learned the languages that still form the basis of a classical education, while they were also held as hostages for the good behavior of their elders. He was not a philanthropist, but a sagacious ruler, and the author of Latin colonies in the West. He was for a time accompanied by a white fawn, which he encouraged the superstitious barbarians to believe was a familiar spirit, by means of which he communicated with the unseen powers and ensured his success.

tants without their trouble or labor; where the yellow-haired Rhadamanthus was refreshed by the whistling breezes of Zephyrus; he longed to find them and live in peace and quiet, far from the rush of war and the groans of the oppressed. From this bright vision he was turned, but perhaps his efforts to establish a merciful government in Spain may be traced to its influence.

Another prominent man on the stage at this time was a leader of the aristocratic party, Marcus Crassus, who lived in a house that is estimated to have cost more than a quarter of a million dollars. Probably he would not have been very prominent if his father had not left him a small fortune, to which he had added very largely by methods that we can hardly consider noble. It is said that when the Sullan proscription was going on, he obtained at ruinously low prices the estates that the proscribed had to give up, and, whenever there was a fire, he would be on the spot ready to buy the burning or ruined buildings for little or nothing. He owned many slaves who were accomplished as writers, silversmiths, stewards, and table-waiters, whom he let out to those who wished their services, and thus added largely to his income. He did not build any houses, except the one in which he lived, for he agreed with the proverb which says that fools build houses for wise men to live in, though "the greatest part of Rome sooner or later came into his hands," as Plutarch observes. He was of that sordid, avaricious character which covets wealth merely for the desire to be considered rich, for the vulgar popularity that accompanies that reputation, and not for ambition or enjoyment. He was said to be uninfluenced by the love of luxury or by the other passions of humanity. He was not a man of extensive learning, though he was pretty well versed in philosophy and in history, and by pains and industry had made himself an accomplished orator. He could thus wield a great influence by his speeches to the people from the rostra.

Among the aristocrats who composed the oligarchy that ruled at about this time were two men born in the same year (106 B.C.): the egotistic, vain, and irresolute, but personally pure orator, Marcus Tullius Cicero; and the cold and haughty soldier, Cneius Pompeius Magnus, commonly known as Pompey the Great. The philosophical, oratorical, and theological writings of Cicero are still studied in our schools as models in their different classes. Inheriting a love of culture from his father, a member of an ancient family, he was afforded every advantage in becoming acquainted with all branches of a polite education; and travelled to the chief seats of learning in Greece and Asia Minor with this end in view. When he was twenty-six years of age, he made his first appearance as a public pleader, and soon gained the reputation of being the first orator at the Roman bar. Besides these pursuits, Cicero had had a brief military experience, during the war between Sulla and Marius.

Pompey, likewise, began to learn the art of war under his father, in the same struggle, but he continued its exercise until he became a consummate warrior. For his success in pursuing the remains of the Marian faction in Africa and Sicily, Pompey was honored with the name Magnus (the Great), and with a triumph, a distinction that had never before been won by a man of his rank who had not previously held public office.

Older than these men there was one whose character is forever blackened on the pages of history by the relentless pen of Cicero, Caius Licinius Verres, who, if we may believe the only records we have regarding him, was the most phenomenal freebooter of all time. The story of his career is a vivid demonstration of the manner in which the people of the Roman provinces were outraged by the officers sent to rule over them, and we shall anticipate our story a little in tracing it. The provincial governors were, as a class, corrupt, and Verres was as vile as any of them, but he was also brutal in his manners and natural instincts, rapacious, licentious, cruel, and fond of low companions. At first, one of the Marian faction, he betrayed his associates, embezzled the funds that had been entrusted to him, and joined himself to Sulla, who sent him to Brundusium, allowing him a share in the confiscated estates. Thence he was transferred to Cilicia, where again he proved a traitor to his superior officer, and stole from cities, private persons, temples, and public places, every thing that his rapacity coveted. One city offered him a vessel as a loan, and he refused to return it; another had a statue of Diana covered with gold, and he scraped off the precious metal to put it in his pocket. Using the money thus gained to ensure his election to office at Rome, Verres enjoyed a year at the Capitol, and then entered upon a still more outrageous career as governor of the island of Sicily. Taking with him a painter and a sculptor well versed in the values of works of art, he systematically gathered together all

POMPEY (CNEIUS POMPEIUS MAGNUS).

that was considered choice in the galleries and temples. Allowing his officers to make exorbitant exactions upon the farmers, he confiscated many estates to his own use, and reaped the crops. Even travellers were attacked to enrich this extraordinary thief, and six vessels were afterward dispatched to Rome with the plunder, which he asserted was sufficient to permit him to revel in opulence the remainder of his life, even if he were obliged to give up two thirds in fines and bribes.

The people Verres had outraged did not, however, suffer in quiet. They engaged Cicero to conduct their case against him, and this the great orator did with overwhelming success.* Though protected by Hortensius, an older advocate, who, during the absence of Cicero, on his travels, had acquired the highest rank as an orator, so terrible was the arraignment in its beginning that, at the suggestion of Hortensius, Verres did not remain to hear its close, but hastened into voluntary exile. He precipitately took ship for Marseilles, and for twenty-seven years was forced to remain in that city. Would that every misdoer among the provincial governors had thus been followed up by the law!

The representative of the Sullan party at this time was Lucius Sergius Catiline, an aristocrat, who, during the proscription, behaved with fiendish atrocity towards those of the opposite party, torturing and killing men with the utmost recklessness.

---

* The orations of Cicero against Verres are based upon information which the orator gathered by personally examining witnesses at the scenes of the rascality he unveiled. The orator showed a true Roman lack of appreciation of Greek art, and exercised his own love of puns to a considerable extent, playing a good deal upon the name Verres, which meant a boar. The extreme corpulence of the defendant, too, offered an opportunity for gross personal allusions. Cicero compared him to the Erymanthean boar, and called him the "drag-net" of Sicily, because his name resembled the word *everriculum*, a drag-net.

His early years had been passed in undisguised debaucheries and unrestrained vice, but in spite of all his acts, he made political progress, was prætor, governor of Africa, and candidate for the consulship by turn. Failing in the last effort, however, he entered into a conspiracy to murder the successful candidates, and was only foiled by his own impatience. We shall find that he was encouraged by this failure which so nearly proved a success.

There was one man among the host of busy figures on the stage at this eventful period who seems to stalk about like a born master, and the lapse of time since his days has not at all dimmed the fame of his deeds, so deep a mark have they left upon the laws and customs of mankind, and so noteworthy are they in the annals of Rome. Caius Julius Cæsar was six years younger than Pompey and Cicero, and was of the popular or Marian party, both by birth and tastes. His aunt Julia was wife of the great Marius himself, and though he had married a young woman of high birth to please his father, he divorced her as soon as his father died, and married Cornelia, daughter of Cinna, the devoted opponent of Sulla, to please himself.

When Sulla returned to Rome from the East, he ordered Pompey to put away his wife, and he obeyed. He ordered Cæsar, a boy of seventeen, to give up his Cornelia, and he proudly replied that he would not. Of course he could not remain at Rome after that, and he fled to the land of the Sabines until Sulla was induced to grant him a pardon. Still, he did not feel secure at Rome, and a second time he sought safety in expatriation. Upon the death of the dictator, he returned, having gained experience in war, and having developed his talents as an orator by study in a school at Rhodes. He plunged immediately into public life and won great distinction by his effective speaking.

These are enough characters for us to remember at present. They represent four groups, all striving for supreme power. There are the men of the oligarchy, represented by Pompey and Cicero, actually holding the reins of government; and Crassus, standing for the aristocrats, who resent their claims; Cæsar, foremost among the Marians, the former opponents of Sulla and his schemes; and Catiline, at the head of the faction which included the host of warriors that Sulla had settled in peaceful pursuits throughout Italy,—in peaceful pursuits that did not at all suit their impetuous spirits, ever eager as they were for some revolution that would plunge them again into strife, and perchance win for them some spoil.

The consuls at the time of the death of Sulla were Lepidus and Catulus, who now fell out with one another, Lepidus taking the part of the Marians, and Catulus holding with the aristocrats. This was the same Lepidus who had opposed the burial of the dictator Sulla in the Campus Martius. As soon as the Marians saw that one consul was ready to favor them, there was great excitement among the portion of the community that looked for gain in confusion. Those who had lost their riches and civic rights, hoped to see them restored; young profligates trusted that in some way they might find means to gratify their love of luxury; and the people in general, who had no other reason, thought that

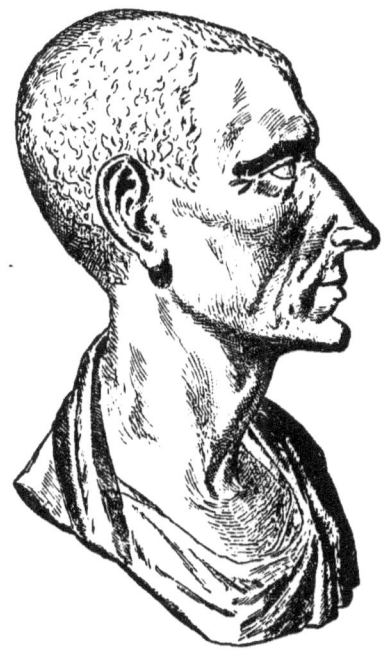

CAIUS JULIUS CÆSAR.

after the three years of the calm of despotism, it would be refreshing to see some excitement in the forum. Lepidus was profuse in promises; he told the beggars that he would again distribute free grain; and the families deprived of their estates, that they might soon expect to enjoy them again. Catulus protested in vain, and the civil strife constantly increased, without any apparent probability that the Senate, now weak and inefficient, would or could successfully interfere. Finally it was decreed that Lepidus and Catulus should each be sent to the provinces under oath not to turn their swords against each other.

Lepidus slowly proceeded to carry out his part of this decree, but Catulus remained behind long enough to complete a great temple, which towered above the forum on the Capitoline Hill. The foundations only remain now, but they bear an inscription placed there by order of the senate, testifying that Catulus was the consul under whom the structure was completed. Lepidus did not consider his oath binding long, and the following year (B.C. 77) he marched straight to Rome again, announcing to the senators that he came to re-establish the rights of the people and to assume the dictatorship himself. He was met by an army under Pompey and Catulus, at a spot near the Mulvian bridge and the Campus Martius, almost on the place where the fate of the Roman Empire was to be determined four centuries later by a battle between Maxentius and Constantine (A.D. 312). Lepidus was defeated and forced to flee. Shortly after, he died on the island of Sardinia, overcome by chagrin and sorrow. One would expect to read of a new proscription, after this success, but the victors did not resort to that terrible vengeance. Thus Pompey found himself at the head of Roman affairs.

His first duty was to march against the remnant of the party of the Marians. They had joined Sertorius in Spain. It was the year 76 when Pompey arrived on the scene of his new operations. He found his enemy more formidable than he had supposed, and it was not until five years had passed, and Sertorius had been assassinated, that he was able to achieve the victory and scatter the army of the Marians. Meantime the Romans had been fearing that Sertorius would actually prove strong enough to march upon the capital and perhaps overwhelm it. Hardly had their fears in this respect been quieted than they found themselves menaced by a still more frightful catastrophe.

We remember how, in the year 264 B.C., two young Romans honored the memory of their father by causing men to fight each other to the death with swords to celebrate his funeral, and hints from time to time have shown how the Romans had become more and more fond of seeing human beings hack and hew each other in the amphitheatres. The men who were to be "butchered to make a Roman holiday," as the poet says, were trained for their horrid work with as much system as is now used in our best gymnasiums to fit men to live lives of happy peace, if not with more. They were divided into classes with particular names, according to the arms they wore, the hours at which they fought, and their modes of fighting, and great were the pains that their instructors took to make them perfect in their bloody work. Down at Capua, that celebrated centre of refinement and luxury, there was a school of gladiators, kept by one Lentulus, who hired his fierce pupils out to the nobles to be used at games and festivals.

While Pompey was away engaged with Sertorius, the enemies of Rome everywhere thought it a favorable moment to give her trouble, and these gladiators conspired in the year 73 to escape to freedom, and thus cheat their captors out of their expected pleasures, and give their own wives and children a little more of their lives. So large was the school that two hundred engaged in the plot, though only seventy-eight were successful in escaping. They hurried away to the mountains, armed with knives and spits that they had been able to snatch from the stalls as they fled, and, directed by one Spartacus who had been leader of a band of robbers, found their way to the crater of Mount Vesuvius, not a comfortable resort one would think; but at that time it was quite different in form from what it is now, the volcano being extinct, so that it afforded many of the advantages of a fortified town. From every quarter the hard-worked slaves flocked to the standard of Spartacus, and soon he found himself at the head of a large army. His plan was to cross the Alps, and find a place of refuge in Gaul or in his native Thrace; but his brutalized followers thought only of the present. They were satisfied if they could now and then capture a rich town, and for a while revel in luxuries; if they could wreak their vengeance by forcing the Romans themselves to fight as gladiators; or, if they had the opportunity to kill those to whom they attributed their former distresses. They cared not to follow their leader to the northward, and thus his wiser plans were baffled; but, in spite of all obstacles, he laid the country waste from the foot of the Alps to the most southern extremity of the toe of the Italian boot. For two years he was able to keep up his war against the Roman people, but at last he was driven to the remotest limits of Bruttium, where his only hope

GLADIATORS.

was in getting over to Sicily, in the expectation of gaining other followers; but his army was signally defeated by Crassus, a small remnant only escaping to the northward, where they were exterminated by Pompey, then returning from Spain (B.C. 71). From Capua to Rome six thousand crosses, each bearing a captured slave, showed how carefully and ruthlessly the man-hunt had been pursued by the frightened and exasperated Romans. Both Crassus and Pompey claimed the credit of the final victory, Pompey asserting that though Crassus had scotched the serpent, he had himself killed it.

On the last day of the year 71 Pompey entered Rome with the honor of a triumph, while Crassus received the less important distinction of an ovation,* as it was called, because his success had been obtained over slaves, less honorable adversaries than those whom Pompey had met. Each desired to be consul, but neither was properly qualified for the office, and therefore they agreed to overawe the senate and win the office for both, each probably thinking that at the first good opportunity he would get the better of the other. In this plan they were successful, and thus two aristocrats came to the head of government, and the oligarchy, to which one of them belonged, went out of power, and soon Pompey, who all the time posed as the friend of the people, proceeded to repeal the most important parts of the legislation of Sulla. The tribunes were restored, and Pompey openly broke with the aristocracy to which by birth he belonged, thus beginning a new era, for the social class of a man's family was no longer to indicate the political party to which he should give his adherence.

* In a triumph in these times, the victorious general, clad in a robe embroidered with gold, and wearing a laurel wreath, solemnly entered the city riding in a chariot drawn by four horses. The captives and spoils went before him, and the army followed. He passed along the Via Sacra on the Forum Romanum, and went up to the Capitol to sacrifice in the temple of Jupiter. In the ovation the general entered the city on foot, wore a simple toga, and a wreath of myrtle, and was in other respects not so conspicuously honored as in the triumph. The two celebrations differed in other respects also.

TRIUMPHAL PROCESSION OF A ROMAN GENERAL.

XV.

PROGRESS OF THE GREAT POMPEY.

THE master spirits of this remarkable age were now in full action on the stage, and it is difficult to keep the eye fixed upon all of them at once. Now one is prominent and now another; all are pushing their particular interests, while each tries to make it appear that he has nothing but the good of the state at heart. Whenever it is evident that a certain cause is the popular one, the various leaders, opposed on most subjects, are united to help it, in the hope of catching the popular breeze. During the consulship of Pompey and Catulus, Pompey was the principal Roman citizen, and he tried to make sure that his prestige should not be lessened when he should step down from his high office.

Crassus, aristocrat by birth and aristocrat by choice, had been a candidate for the senate in opposition to Pompey, but he soon found that his interest demanded that he should make peace with his powerful colleague, and as he did it, he told the people that he did not consider that his action was in any degree base or humiliating, for he simply made advances to one whom they had themselves named the Great. Crowds daily courted Pompey on account of his

INTERIOR OF A ROMAN HOUSE.

power; but a multitude equally numerous surrounded Crassus for his wealth, and Cicero on account of his wonderful oratory. Even Julius Cæsar, the strong Marian, who pronounced a eulogy upon his aunt, the widow of Marius, seemed also to pay homage to Pompey, when, a year later, he took to wife Pompeia, a relative of the great soldier (B.C. 67).

Both Cæsar and Pompey saw that gross corruption was practised by the chiefs of the senate when they had control of the provinces, and knew that it ought to be exposed and effectually stopped, but Cæsar was the first to take action. He was quickly followed by Pompey, however, who encouraged Cicero to denounce the crimes of Verres with the success that we have already noticed. Cicero loftily exclaimed that he did not seek to chastise a single wicked man who had abused his authority as governor, but to extinguish and blot out all wickedness in all places, as the Roman people had long been demanding; but with all his eloquence he was not able to make the people appreciate the fact that the interests of Rome were identical with the well-being and prosperity of her allies, distant or near at hand.

Both Crassus and Pompey retired from the consulship amid the plaudits of the people and with the continued friendship of the optimates. Crassus, out of his immense income, spread a feast for the people on ten thousand tables; dedicated a tenth of his wealth to Hercules; and distributed among the citizens enough grain to supply their families three months. With all his efforts, however, he could not gain the favor which Pompey apparently held with ease. For two years Pompey assumed royal manners, and gave himself up to the enjoyment of his popularity, but then beginning to fear that without some new evidence of genius he might lose the admiration of the people, he began to make broad plans to astonish them.

For years the Mediterranean Sea had been infested by daring pirates, who at last made it unsafe for a Roman noble even to drive to his sea-side villa, or a merchant to venture abroad for purposes of trade. Cities had been ravaged, and the enemies of Rome had from time to time made alliances with the marauders. The pirates dyed their sails with Tyrian purple, they inlaid their oars with silver, and they spread gold on their pennants, so rich had their booty made them. Nor were they less daring than rich; they had captured four hundred towns of importance, they had once kidnapped Cæsar himself, and held him for enormous ransom,* and now they threatened to cut off the entire supply of grain that came from Africa, Sardinia, and Sicily.

The crisis was evident to all, and in it Pompey saw

---

* This occurred in the year 76 B.C., when Cæsar, at the age of twenty-four, was on his way to Rhodes, intending to perfect himself in oratory at the school of Apollonius Molo, the teacher of Cicero. He was travelling as a gentleman of rank, and was captured off Miletus. After a captivity of six weeks, during which he mingled freely with the games and pastimes of the pirates, though plainly assuring them that he should one day hang them all, Cæsar was liberated, on payment of a ransom of some fifty thousand dollars. Good as his word, he promptly collected a fleet of vessels, returned to the island, seized the miscreants as they were dividing their plunder, carried them off to Pergamos, and had them crucified. He then went on to Rhodes, and practised elocution for two years.

his opportunity. In the year 67, he caused a law to be introduced by the tribune Gabinius, ordaining that a commander of consular rank should be appointed for three years, with absolute power over the sea and the coasts about it for fifty miles inland, together with a fleet of two hundred sail, with officers, seamen, and supplies. When the bill had passed, Gabinius declared that there was but one man fit to exercise such remarkable power, and it was conferred with acclamations upon Pompey, whom he nominated. The price of grain immediately fell, for every one had confidence that the dread crisis was passed. The people were right, for in a few weeks the pirates had all been brought to terms. Pompey had divided the sea into thirteen parts, and in each of them the freebooters had been encountered in open battle, driven into creeks and captured, or forced to take refuge in their castles and hunted out of them, so that those who were not taken had surrendered.

The next move among the master spirits led to the still greater advancement of Pompey. His supporters at Rome managed to have him appointed to carry on a war in the East. In the year 74, when other enemies of the republic seized the opportunity to rise against Rome, Mithridates, never fully conquered, entered upon a new war. Lucius Licinius Lucullus, who had gained fame in the former struggle with Mithridates, was sent again to protect Roman interests in Pontus. He completely broke the power of the great monarch, in spite of his vast preparations for the struggle, but, under a pretext, he was now superseded by Pompey, who went out with a feigned appearance of reluctance, to pluck the fruit just ready to drop (B.C. 66). Cicero urged Pompey to accept this new honor,* and Cæsar, who enjoyed the precedents that Pompey had established, in adopting monarchical style, was now glad to have a

A ROMAN POETESS.

rival removed from the country, that he might have better opportunity to perfect his own plans.

* When the Manilian law which enlarged the powers of Pompey was under discussion, Cicero made his first address to the Roman people, and though vigorously opposed by Hortensius and Catulus, carried the day against the senate and the optimates whom they represented. This oration contains a panegyric of Pompey for suppressing piracy, and argues that a public servant who has done well once deserves to be trusted again.

The third or great Mithridatic war lasted from the year 74, when Lucullus was sent out, to 61. By the terms of the Manilian law, Pompey went out with unlimited power over the whole of Asia, as far as Armenia, as well as over the entire Roman forces; and as he already was supreme over the region about the Mediterranean Sea, he was practically dictator throughout all of the dominions of the republic. He planned his first campaign with so much skill that he cut Mithridates off from all help by sea, and destroyed every hope of alliances with other rulers. So clearly did it appear to the Pontic monarch that resistance would be vain, that he sued for peace. Pompey would accept no terms but unconditional surrender, however, and negotiations were broken off. Mithridates determined to avoid battle, but Pompey finally surprised and defeated him in Lesser Armenia, forcing him to flight. He found a retreat in the mountainous region north of the Euxine Sea, where Pompey was unable to follow him. There he meditated grand schemes against the Romans, which he was utterly unable to carry out, and at last he fell a victim to the malevolence of one of his former favorites (B.C. 63).

Pompey continued his conquering progress throughout Asia Minor, and did not return to Rome until he had subdued Armenia, Syria, Phœnicia, and Palestine,* had established many cities, and had organized

---

* There was civil war in Palestine at the time, and the king surrendered to Pompey, but the people refused, took refuge in the stronghold of the temple, and were only overcome after a seige of three months. Pompey explored the temple, examined the golden vessels, the table of shew bread, and the candlesticks in their places, but was

the frontier of the Roman possessions from the Euxine to the river Jordan. When he arrived at Rome, on the first of January, 61, he found that affairs had considerably changed during his absence, and it was not easy for him to determine what position he should assume in relation to the political parties. Cicero offered him his friendship; Cato, grandson of the stern old censor, and an influential portion of the senate opposed him; Crassus and Lucullus, too, were his personal enemies; and Cæsar, who appeared to support him, had really managed to prepare for him a secondary position in the state. On the 1 ist day of September, Pompey celebrated the most splendid triumph that the city had ever seen, and with it the glorious part of his life ended. Over three hundred captive princes walked before his chariot, and brazen tablets declared that he had captured a thousand fortresses, many small towns, and eight hundred ships; that he had founded thirty-nine cities, and vastly raised the public revenue.

The year following the departure of Pompey for the East was rendered noteworthy by the breaking out of a conspiracy that will never be forgotten so long as the writings of Cicero and Sallust remain. These were times of treasons, stratagems, and greed for spoils. Vice and immorality were rampant, and among the vicious and dabased none had fallen lower than Lucius Sergius Catiline, a ferocious man of powerful body and strong mind, who first appears as

surprised to find the Holy of Holies empty, there being no representation of a deity. He reverently refrained from touching the gold, the spices, and the money that he saw, and ordered the place to be cleansed and purified that service might be resumed.

a partisan of Sulla and an active agent in his proscription. All his powers were perverted to evil, and when to his natural viciousness there was added the intensity of disappointed political ambition, he was ready to plunge his country into the most desperate strife to gratify his hate. He stands for the worst vices of this wretched age. He had been a provincial governor, and in Africa had perpetrated all the crimes that Cicero could impute to a Verres, and thus had proclaimed himself a villain of the deepest dye, both abroad and at home.

Gathering about him the profligate nobles and the criminals who had nothing to lose and everything to gain by revolution, Catiline plotted to murder the consuls and seize the government; but his attempt was foiled, and he waited for a more favorable opportunity. Two years later he was defeated by Cicero as candidate for the consulship, and the plot was renewed, it being then determined to add the burning of the city to the other atrocities contemplated. Cicero discovered the scheme, and unveiled its horrid details in four orations; but again the miserable being was permitted to escape justice. He was present and listened in rage to the invective of Cicero until he could bear it no longer, and then rushed wildly out and joined his armed adherents, an open enemy of the state. His plot failed in the city through imprudence of the conspirators and the skill of Cicero, and he himself fled, hoping to reach Gaul. He was, however, hemmed in by the Roman army and killed in a battle. Catiline's head was sent to Rome to assure the government that he was no more. Cicero, who had caused nine of the conspirators to be put to death,* now laid down his consular authority amid the plaudits of the people, who, under the lead of Cato and Catulus, hailed him as the Father of his Country.

Cicero was apparently spoiled by his success. Carried away by his own oratorical ability, he too often reminded the people in his long and eloquent speeches of the great deeds that he had done for the country. They cheered him as he spoke, but after this they never raised him to power again.

Just about this time a noble named Publius Clodius Pulcher, who was a demagogue of the worst moral character, in the pursuance of his base intrigues, committed an act of sacrilege by entering the house of Cæsar, disguised as a woman, during the celebration of the mysteries of the Bona Dea, to which men were never admitted. He was tried for the impiety, and, through the efforts of Cicero, was almost convicted, though he managed to escape by bribery. He was ever afterward a determined enemy of the great orator, and, by the aid of Pompey, Cæsar, and Crassus, finally succeeded in having him condemned for putting to death the Catilinian conspirators without due process of law. Cicero does not appear manly in the story of this affair. He left Rome, fearing to face the result ; and after he had

* Under Roman law no citizen could legally be put to death except by the sanction of the Comitia Curiata, the sovereign assembly of the people, though it often happened that the regulation was ignored. If nobody dared or cared to object, no notice was taken of the irregularity, but we shall see that Cicero paid dearly for his action at this time.

gone Clodius caused a bill to be passed by which he was declared a public enemy, and every citizen was forbidden to give him fire or water within four hundred miles of Rome (spring of 58). He found his way to Brundusium and thence to Greece, where he passed his time in the most unmanly wailings and gloomy forebodings. His property was confiscated, his rich house on the Palatine Hill and his villas being given over to plunder and destruction. Strange as it appears, Cicero was recalled the next year, and entered the city amid the hearty plaudits of the changeful people, though his self-respect was gone and his spirit broken.

Meantime, Cæsar had been quietly pushing himself to the front. He had returned from Spain, where he had been governor, at about the time that Pompey had returned from the East. He reconciled that great warrior to Crassus (called from his immense wealth *Dives*, the rich), and with the two made a secret arrangement to control the government. This was known as the *First Triumvirate*,* or government of three men, though it was only a coalition, and did not strictly deserve the name given it (B.C. 60). Cæsar reaped the first-fruits of the league, as he intended, by securing the office of consul, through the assistance of his colleagues, whose influence proved irresistible.

Entering upon his office in the year 59, Cæsar very soon obtained the good-will of all,—first win-

---

* Each of the three pledged himself not to speak nor to act except to subserve the common interest of all, though of course they were not sincere in their promises of mutual support.

THE FORUM ROMANUM IN MODERN TIMES.

ning the people by proposing an agrarian law dividing the public lands among them. This was the last law of this sort, as that of Cassius (B.C. 486) had been the first.* He rewarded Crassus by means of a law remitting one third of the sum that the publicans who had agreed to farm the revenues in Asia Minor had contracted to pay to the state ; and satisfied Pompey by a ratification of all his acts in the East. The distribution of the lands among the people was placed in the hands of Pompey and Crassus.

At the end of his term of office Cæsar was made governor of Gaul, an office which he sought no more for the opportunity it afforded of gaining renown by conquering those ancient enemies who had formerly visited Rome with such dire devastation, than because he hoped to win for himself an army and partisans who would be useful in carrying out further ambitious ends.

Cæsar now entered upon a wonderful career of conquest, which lasted nine years. The story of what he accomplished during the first seven is given in his "Commentaries," as they are called, which are still read in schools, on account of the incomparable simplicity, naturalness, and purity of the style in which they are written, as well as because they seem to give truthful accounts of the events they describe. Sixty years before this time the Romans had possessed themselves of a little strip of Gaul south of the Alps, which was known as the Province,† and though they had ever since thought that there was a very important region to the north and west that

* See page 83.   † See pages 166 and 182.

might be conquered, they made no great effort to gain it. Cæsar was now to win imperishable laurels by effecting what had been before only vaguely dreamed of. He first made himself master of the country of the Helvetii (modern Switzerland), defeated the Germans under their famous general Ariovistus, and subjected the Belgian confederacy. The frightful carnage involved in these campaigns cannot be described, and the thousands upon thousands of brave barbarians who were sacrificed to the extension of Roman civilization are enough to make one shudder. When the despatches of Cæsar announcing his successes reached Rome, the senate, on motion of Cicero, though against the protestations of Cato, ordained that a grand public thanksgiving, lasting fifteen days, should be celebrated (B.C. 57). This was an unheard-of honor, the most ostentatious thanksgiving of the kind before—that given to Pompey, after the close of the war against Mithridates— having lasted but ten days.

Pompey and Crassus had fallen out during the absence of Cæsar, and he now invited them to meet and consult at Lucca, at the foot of the Apennines, just north of Pisa, where (April, 56) he held a sort of court, hundreds of Roman senators waiting upon him to receive the bribes with which he ensured the success of his measures during his absences in the field.* Here the three agreed that Pompey should

* Pompey had left Rome ostensibly for the purpose of arranging for supplies of grain from Africa and Sardinia. He was followed by many of his most noted adherents, the conference counting more than two hundred senators and sixscore lictors. Cæsar, like a mighty

rule Spain, Crassus Syria, and Cæsar Gaul, which he had made his own. Cæsar still kept on with his conquests, meeting desperate resistance, however, from the hordes of barbarians, who would not remain conquered, but engaged in revolts that caused him vast trouble and the loss of large numbers of soldiers. Incidentally to his other wars, he made two incursions into Britain, the home of our forefathers (B.C. 55 and 54), and nominally conquered the people, but it was not a real subjugation. Shakespeare did not make a mistake when he put into the mouth of the queen-wife of Cymbeline the words:

> * * * "A kind of conquest
> Cæsar made here ; but made not here his brag
> Of ' came' and ' saw' and ' overcame,'"

and certainly the brave Britons did not continue to obey their self-styled Roman " rulers."

In the sixth year of Cæsar's campaigns in Gaul, it seemed as if all was to be lost to the Romans. There arose a young general named Vercingetorix, who was much abler than any leader the Gauls had ever opposed to their enemies, and he united them as they had never been united before. This man persuaded his countrymen to lay their own country waste, in order that it might not afford any abiding place for the Romans, but contrary to his intentions one town that was stongly fortified was left, and to that Cæsar

magician, caused the discordant spirits to act in concert. The power of the triumvirs is shown by the change that came over public opinion, and the calmness with which their acts were submitted to, though it was evident that the historic form of government was to be overturned, and a monarchy established.

laid siege, finally taking it and butchering all the men, women, and children that it contained. Vercingetorix then fortified himself at Alesia (southeast of Paris), where he was, of course, besieged by the Romans, but soon Cæsar found his own forces attacked in the rear, and surrounded by a vast army of Gauls, who had come to the relief of their leader. In the face of such odds, he succeeded in vanquishing the enemy, and took the place, achieving the most wonderful act of his genius. The conquered chief was reserved to grace a Roman triumph, and to die by the hand of a Roman executioner.* The fate of Gaul was now certain, and Cæsar found comparatively little difficulty in subduing the remaining states, the last of which was Aquitania, the flat and uninteresting region in the southwest of modern France, watered by the Garonne and washed by the Atlantic. The conqueror treated the Gauls with mildness, and endeavored in every way to make them adopt Roman habits and customs. As they had lost all hope of resisting him, they calmly accepted the situation, and the foundation of the subsequent Romanizing of the west of Europe was laid. Three million Gauls had been conquered, a

* The historian Mommsen says of this unfortunate "barbarian": "As after a day of gloom the sun breaks through the clouds at its setting, so destiny bestows on nations in their decline a last great man. Thus Hannibal stands at the close of the Phœnician history and Vercingetorix at the close of the Celtic. They were not all to save the nations to which they belonged from a foreign yoke, but they spared them the last remaining disgrace—an ignominious fall. . . . The whole ancient world presents no more genuine knight [than Vercingetorix], whether as regards his essential character or his outward appearance."

million had been butchered, and another million taken captive, while eight hundred cities, centres of active life and places of the enjoyment of those social virtues for which the rough inhabitants of the region were noted, had been destroyed. Legions of Roman soldiers had been cut to pieces in accomplishing this result, the influence of which upon the history of Europe can hardly be over-estimate. Cæsar had completely eclipsed the military prestige of his rival, Pompey the Great.

XVI.

HOW THE TRIUMVIRS CAME TO UNTIMELY ENDS.

It was agreed at the conference of Lucca that Pompey should rule Spain, but it did not suit his plans to go to that distant country. He preferred to remain at Rome, where he thought that he might do something that would establish his influence with the people, and give him the advantage over his colleagues that they were each seeking to get over him. In order to court popularity, he built the first stone theatre that Rome had ever seen, capable of accommodating the enormous number of forty thousand spectators, and opened it with a splendid exhibition (B.C. 55).* Day after day the populace were ad-

* This theatre was built after the model of one that Pompey had seen at Mitylene, and stood between the Campus Martius and Circus Flaminius. Adjoining it was a hall affording shelter for the spectators in bad weather, in which Julius Cæsar was assassinated. The Roman theatres had no roofs, and, in early times, no seats. At this period there were seats of stone divided by broad passages for the convenience of the audience in going in and out. A curtain, which was drawn down instead of up, served to screen the actors from the spectators. Awnings were sometimes used to protect the audience from rain and sun. A century before this time the Senate had stopped the construction of a theatre, and prohibited dramatic exhibitions as subversive of good morals. The actors usually wore masks. See page 159.

mitted, and on each occasion new games and plays were prepared for their gratification. For the first time a rhinoceros was shown; eighteen elephants were killed by fierce Libyan hunters, and five hundred African lions lost their lives in the combats to which they were forced; the vehement, tragic actor Æsopus, then quite aged, came out of his retirement for the occasion, and uttered his last words on the stage, the juncture being all the more remarkable from the fact that his strength failed him in the midst of a very emphatic part; gymnasts contended, gladiators fought to the death, and the crowd cheered, but, alas for Pompey! the cheers expressed merely temporary enjoyment at the scenes before them, and did not at all indicate that he had been received to their hearts.

Crassus, in the meantime, was thinking that he too must accomplish something great or he would be left behind by both of his associates. He reflected that Cæsar had won distinction in Gaul, and Pompey by overcoming the pirates and conquering the East, and determined to show his skill as a warrior in his new province, Parthia. There was no cause for war against the people of that distant land, but a cause might easily be found, or a war begun without one, the great object aimed at being the extension of the sovereignty of Rome, and marking the name of Crassus high on the pillar of fame. This would surely, he thought, give him the utmost popularity. Thus, in the year 54, he set out for Syria, and the world saw each of the triumvirs busily engaged in pushing his own cause in his own way. Ten years later not

AN ELEPHANT IN ARMOR. (See page 122.)

one of them was alive to enjoy that which they had all so earnestly sought.

It is not necessary to follow Crassus minutely in his campaign. He spent a winter in Syria, and in the spring of 53 set out for the still distant East, crossing the Euphrates, and plunging into the desert wastes of old Mesopotamia, where he was betrayed into the hands of the enemy, and lost, not far from Carrhæ (Charran or Haran), the City of Nahor, to which the patriarch Abraham migrated with his family from Ur of the Chaldees. Thus there remained but two of the three ambitious seekers of popular applause.

Pompey had been in some degree attached to Cæsar through his daughter Julia, whom he had married; but she died in the same year that Crassus went to the East, and from that time he gravitated toward the aristocrats, with whom his former affiliations had been. The ten years of Cæsar's government were to expire on the 1st of January, 48, and it became important for him to obtain the office of consul for the following year; but the senate and Pompey were equally interested to have him deprived of the command of the army before receiving any new appointment. The reason for this was that Cato[*] had declared that as soon as Cæsar should

---

[*] This Cato was great-grandson of Cato the Censor (see page 152), was a man who endeavored to remind the world constantly of his illustrious descent by imitating the severe independence of his great ancestor, and by assuming marked peculiarity of dress and behavior. His life, blighted by an early disappointment in love, was unfortunate to the last. He was a consistent, but often ridiculous, leader of the minority opposed to the triumvirs.

become a private citizen he would bring him to trial for illegal acts of which his enemies accused him; and it was plain to him, no less than to all the world, that if Pompey were in authority at the time, conviction would certainly follow such a trial. One of Cicero's correspondents said on this subject: "Pompey has absolutely determined not to allow Cæsar to be elected consul on any terms except a previous resignation of his army and his government, while Cæsar is convinced that he must inevitably fall if he has once let go his army."

In the year 50, Cæsar went into Cisalpine Gaul, that is, into the region which is now known as Northern Italy, and was received as a great conqueror. He then went over the mountains to Farther Gaul and reviewed his army—the army that he had so often led to victory. He did not lose sight of the fact that it was now, more than ever before, necessary for him to have some one in Rome who would look out for his interests in his absences, and he bethought himself of a man whom he had known from his youth, Caius Scribonius Curio by name, a spendthrift whom he had vainly tried to inspire with higher ambition than the mere gratification of his appetites. He was married to Fulvia, a scheming woman of light character, widow of Clodius (who afterwards become wife of Marc Antony), and he was harassed by enormous debts. Though Curio was allied to the party of Pompey, Cæsar won him over by paying his debts,* and he then began cautiously

---

* The debts of this young man have been estimated as high as $2,500,000, and their vastness shows by contrast how wealthy private citizens sometimes became at this epoch.

to turn his back upon his former associates. At first, he pretended to act against Cæsar as usual; then he cautiously assumed the appearance of neutrality; and, when the proper opportunity arrived, he threw all the weight of his influence in favor of the master to whom he had sold himself. Curio was not the only person whom Cæsar bought, for he distributed immense sums among other citizens of influence, as he had not hesitated to do before, and they quietly interposed objections to any movement against him, though outwardly holding to Pompey's party.

The senate, assisted by the solemn jugglery of the pontiffs, who had charge of the calendar and were accustomed to shorten or lengthen the year according as their political inclinations impelled them, proposed to weaken Cæsar's position by obliging him to resign his authority November 13th, though his term did not expire, as we know, until the following January.

Under these circumstances, Curio, then one of the tribunes of the people, began his tactics by plausibly urging that it would be only fair that Pompey, who was not far from the city at the head of an army, should also give up his authority at the same time before entering the city. Pompey had no intention of doing this, though everybody saw that it was reasonable, and Curio took courage and went a step farther, denouncing him as evidently designing to make himself tyrant.* However, in order to keep

---

* A tyrant was simply a ruler with dictatorial powers, and it was not until he abused his authority that he became the odious character indicated by the modern meaning of the title; but any thing that looked like a return to the government of a king was hateful to the Romans.

up his appearance of impartiality, he approved a declaration that unless both generals should lay down their authority, they ought to be denounced as public enemies, and that war should be immediately declared against them. Pompey became indignant at this. Finally it was decided that each commander should be ordered to give up one legion, to be used against the Parthians, in a war which it was pretended would soon open. Pompey readily assented, but craftily managed to perform his part without any loss; for he called upon Cæsar to return to him a legion that he had borrowed three years before. The senate then sent both legions to Capua instead of to Asia, intending, in due time, to use them against Cæsar. Cæsar gave up the two legions willingly, because he thought that with the help of the army that remained, and with the assistance of the citizens whom he had bribed, he would be able to take care of himself in any emergency, but nevertheless he endeavored to bind the soldiers of these legions more firmly to him by giving a valuable present to each one as he went away.* Not long after this Curio went to Ravenna to consult Cæsar.

* One of Cicero's correspondents writing in January, 50, says in a postscript: "I told you above that Curio was freezing, but he finds it warm enough just at present, everybody being hotly engaged in pulling him to pieces. Just because he failed to get an intercalary month, without the slightest ado he has stepped over to the popular side, and begun to harangue in favor of Cæsar."

In replying to this, Cicero wrote: "The paragraph you added was indeed a stab from the point of your pen. What! Curio now become a supporter of Cæsar. Who could ever have expected this but myself? for, upon my life, I really did expect it. Good heavens! how I miss our laughing together over it."

We see on our maps a little stream laid down as the boundary between Italy and Gaul. It is called the Rubicon ; but when we go to Italy and look for the stream itself we do not find it so easily, because there are at least two rivers that may be taken for it. However, it is not of much importance for the purposes of history which was actually the boundary. North of the Rubicon we see the ancient city of Ravenna, which stood in old times like Venice, on islands, and like it was intersected in all directions by canals through which the tide poured volumes of purifying salt water twice every day. Now the canals are all filled up, and the city is four miles from the sea, so large have been the deposits from the muddy waters that flow down the rivers into the Adriatic at that place. Thirty-three miles south of Ravenna and nine miles from the Rubicon, the map shows us another ancient town called Ariminum, connected directly with Rome by the Flaminian road, which was built some two hundred years before the time of which we are writing. Ravenna was the last town in the territory of Cæsar on the way to Rome, and there he took his position to watch proceedings, for it was not allowed him to leave his province.

On the first of January, 49, Curio arrived at Rome with a letter from Cæsar offering to give up his command provided Pompey would do the same. The consuls at that time were partisans of Pompey, and they at first refused to allow the letter to be read ; but the tribunes of the people were in favor of Cæsar, and they forced the senators to listen to it.

Roman Trumpeter. Roman Hornblower. Commanders of Allies. Samnite. African. British Warrior. German Confederates.

ITALIAN AND GERMAN ALLIES, COSTUMES, AND ARMOR.

A violent debate followed, and it was finally voted that unless Cæsar should disband his army within a certain time he should be considered an enemy of the state, and be treated accordingly. On the sixth of the same month the power of dictators was given to the consuls, and the two tribunes who favored Cæsar—one of whom was Marc Antony—fled to him in disguise, for there was no safety for them in Rome.

Now there was war. On the one side we have Pompey, proud and confident, but unprepared because he was so confident; and on the other, Cæsar, cool and unperturbed, relying not only on his army, but also upon the friends that his money and tact had made among the soldiers with him, no less than among those at Capua and elsewhere, upon which his opponent also depended.

The moment is one that has been fixed in the memory of men for all time by a proverbial expression based upon an apochryphal event that might well have happened upon the banks of the little Rubicon. As soon as Cæsar heard of the action of the senate he assembled his soldiers and asked them if they would support him. They replied that they would follow him wherever he commanded. The story runs that he then ordered the army to advance upon Ariminum, but that when he arrived at the little dividing river he ordered a halt, and meditated upon his course. He knew that when he crossed that line blood would surely flow from thousands of Romans, and he asked himself whether he was right in bringing such woes upon his countrymen, and how his act would be represented in history.

It is not improbable that the great conqueror entertained thoughts like these, for he was a writer of history as well as one of the mightiest makers of it; but he mentions nothing of the sort in his own story of the advance, and we may well doubt whether it was not invented by Suetonius, or some other historian, who wished to make his account as picturesque as possible. It is said that after these thoughts Cæsar exclaimed: "The die is cast; let us go where the gods and the injustice of our enemies direct us!" He then urged his charger through the stream.

There had been confusion in the capital many a time before, but probably never was there such a commotion as arose when it was known that the conqueror of Gaul, the man who had for years marched through that great region as a mighty monarch, was on the way towards it. That the consuls were endowed with dictatorial power for the emergency, availed little. A few days before, some one had asked Pompey what he should do for an army if Cæsar should leave his province with his soldiers, and he replied haughtily that he should need but to stamp on the ground and soldiers would spring up. Now he stamped, and stamped in vain; no volunteers came at his call. The venerable senators, successors of those who had remained in their seats when the barbarians were coming, hastened away for dear life; they did not make the usual sacrifices; they did not take their goods and chattels; they even forgot the public treasure, which would have been of the utmost use to them and to the cause of Pompey.

Cæsar's army supported him as a whole, but there was one self-important man among the leaders of it who proved an exception. Titus Labienus, who had been with Cæsar in Spain, who had performed some brilliant feats when Vercingetorix revolted, and who was in all his master's confidence, had allowed his little mind to become filled with pride and ambition until he began to believe that he was at the bottom of Cæsar's success, and probably as great a general as he! He was ready to allow the Pompeians to beguile him from his allegiance, and at last went over to them. Cæsar, to show how little he cared for the defection of Labienus, hastened to send his baggage after him; but in Rome he was welcomed with acclamations. Cicero, the trimmer, exclaimed: "Labienus has behaved quite like a hero!" and believed that Cæsar had received a tremendous blow by his defection. This deserter's act had, however, no effect whatever on the progress of Cæsar, who, though it was the middle of winter, marched onwards, receiving the surrender of city after city, giving to all the conquered citizens the most liberal terms, and thus binding them firmly to his cause.*

Pompey did not even attempt to interrupt the triumphant career of his enemy, but determined to find safety out of Italy, and hastened to Brundusium

---

* As Cæsar approached Rome, Cato took flight, and, determined to mourn until death the unhappy lot of his country, allowed his hair to grow, and resigned himself to unavailing grief. Too weak and perplexed to stand against opposing troubles, he fondly thought that resolutions and laws and a temporizing policy might avail to bring happiness and order to a distraught commonwealth.

as fast as possible. After mastering the whole country, Cæsar reached the same port before Pompey was able to get away, and began a siege, in the progress of which Pompey escaped. Cæsar was not able to follow, on account of a want of vessels. He therefore turned back to Rome, where he encountered no opposition, except from Metellus, a tribune of the people, who attempted to keep him from taking possession of the gold in the temple of Saturn, traditionally supposed to have been that which Camillus had recovered from Brennus. It was intended for use in case the Gauls should make another invasion, but Cæsar said that he had conquered the Gauls, and they need be feared no more. "Stand aside, young man!" he exclaimed; "it is easier for me to do than to say!" Metellus saw that it was not worth while to discuss the question with such a man, and prudently stepped aside.

Cæsar did not remain at Rome at this time, but hastened to Spain, where partisans of Pompey were in arms, leaving Marc Antony in charge of Italy in general, and Marcus Lepidus responsible for order in the city. Both of these men were destined to become more prominent in the future. At the same time, legions were sent to Sicily and Sardinia, and their success, which was easily gained, preserved the city from a scarcity of grain. Cæsar himself overcame the Pompeians in Spain, and, in accordance with his policy in Italy, dismissed them unharmed. Most of their soldiers were taken into his own army. He then felt free to continue his movements against Pompey himself, and returned to the capital.

For eleven days Cæsar was dictator of Rome, receiving the office from Lepidus, who had been authorized to give it by those senators who had not fled with Pompey. In that short period he passed laws calling home the exiles; giving back their rights as citizens to the children of those who had suffered in the Sullan proscription; and affording relief to debtors. Then, causing the senate to declare him consul, he started for Brundusium to pursue his rival. It was the fourth of January, 48, when he sailed for the coast of Epirus, and the following day he landed on the soil of Greece. He met Pompey at Dyrrachium, but his force was so small that he was defeated. He then retreated to the southeast, and another battle was fought on the plain of Pharsalia, in Thessaly, June 6, 48. The forces were still very unequal, Pompey having more than two soldiers to one of Cæsar's; but Cæsar's were the better warriors, and Pompey was totally defeated. Feeling that every thing was now lost, Pompey sought an asylum in Egypt; and there he was assassinated by order of the reigning monarch, who hoped to win the favor of Cæsar in his contest with his sister, Cleopatra, who claimed the throne.

Cæsar followed his adversary with his usual promptness, and when he had reached Egypt was shown his rival's severed head, from which he turned with real or feigned sadness and tears. This alarmed the king and his partisans, and they still further lost heart when Cleopatra won Cæsar to her support by the charms of her personal beauty.

After a brief struggle known as the Alexandrine

War, which closed in March, 47, Cæsar placed the queen and her brother on the throne. It was at this time that the great Library and Museum at Alexandria were destroyed by fire. Four hundred thousand volumes were said to have been burned. The next month Cæsar was called from Egypt to Pontus, where a son of Mithridates was in arms, and, after a campaign of five days, he gained a decisive victory at a place called Zela, boastfully announcing his success to the senate in three short words: "*Veni, vidi, vici*" (I came, I saw, I overcame). In September, Cæsar was again in Rome, where he remained only three months, arranging affairs. There were fears lest he should make a proscription, but he proceeded to no such extremity, exercising his characteristic clemency towards those who had been opposed to him. A revolt occurred at this time among the soldiers at Capua, and they marched to Rome, but Cæsar cowed them by a display of haughty coolness.

The remnant of the adherents of Pompey gathered together and went to Africa, whither Cæsar followed, and after a short campaign defeated them on the field of Thapsus, April 6, 46. They were commanded by Scipio, father-in-law of Pompey, and by Cato, who had accepted the position after it had been declined by Cicero, his superior in rank. After the defeat of Thapsus Cato retreated to Utica, where he deliberately put an end to his life after occupying several hours in reading Plato's *Phædo*, a dialogue on the immortality of the soul. From the place of his death he is known in history as Cato of Utica.

When the news of this final victory reached Rome

Cæsar was appointed dictator for ten years, and a thanksgiving lasting forty days was decreed. He was also endowed with a newly created office—that of Overseer of Public Morals (*Præfectus Morum*). Temples and statues were dedicated to his honor; a golden chair was assigned for his use when he sat in the senate; the month Quintilis was renamed after him Julius (July); and other unheard of honors were thrust upon him by a servile senate. He was also called the Father of his Country (a title that had been before borne by Camillus and Cicero), and four triumphs were celebrated for him. On his own part, Cæsar feasted the people at twenty-two thousand tables, and caused combats of wild animals and gladiators to be celebrated in the arenas beneath awnings of the richest silks.

The great conqueror now prepared to carry out schemes of a beneficent nature which would have been of great value to the world; but their achievement was interfered with, first by war and then by his own death. He intended to unify the regions controlled by the republic by abolishing offensive political distinctions, and to develop them by means of a geographical survey which would have occupied years to complete under the most competent management; and he wished to codify the Roman law, which had been growing up into a universal jurisprudence, a work which Cicero looked upon as a hopeless though brilliant vision, and one that Justinian actually accomplished, though not until six hundred years later. He contemplated also the erection of vast public works. His knowledge of astronomy

THE CALENDAR REFORMED.

led him to accomplish one important change, for which we have reason to remember him to-day. He reformed the calendar, substituting the one used until 1582 (known from him as the Julian calendar) for that which was then current.* Three hundred and fifty-five days had been called a year from the time of Numa Pompilius, but as that number did not correspond with the actual time of the revolution of the earth around the sun, it had been customary to intercalate a month, every second year, of twenty-two and twenty-three days alternately, and one day had also been added to make a fortunate number. This made the adaptation of the nominal year to the actual a matter of great intricacy, the duty being intrusted to the chief pontiffs. These officers were often corrupted, and managed to effect political ends from time to time by the addition or omission of the intercalary days and months. At this time the civil calendar was some weeks in advance of the actual time, so that the consuls, for example, who should have entered office January 1, 46, really assumed their power October 13, 47. The Julian calendar made the year to consist of 365 days and six hours, which was correct within a few minutes; but, by the time of Pope Gregory XIII., this had amounted to ten days, and a new reform was instituted. Cæsar now added ninety days to the year in order to make the year 45 begin

* The Gregorian calendar was introduced in the Catholic states of Europe in 1582, but owing to popular prejudice England did not begin to use it until 1752, in which year September 3d became, by act of Parliament, September 14th. Usage in America followed that of the mother country.

at the proper time, inserting a new month between the 23d and 24th of February, and adding two new months after the end of November, so that the long year thus manufactured (445 days) was very justly called the "year of confusion, or "the last year of confusion."

Cæsar had also in mind plans of conquest. He had not forgotten that the Roman arms had been unsuccessful at Carrhæ, and he wished to subdue the Parthians, but the ghost of Pompey would not down. His sons raised the banner of revolt in Spain, and the officers sent against them did not succeed in their efforts to assert the supremacy of Rome. It was necessary that Cæsar himself should go there, and accordingly he set out in September. Twenty-seven days later he was on the ground, and though he found himself in the face of greater difficulties than he had anticipated, a few months sufficed to completely overthrow the enemy, who were defeated finally at the battle of Munda, not far from Gibraltar (March, 17, 45). Thirty thousand of them perished. Cæsar did not return to Rome until September, because affairs of the province required attention. Again he celebrated a triumph, marked by games and shows, and new honors from the senate.

Cæsar's ambition now made him wish to continue the supreme power in his family, and he fixed upon a great-nephew named Octavius as his successor. In the fifth year of his consulate (B.C. 44), on the feast of Lupercalia (Feb. 15th), he attempted to take a more important step. He prevailed upon Marc Antony to make him an offer of the kingly diadem, but as he immediately saw that it was not pleasing to the people that he should accept it, he pushed the glittering coronet from him, amid their plaudits, as though he would not think of assuming any sign of authority that the people did not freely offer him themselves.* Cæsar still longed for the name of king, however, and became irritated because it was not given him. This was shown in his intercourse with the nobles, and they were now excited against him by one Caius Cassius Longinus (commonly called simply Cassius), who had wandered and fought with Crassus in Parthia, but had escaped from that disastrous campaign. He had been a follower of Pompey, and had fallen into Cæsar's hands shortly after the battle of Pharsalia. Though he owed his life to Cæsar, he was personally hostile to him, and his feelings were so strong that he formed a plot for his destruction, in which sixty or eighty persons were involved. Among these was Marcus Junius Brutus, then about forty years of age, who had also been with Pompey at Pharsalia. He was of illustrious pedigree, and claimed to be descended from the shadowy hero of his name, who is said to have pur-

---

* "I saw Mark Antony offer him a crown; yet 't was not a crown neither, 't was one of these coronets; and, as I told you, he put it by once; but for all that, to my thinking, he would fain have had it. Then he offered it to him again; then he put it by again; but to my thinking, he was very loth to lay his fingers off it. And then he offered it the third time; he put it the third time by, and still as he refused it, the rabblement shouted and clapped their chapped hands, and threw up their sweaty night-caps, and uttered such a deal of stinking breath because Cæsar refused the crown, that it had almost choked Cæsar; for he swooned and fell down at it." Casca's account, in Shakespeare's *Julius Cæsar*, act i., sc. 2.

sued the Tarquins with such patriotic zeal. His life also had been spared by Cæsar at Pharsalia, and he had made no opposition to his acts as dictator. Cato was his political model, and at about this time, he divorced his wife to marry Portia, Cato's daughter. Cassius had married Junia Tertulla, half-sister of Brutus, and now offered him the place of chief adviser of the conspirators, who determined upon a sudden and bold effort to assassinate the dictator. They intended to make it appear that patriotism gave them the reason for their act, but in this they failed.

The senate was to convene on the Ides of March, and Cæsar was warned that danger awaited him; but he was not to be deterred, and entered the chamber amid the applause of the people. The conspirators crowded about him, keeping his friends at a distance, and at a concerted signal he was grasped by the hands and embraced by some, while others stabbed him with their fatal daggers. He fell at the base of the statue of Pompey, pierced with more than a score of wounds. It is said that when he noticed Brutus in the angry crowd, he exclaimed in surprise and sorrow: "*Et tu Brute!*" (And thou, too, Brutus!).

Brutus had prepared a speech to deliver to the senate, but when he looked around, he found that senators, centurions, lictors, and attendants, all had fled, and the place was empty. He then marched with his accomplices to the forum. It was crowded with an excited multitude, but it was not a multitude of friends. The assassins saw that there was no safety for them in the city. Lepidus was at the gates with an army, and Antony had taken possession of the papers and treasures of Cæsar, which gave him additional power; but all parties were in doubt as to the next steps, and a reconciliation was determined upon as giving time for reflection. Cassius went to sup with Antony, and Brutus with Lepidus. This shows plainly that the good of the republic was not the cause nearest the hearts of the principal actors; but that each, like a wary player at chess, was only anxious lest some adversary should get an advantage over him.

The senate was immediately convened, and under the direction of Cicero, who became its temporary leader, it was voted that the acts of Cæsar, intended as well as performed, should be ratified, and that the conspirators should be pardoned, and assigned to the provinces that Cæsar had designated them for.

Antony now showed himself a consummate actor, and a master of the art of moving the multitude. He prepared for the obsequies of the dictator, at which he was to deliver the oration, and, while pretending to endeavor to hold back the people from violence against the murderers, managed to excite them to such an extent that nothing could restrain them. He brought the body into the Campus Martius for the occasion, and there in its presence displayed the bloody garment through which the daggers of the conspirators had been thrust; identified the rents made by the leader, Cassius, the "envious Casca," the "well-beloved Brutus," and the others; and displayed a waxen effigy that he had prepared for the occasion, bearing all the wounds. He called upon the crowd the while, as it swayed to and fro in its threatening violence, to listen to reason, but at the same time told them that if he possessed the eloquence of a Brutus he would ruffle up their spirits and put a tongue in every wound of Cæsar that would move the very stones of Rome to rise in mutiny. He said that if the people could but hear the last will of the dictator, they would dip their kerchiefs in his blood—yea, beg a hair of him for memory, and, dying, mention it in their wills as a rich legacy to their children.

The oration had its natural effect. The people, stirred from one degree of frenzy to another, piled up chairs, benches, tables, brushwood, even ornaments and costly garments for a funeral pile, and burned the whole in the forum. Unable to restrain themselves, they rushed with brands from the fire towards the homes of the conspirators to wreak vengeance upon them. Brutus and Cassius had fled from the city, and the others could not be found, so that the fury of their hate died out for want of new fuel upon which to feed.

Antony was now the chief man of Rome, and it was expected that he would demand the dictatorship. To the astonishment of all, he proposed that the office itself should be forever abolished, thus keeping up his pretence of moderation; but, on the other hand, he asked for a body-guard, which the senate granted, and he surrounded himself with a force of six thousand men. He appointed magis-

INTERIOR OF THE FORUM ROMANUM.

trates as he wished, recalled exiles, and freed any from prison whom he desired, under pretence of following the will of Cæsar.

It soon became apparent that, in the words of Cicero addressed to Cassius, the state seemed to have been "emancipated from the king, but not from the kingly power," for no one could tell where Antony would stop his pretence of carrying out the plans of Cæsar. The republic was doubtless soon to end, and it was not plain what new misery was in store for the distracted people.

XVII.

HOW THE REPUBLIC BECAME AN EMPIRE.

WHEN Cæsar had planned to go to Parthia, he sent in that direction some of his legions, which wintered at Apollonia, just over the Adriatic, opposite Brundusium, and with them went the young and sickly nephew whom Cæsar had mentioned in his will as his heir. While the young man was engaged in familiarizing himself with the soldiers and their life, a freedman arrived in camp to announce from his mother the tragedy of the Ides of March. The soldiers offered to go with him to avenge his uncle's death, but he decided to set out at once and alone for the capital. At Brundusium he was received by the army with acclamations. He did not hesitate to assume the name Cæsar, and to claim the succession, though he thus bound himself to pay the legacies that Cæsar had made to the people. He was known as Caius Julius Cæsar Octavianus, or, briefly, as Octavius.* Cæsar had bequeathed his magnificent

* Octavius was son of Caius Octavius and Atia, daughter of Julia, sister of Julius Cæsar, and was born Sept. 23, B.C. 63. His true name was the same as that of his father, but he is usually mentioned in history as Augustus, an untranslatable title that he assumed when he became emperor. His descent was traced from Atys, son of Alba, an old Latin hero.

gardens on the opposite side of the Tiber to the public as a park, and to every citizen in Rome a gift of three hundred sesterces, equal to ten or fifteen dollars. These provisions could not easily be carried out except by Antony, who had taken possession of Cæsar's moneys, and who was at the moment the most powerful man in the republic. Next to him stood Lepidus, who was in command of the army. These two seemed to stand between Octavius and his heritage.

Octavius understood the value of money, and took possession of the public funds at Brundusium, captured such remittances from the provinces as he could reach, and sent off to Asia to see how much he could secure of the amount provided for the Parthian expedition, just as though all this had been his own personal property.

Thus the timid but ambitious youth began to prepare himself for supreme authority. When he reached Rome his mother and other friends warned him of the risks involved in his course, but he was resolute. He had made the acquaintance at Apollonia of Marcus Vipsanius Agrippa, then twenty years of age, who afterwards became a skilful warrior and always was a valuable adviser, and now he determined to make a friend of Cicero. This remarkable orator had already been intimate with all the prominent men of his day; had at one time or another flattered or cajoled Curio, Cassius, Crassus, Pompey, Antony, and Cæsar, and now, after thorroughly canvassing the probabilities, he decided to take the side of Octavius, though he was loth to break with either Brutus or Antony. His weakness is plainly and painfully presented by his own hand in his interesting letters, which add much light to the story of this period. *

Octavius gathered together enough money to pay the legacies of Cæsar by sales of property, and by loans, in spite of the fact that Antony refused to give up any that he had taken. He artfully won the soldiers and the people by his liberality (that could not fail to be contrasted with the grasping action of Antony), and by the shows with which he amused them. Thus with it all he managed to make the world believe that he was not laying plans of ambition, but simply wished to protect the state from the selfish designs of his rival. In this effort he was supported by the oratory of Cicero, who began to compose and deliver or publish a remarkable series of fourteen speeches known as Philippics, from their resemblance to the four acrimonious invectives against Philip of Macedon which the great Demosthenes launched at Athens during the eleven years in which he strove to arouse the weakened Greeks from inactivity and pusillanimity (352–342 B.C.).

* James Anthony Froude says : " In Cicero, Nature half-made a great man and left him uncompleted. Our characters are written in our forms, and the bust of Cicero is the key to his history. The brow is broad and strong, the nose large, the lips tightly compressed, the features lean and keen from restless intellectual energy. The loose, bending figure, the neck too weak for the weight of the head, explain the infirmity of will, the passion, the cunning, the vanity, the absence of manliness and veracity. He was born into an age of violence with which he was too feeble to contend. The gratitude of mankind for his literary excellence will forever preserve his memory from too harsh a judgment."—" Cæsar, a Sketch," chapter xxvii.

Cicero entered Rome on the first of September, and delivered his first Philippic the next day, in the same Temple of Concord in which he had denounced Catiline twenty years before. He then retired from the city, and did not hear the abusive tirade with which Antony attempted to blacken his reputation. In October he prepared a second speech, which was not delivered, but was given to the public in November. This is the most elaborate and the best of the Philippics, and it is also much more fierce than the former. The last of the series was delivered April 22, 43. Antony was soon declared a public enemy, and Cicero in his speeches constantly urged a vigorous prosecution of the war against him.

Octavius gained the confidence of the army, and then demanded the consulate of the senate. When that powerful office had been obtained, he broke with the senate, and marched to the northward, ostensibly to conquer Antony and Lepidus, who were coming down with another great army. Instead of precipitating a battle, Lepidus contrived to have a meeting on a small island in a tributary of the Po, not far from the present site of Bologna, and there, toward the end of October, it was agreed that the government of the Roman world should be peaceably divided between the three captains, who were to be called Triumvirs for the settlement of the affairs of the republic. They were to retain their offices until the end of December, 38, Lepidus ruling Spain; Octavius, Sicily, Sardinia, and Africa; and Antony, the two Gauls; while Italy was to be governed by the three in common, their authority being

paramount to senate, consuls, and laws. This is
known as the Second Triumvirate, though we must
remember that the former arrangement, made by

MARCUS TULLIUS CICERO.

Cæsar, Pompey, and Crassus, was simply a private
league without formal sanction of law. The second
triumvirate was proclaimed November, 27, 43 B.C.

The first work of the three rulers was to rid themselves of all whom they feared as enemies, and we have to imagine them sitting down to make out a list of those who, like the sufferers at the dreadful time of Marius and Sulla, were proscribed. Among the prominent men seventeen were first chosen to be butchered, and on the horrid list are found the names of a cousin of Octavius, a brother of Lepidus, and an uncle of Antony. To the lasting execration of Octavius, he consented that Cicero, who had so valiantly fought for him, should be sacrificed to the vengeance of Antony, whom the orator had scarified with his burning words.

This was but the beginning of blood-shedding, for when the triumvirs reached Rome they issued list after list of the doomed, some names being apparently included at the request of daughters, wives, and friends to gratify private malice. The head and hands of Cicero were cut off and sent to be affixed to the rostra, where they had so often been seen during his life. It is said that on one occasion a head was presented to Antony, and he exclaimed: "I do not recognize it, show it to my wife"; and that on another, when a man begged a few moments of respite that he might send his son to intercede with Antony, he was told that it was that son who had demanded his death. The details are too horrible for record, and yet it is said that the massacre was not so general as in the former instance. In this reign of terror, three hundred senators died, and two thousand knights.

While these events had occurred in Rome, Brutus and Cassius had been successfully pursuing their conquests in Syria and Greece, and were now masters of the eastern portion of the Roman world. When they heard of the triumvirate and the proscription, they determined to march into Europe; but Antony and Octavius were before them, and the opposed forces met on the field of Philippi, which lies nine miles from the Ægean Sea, on the road between Europe and Asia, the Via Egnatia, which ran then as now from Dyrrachium and Apollonia in Illyricum, by way of Thessalonica to Constantinople, or Byzantium, as it was then called. Brutus engaged the forces of Octavius, and Cassius those of Antony. Antony made head against his opponent; but Octavius, who was less of a commander, and fell into a fit of illness on the beginning of the battle, gave way before Brutus, though in consequence of misinformation of the progress of the struggle, Cassius killed himself just before a messenger arrived to tell him of his associate's success. Twenty days afterwards the struggle was renewed on the same ground, and Brutus was defeated, upon which he likewise put an end to his own life. If the murderers of Cæsar had fought for the republic, there was no hope for that cause now. The three rulers were reduced to two, for Lepidus was ignored after the victory of his associates, and it only remained to eliminate the second member of the triumvirate to establish the monarchy. For the present, Octavius and Antony divided the government between them, Antony taking the luxurious East, and leaving to Octavius the invidious task of governing Italy and allotting lands to the veterans.

Thousands of the inhabitants of Cisalpine Gaul were expelled from their homes to supply the soldiers with farms, but still they remained unsatisfied, and Italy was filled with complaints which Octavius was unable to allay. Antony, on the other hand, gave himself up to the grossest dissipation, careless of consequences. At Tarsus, he had an interview with Cleopatra, then twenty-eight years of age, whom he had seen years before when he had accompanied Gabinius to Alexandria, and later, when she had lived at Rome the favorite of Cæsar. Henceforth he was her willing slave. She sailed up the river Cydnus in a vessel propelled by silver oars that moved in unison with luxurious music, and filled the air with fragrance as she went, while beautiful slaves held the rudder and the ropes. The careless and pleasure-loving warrior forgot every thing in his wild passion for the Egyptian queen. He forgot his wife, Fulvia, but she was angry with Octavius because he had renounced his wife Claudia, her daughter, and stirred up a threatening revolt against him, which she fondly hoped might also serve to recall Antony from the fascinations of Cleopatra. With her supporters she raised a considerable army, by taking the part of the Italians who had been dispossessed to give farms to the veterans, and by pretending also to favor the soldiers, to whom rich spoils from Asia were promised. They were, however, pushed from place to place until they found themselves shut up in the town of Perusia, in Etruria, where they were besieged and forced to surrender, by the military skill of Agrippa, afterwards known as one of the ablest generals of antiquity.

ANTONY'S FAILING FORTUNES. 263

Meantime, Antony's fortunes in the East were failing, and he determined upon a brave effort to overthrow Octavius. He sailed for Brundusium, and laid siege to it; but the soldiers on both sides longed for peace. Fulvia had died, and mutual friends prevailed upon Octavius and Antony to make peace and portion out the world anew. Again the East fell to Antony and the West to his colleague.

CLEOPATRA'S SHOW-SHIP.

Antony married Octavia, sister of Octavius, and both repaired to the capital, where they celebrated games and festivities in honor of the marriage and the reconciliation. This was at the end of the year 40 B.C.

The next year peace was effected with Sextus, a son of the great Pompey, who had been proscribed as one of the murderers of Cæsar, though he had really had no share in that deed. He had been engaged in marauding expeditions having for their purpose the injury of the triumvirs, and at this time had been able to cut off a considerable share of the supply of grain from Sicily and Africa. He was indemnified for the loss of his private property and was given an important command for five years. This agreement was never consummated, for Antony had not been consulted and refused to carry out a portion of it that depended upon him. Again Pompey entered upon his marauding expeditions, and the price of grain rose rapidly at Rome. Two years were occupied in preparing a fleet, which was placed under command of Agrippa, who defeated Pompey off Naulochus, on the northwestern coast of Sicily (Sept. 3, 36.)

In the midst of the preparations for the war with Pompey, (B.C. 37) discord had arisen between Antony and Octavius, and the commander of the Eastern army set out for Italy with a fleet of three hundred sail. Octavius forbade his landing, and he kept on his course to Tarentum, where a conference was held. There were present on this memorable occasion, besides the two triumvirs, Agrippa, the great general; Octavia, sister of one triumvir and wife of the other, one of the noblest women of antiquity; and Caius Cilnius Mæcenas, a wealthy patron of letters, who had also been present when the negotiations were made previous to the peace of Brundusium, three years before. Probably the satiric poet Horace was also one of the group, for he gives, in one of his satires, an account of a journey from Rome to Brundusium, which he is supposed to have made at the time that Mæcenas was hurrying to the conference.

Horace says that he set out from Rome accompanied by Heliodorus, a rhetorician whom he calls by far the most learned of the Greeks, and that they found a middling inn at Aricia, the first stopping-place, on the Appian Way, sixteen miles out, at the foot of the Alban mount.

Next they rested, or rather tried to rest, at Appii Forum, a place stuffed with sailors, and then took a boat on the canal for Tarracina. He gives a vivid picture of the confusion of such a place, where the watermen and the slaves of the travellers were mutually liberal in their abuse of each other, and the gnats and frogs drove off sleep. Drunken passengers, also, added to the din by the songs that their potations incited them to. At Feronia the passengers left the boat, washed their faces and hands, and crawled onward three miles up to the heights of Anxur, where Mæcenas and others joined the party. Slowly they made their way past Fundi, and Formiæ, where they seem to have been well entertained. The next day they were rejoiced by the addition of the poet Virgil and several more friends to the party, and pleasantly they jogged onwards until their mules deposited their pack-saddles at Capua, where Mæcenas was soon engaged in a game of tennis, while Horace and Virgil sought repose. The next stop was not far from the celebrated Caudine Forks, at a friend's villa, where they were very hospitably entertained, and supplied with a bountiful supper, at which buffoons performed some droll raillery. Thence they went directly to Beneventum, where the bustling landlord almost burned

himself and those he entertained in cooking their
dainty dinner, the kitchen fire falling through the
floor and spreading the flames towards the highest
part of the roof. It was a ludicrous moment, for
the hungry guests and frightened slaves hardly knew
whether to snatch their supper from the flames or to
try to extinguish the fire.

From Beneventum the travellers rode on in sight
of the Apuleian mountains to the village of Trivicum,
where the poet gives us a glimpse of the customs of
the times when he tells us that tears were brought
to their eyes by the green boughs with the leaves
upon them with which a fire was made on the hearth.
Hence for twenty-four miles the party was bowled
away in chaises to a little town that the poet does
not name, where water was sold, the worst in the
world, he thought it, but where the bread was very
fine. Through Canusium they went to Rubi, reaching that place fatigued because they had made a
long journey and had been troubled by rains. Two
days more took them through Barium and Egnatia
to Brundusium, where the journey ended.

At this conference it was agreed that the triumvirate should continue five years longer, Antony agreeing to assist Octavius with 120 ships against Pompey,
and Octavius contributing a large land force to help
Antony against the Parthians. After Pompey had
been overcome, Lepidus claimed Sicily, but Octavius
seduced his soldiers from him, and obliged him to
throw himself upon his rival's mercy. He was permitted to retire into private life, but was allowed to
enjoy his property and dignities. He lived in the

ease that he loved until 13 B.C., first at Circeii, not far from Tarracina, and afterwards at Rome, where he was deprived of honors and rank. Lepidus had not been a strong member of the triumvirate for a long time, but after this he was not allowed to interfere even nominally in affairs of government. Antony and Octavius were now to wrestle for the supremacy, and the victor was to be autocrat.

For three years after his marriage with Octavia, Antony seems to have been able to conquer the fascinations of the Egyptian queen, but then, when he was preparing to advance into Parthia, he allowed himself to fall again into her power, and the chances that he could hold his own against Octavius were lessened (B. C. 37). He advanced into Syria, but called Cleopatra to him there, and delayed his march to remain with her, overwhelming her with honors. When at last he did open the campaign, he encountered disaster, and, hardly escaping the fate of Crassus, retreated to Alexandria, where he gave himself up entirely to his enchantress. He laid aside the dress and manners of a Roman, and appeared as an Eastern monarch, vainly promising Cleopatra that he would conquer Octavius and make Alexandria the capital of the world. The rumors of the mad acts of Antony were carried to Rome, where Octavius was growing in popularity, and it was inevitable that a contrast should be made between the two men. Octavius easily made the people believe that they had every thing to fear from Antony. The nobles who sided with Antony urged him to dismiss Cleopatra, and enter upon a contest with his rival untrammelled; but, on the contrary, in his infatuation he divorced Octavia.

War was declared against Cleopatra, for Antony was ignored, and Octavius as consul was directed to push it. Mæcenas was placed in command at Rome, Agrippa took the fleet, and the consul himself the land forces. The decisive struggle took place off the west coast of Greece, north of the islands of Samos and Leucas, near the promontory of Actium, which gained its celebrity from this battle (September 2, B.C. 31). The ships of Agrippa were small, and those of Antony large, but difficult of management, and Cleopatra soon became alarmed for her safety. She attempted to flee, and Antony sailed after her, leaving those who were fighting for them. Agrippa obtained a decisive victory, and Octavius likewise overcame the forces on land.

Agrippa was sent back to Rome, and for a year Octavius busied himself in Greece and Asia Minor, adding to his popularity by his mildness in the treatment of the conquered. He had intended to pass the winter at Samos, but troubles among the veterans called him to Italy, where he calmed the rising storm, and returned again to his contest, after an absence of only twenty-seven days.

Both Cleopatra and Antony sent messengers to solicit the favor of Octavius, but he was cold and did not satisfy them, and calmly pushed his plans. An effort was made by Cleopatra to flee to some distant Arabian resort, but it failed: Antony made a show of resistance, but found that his forces were not to be trusted, and both then put an end to their

ANCIENT STATUE OF AUGUSTUS. (THE RIGHT ARM IS A RESTORATION.)

lives, leaving Octavius master of Egypt, as he was of the rest of the world. He did not hasten back to Rome, where he knew that Mæcenas and Agrippa were faithfully attending to his interests, but occupied himself another year away from the capital in regulating the affairs of his new province.

In the summer of the year 29, however, Octavius left Samos, where he had spent the winter in rest, and entered Rome amid the acclamations of the populace, celebrating triumphs for the conquest of Dalmatia, of Actium, and of Egypt, and distributing the gold he had won with such prodigality that interest on loans was reduced two thirds and the price of lands doubled. Each soldier received a thousand sesterces (about $40), each citizen four hundred, and a certain sum was given to the children, the whole amounting to some forty million dollars.

Octavius marked the end of the old era by himself closing the gates of the temple of Janus for the third time in the history of Rome, and by declaring that he had burned all the papers of Antony. Several months later, by suppressing all the laws of the triumvirate he emphasized still more the fact which he wished the people to understand, that he had broken with the past.

The Roman Republic was ended. The Empire was not established in name, but the government was in reality absolute. The chief ruler united in himself all the great offices of the state, but concealed his strength and power, professing himself the minister of the senate, to which, however, he dictated the decrees that he ostentatiously obeyed.

CHAPTER XVIII.

SOME MANNERS AND CUSTOMS OF THE ROMAN PEOPLE.

We have now traced the career of the people of Rome from the time when they were the plain and rustic subjects of a king, through their long history as a conquering republic, down to the period when they lost the control of government and fell into the hands of a ruler more autocratic than their earlier tyrants. The heroic age of the republic had now long since passed away, and with it had gone even the admiration of those personal qualities which had lain at the foundation of the national greatness.

History at its best is to such an extent made up of stories of the doings of rulers and fighting-men, who happen by their mere strength and physical force to have made themselves prominent, that it is often read without conveying any actual familiarity with the people it is ostensibly engaged with. The soldiers and magistrates of whom we have ourselves been reading were but few, and we may well ask what the millions of other citizens were doing all these ages. How did they live? What were their joys and griefs? We have, it is true, not failed to get an occasional glimpse of the intimate life of the people who were governed, as we have seen a Virginia passing through the forum to her school, and a Lucretia spinning among her maidens, and we have learned that in the earliest times the workers were honored so much that they were formed into guilds, and had a very high position among the centuries (see pages 31 and 50), but these were only suggestions that make us all the more desirous to know particulars.

Rome had not become a really magnificent city, even after seven hundred years of existence. We know that it was a mere collection of huts in the time of Romulus, and that after the burning of the principal edifices by the Gauls, it was rebuilt in a hurried and careless manner, the houses being low and mean, the streets narrow and crooked, so that when the population had increased to hundreds of thousands the crowds found it difficult to make their way along the thoroughfares, and vehicles with wheels were not able to get about at all, except in two of the streets. The streets were paved, it is true, and there were roads and aqueducts so well built and firm that they claim our admiration even in their ruins.

The Roman house at first was extremely simple, being of but one room called the *atrium*, or darkened chamber, because its walls were stained by the smoke that rose from the fire upon the hearth and with difficulty found its way through a hole in the roof. The aperture also admitted light and rain, the water that dripped from the roof being caught in a cistern that was formed in the middle of the room. The

THE HOUSE-PHILOSOPHER. (See page 277.)

atrium was entered by way of a vestibule open to the sky, in which the gentleman of the house put on his toga as he went out.* Double doors admitted the visitor to the entrance-hall or *ostium*. There was a threshold, upon which it was unlucky to place the left foot; a knocker afforded means of announcing one's approach, and a porter, who had a small room at the side, opened the door, showing the caller the words *Cave canem* (beware of the dog), or *Salve* (welcome), or perchance the dog himself reached out toward the visitor as far as his chain would allow. Sometimes, too, there would be noticed in the mosaic of the pavement the representation of the faithful domestic animal which has so long been the companion as well as the protector of his human friend. Perhaps myrtle or laurel might be seen on a door, indicating that a marriage was in process of celebration, or a chaplet announcing the happy birth of an heir. Cypress, probably set in pots in the vestibule, indicated a death, as a crape festoon does upon our own door-handles, while torches, lamps, wreaths, garlands, branches of trees, showed that there was joy from some cause in the house.

In the "black room" the bed stood; there the meals were cooked and eaten, there the goodman received his friends, and there the goodwife sat in the midst of her maidens spinning. The original house grew larger in the course of time: wings were built on the sides,—and the Romans called them wings as well as we (*ala*, a wing). Beyond the

* When Cincinnatus went out to work in the field, he left his toga at home, wearing his tunic only, and was "naked" (*nudus*), as the Romans said. The custom illustrates MATT. xxiv., 18. (See p. 86.)

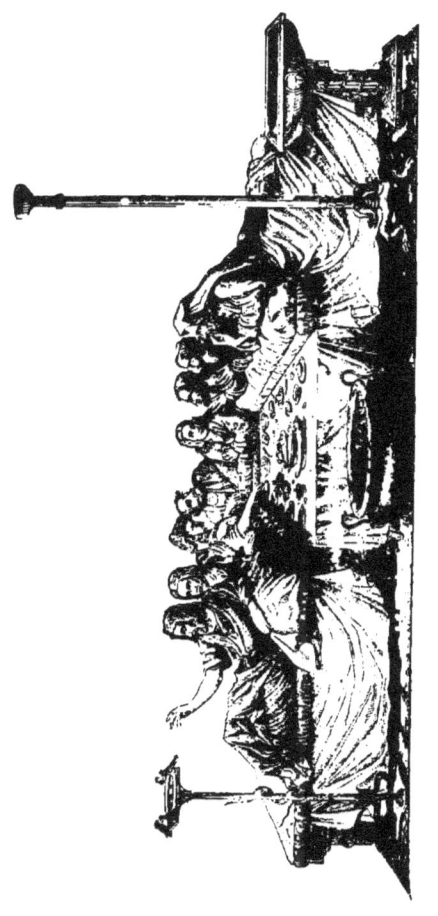

DINING TABLE AND COUCHES.

black room a recess was built in which the family records and archives were preserved, but with it for a long period the Roman house stopped its growth.

Before the empire came, however, there had been great progress in making the dwelling convenient as well as luxurious. Another hall had been built out from the room of archives, leading to an open court, surrounded by columns, known as the *peristylum* (*peri* about, *stulos*, a pillar), which was sometimes of great magnificence. Bedchambers were made separate from the atrium, but they were small, and would not seem very convenient to modern eyes.

The dining-room, called the *triclinium* (Greek, *kline*, a bed) from its three couches, was a very important apartment. In it were three lounges surrounding a table, on each of which three guests might be accommodated. The couches were elevated above the table, and each man lay almost flat on his breast, resting on his left elbow, and having his right hand free to use, thus putting the head of one near the breast of the man behind him, and making natural the expression that he lay in the bosom of the other.* As the guests were thus arranged by threes, it was natural that the rule should have been made that a party at dinner should not be less in number than the Graces nor more than the Muses, though it has remained a useful one ever since.

Spacious saloons or parlors were added to the houses, some of which were surrounded with gal-

---

* In the earliest times the Romans sat at table on benches. The habit of reclining was introduced from Greece, but Roman women sat at table long after the men had fallen into the new way.

leries and highly adorned. In these the dining-tables were spread on occasions of more ceremony than usual. After the capture of Syracuse, and the increase of familiarity with foreign art, picture-rooms were built in private dwellings; and after the second Punic war, book-rooms became in some sort a necessity. Before the republic came to an end, it was so fashionable to have a book-room that ignorant persons who might not be able to read even the titles of their own books endeavored to give themselves the appearance of erudition by building book-rooms in their houses and furnishing them with elegance. The books were in cases arranged around the walls in convenient manner, and busts and statues of the Muses, of Minerva, and of men of note were used then as they are now for ornaments.* House-philosophers were often employed to open to the uninstructed the stores of wisdom contained in the libraries.

As wealth and luxury increased, the Romans added the bath-room to their other apartments. In the early ages they had bathed for comfort and cleanliness once a week, but the warm bath was apparently unknown to them. In time this became very common, and in the days of Cicero there were hot and cold baths, both public and private, which were well patronized. Some were heated by fires in flues, directly under the floors, which produced a vapor bath. The bath was, however, considered a

---

* The books were rolls of the rind *(liber)* of the Egyptian papyrus, which early became an article of commerce, or of parchment, written on but one side and stained of a saffron color on the other. Slaves were employed to make copies of books that were much in demand, and booksellers bought and sold them.

luxury, and at a later date it was held a capital offence to indulge in one on a religious holiday, and the public baths were closed when any misfortune happened to the republic.

Comfort and convenience united to take the cooking out of the atrium (which then became a reception-room) into a separate apartment known as the *culina*, or kitchen, in which was a raised platform on which coals might be burned and the processes of broiling, boiling, and roasting might be carried on in a primitive manner, much like the arrangement still to be seen at Rome. On the tops of the houses, after a while, terraces were planned for the purpose of basking in the sun, and sometimes they were furnished with shrubs, fruit-trees, and even fish-ponds. Often there were upwards of fifty rooms in a house on a single floor; but in the course of time land became so valuable that other stories were added, and many lived in flats. A flat was sometimes called an *insula*, which meant, properly, a house not joined to another, and afterwards was applied to hired lodgings. *Domus*, a house, meant a dwelling occupied by one family, whether it were an *insula* or not.

The floors of these rooms were sometimes, but not often, laid with boards, and generally were formed of stone, tiles, bricks, or some sort of cement. In the richer dwellings they were often inlaid with mosaics of elegant patterns. The walls were often faced with marble, but they were usually adorned with paintings; the ceilings were left uncovered, the beams supporting the floor or the roof above being visible, though it was frequently arched over. The means of lighting, either by day or night, were defective. The atrium was, as we have seen, lighted from above, and the same was true of other apartments—those at the side being illuminated from the larger ones in the middle of the house. There were windows, however, in the upper stories, though they were not protected by glass, but covered with shutters or lattice-work, and, at a later period, were glazed with sheets of mica. Smoking lamps, hanging from the ceiling or supported by candelabra, or candles, gave a gloomy light by night in the houses, and torches without.

The sun was chiefly depended upon for heat, for there were no proper stoves, though braziers were used to burn coals upon, the smoke escaping through the aperture in the ceiling, and, in rare cases, hot-air furnaces were constructed below, the heat being conveyed to the upper rooms through pipes. There has been a dispute regarding chimneys, but it seems almost certain that the Romans had none in their dwellings, and, indeed, there was little need of them for purposes of artificial warmth in so moderate a climate as theirs.

Such were some of the chief traits of the city houses of the Romans. Besides these, there were villas in the country, some of which were simply farm-houses, and others places of rest and luxury supported by the residents of cities. The farm villa was placed, if possible, in a spot secluded from visitors, protected from the severest winds, and from the malaria of marshes, in a well-watered place near the foot of a well-wooded mountain. It had accommodations for the kitchen, the wine-press, the farm-superintendent, the slaves, the animals, the crops, and the other products of the farm. There were baths, and cellars for the wine and for the confinement of the slaves who might have to be chained.

Varro thus describes life at a rural household: "Manius summons his people to rise with the sun, and in person conducts them to the scene of their daily work. The youths make their own bed, which labor renders soft to them, and supply themselves with water-pot and lamp. Their drink is the clear fresh spring; their fare, bread, with onions as a relish. Every thing prospers in house and field. The house is no work of art, but an architect might learn symmetry from it. Care is taken of the field that it shall not be left disorderly, and waste or go to ruin through slovenliness or neglect; and, in return, grateful Ceres wards off damage from the produce, that the high-piled sheaves may gladden the heart of the husbandman. Here hospitality still holds good; every one who has but imbibed mother's milk is welcome. The bread-pantry, the wine-vat, and the store of sausages on the rafter,—lock and key are at the service of the traveller, and piles of food are set before him; contented, the sated guest sits, looking neither before him nor behind, dozing by the hearth in the kitchen. The warmest double-wool sheepskin is spread as a couch for him. Here people still, as good burgesses, obey the righteous law which neither out of envy injures the innocent, nor out of favor pardons the guilty. Here they speak no evil against their neighbors. Here they trespass not with their feet on the sacred hearth, but honor the gods with devotion and with sacrifices; throw to the familiar spirit his little bit of flesh into his appointed little dish, and when the master of the household dies accompany the bier with the same prayer with which those of his father and of his grandfather were borne forth."

The pleasure villa had many of the appointments of the town house, but was outwardly more attractive, of course. It stood in the midst of grassy slopes, was approached through avenues of trees leading to the portico, before which was a terrace and ornaments made of box-trees cut into fantastic forms representing animals. The dining-room stood out from the other buildings, and was light and airy. Perhaps a grand bedchamber was likewise built out from the others, so that it might have the warmth of the sun upon it through the entire day. Connected with the establishment were walks ornamented with flower-beds, closely clipped hedges, and trees tortured into all sorts of unnatural shapes. There were shaded avenues for gentle exercise afoot or in litters; there were fountains, and perhaps a hippodrome formed like a circus, with paths divided by hedges and surrounded by large trees in which the luxurious owner and his guests might run or exercise themselves in the saddle.*

* Roman extravagance ran riot in the appointments of the villa. One is mentioned that sold for some $200,000, chiefly because it comprised a desirable fish-pond. A late writer says of the site of Pompey's villa on a slope of the Alban hills : " It has never ceased in all the in-

In such houses the Roman family lived, composed as families must be, of parents and children, to which were usually added servants, for after the earlier times of simplicity had passed away it became so fashionable to keep slaves to perform all the different domestic labors, that one could hardly claim to be respectable unless he had at least ten in his household. The first question asked regarding a stranger was: "How many slaves does he keep?" and upon its answer depended the social position the person would have in the inquirer's estimation. The son did not pass from his father's control while that parent lived, but the daughter might do so by marriage. The power of the father over his children and grandchildren, as well as over his slaves was very great, and the family spirit was exceedingly strong.

When a man and a woman had agreed to marry, and the parents and friends had given their consent, there was sometimes a formal meeting at the maiden's house, at which the marriage-agreement was written out on tablets and signed by the engaged persons. It seems, too, that in some cases the man placed a ring on the hand of his betrothed. It was no slight affair to choose the wedding-day, for no day

tervening ages to be a sort of park, and very fine ruins, from out of whose massive arches grow a whole avenue of live oaks, attest to the magnificence which must once have characterized the place. The still beautiful grounds stretch along the shore of the lake as far as the gate of the town of Albano. . . . The house in Rome I occupy, stands in the old villa of Mæcenas, an immense tract of land comprising space enough to contain a good-sized city. . . . Where did the Plebs live? and what air did they and their children breathe? Who cared or knew, so long as Pompey or Cæsar fared sumptuously? What marvel that there were revolutions!"

that was marked *ater* on the calendar would be considered fit for the purpose of the rites that were to accompany the ceremony. The calends (the first day of the month), the nones (the fifth or seventh), and the ides (the thirteenth or fifteenth), would not do, nor would any day in May or February, nor many of the festivals.

In early times, the bride dressed herself in a long white robe, adorned with ribbons, and a purple fringe, and bound herself with a girdle on her wedding day. She put on a bright yellow veil and shoes of the same color, and submitted to the solemn religious rites that were to make her a wife. The pair walked around the altar hand in hand, received the congratulations of their friends, and the bride, taken with apparent force from the arms of her mother, as the Sabine women were taken in the days of Romulus, was conducted to her new home carrying a distaff and a spindle, emblems of the industry that was thought necessary in the household work that she was to perform or direct. Strong men lifted her over the threshold, lest her foot should trip upon it, and her husband saluted her with fire and water, symbolic of welcome, after which he presented her the keys. A feast was then given to the entire train of friends and relatives, and probably the song was sung of which *Talasia* was the refrain.* Sometimes the husband gave another entertainment the next day, and there were other religious rites after which the new wife took her proud position as mater-familias, sharing the honors of her husband, and presiding over the household.

* See page 22.

The wives and daughters made the cloth and the dresses of the household, in which they had ample occupation, but their labors did not end there.* The grinding of grain and the cooking was done by the servants, but the wife had to superintend all the domestic operations, among which was included the care of the children, though old Cato thought it was necessary for him to look after the washing and swaddling of his children in person, and to teach them what he thought they ought to know. The position of the woman was entirely subordinate to the husband, though in the house she was mistress. She belonged to the household and not to the community, and was to be called to account for her doings by her father, her husband, or her near male relatives, not by her political ruler. She could acquire property and inherit money the same as a man could, however. When the pure and noble period of Roman history had passed, women became as corrupt as the rest of the community. The watering-places were scenes of unblushing wickedness; women of quality, but not of character, masquerading before the gay world with the

* Varro contrasts the later luxury with past frugality, setting in opposition the spacious granaries, and simple farm arrangements of the good old times, and the peacocks and richly inlaid doors of a degenerate age. Formerly even the city matron turned the spindle with her own hand, while at the same time she kept her eye upon the pot on the hearth ; now the wife begs the husband for a bushel of pearls, and the daughter demands a pound of precious stones : then the wife was quite content if the husband gave her a trip once or twice in the year in an uncushioned wagon ; now she sulks if he go to his country estate without her, and as she travels my lady is attended to the villa by the fashionable host of Greek menials and singers.

most reckless disregard of all the proprieties of life.*

The garments of Roman men and women were of extreme simplicity for a long period, but the desire of display and the love of ornament succeeded in making them at last highly adorned and varied. Both men and women wore two principal garments, the tunic next to the body, and the pallium which was thrown over it when going abroad; but they also each had a distinctive article of dress, the men wearing the *toga* (originally worn also by women), a flowing outer garment which no foreigner could use,

COVERINGS FOR THE FEET.

and the women the *stola*, which fell over the tunic to the ankles and was bound about the waist by a girdle. Boys and girls wore a toga with a broad border of purple, but when the boy became a man he threw this off and wore one of the natural white color of the wool.

Sometimes the stola was clasped over the shoulder, and in some instances it had sleeves. The *pallium*

* Cato the Elder, who enjoyed uttering invectives against women, was free in denouncing their chattering, their love of dress, their ungovernable spirit, and condemned the whole sex as plaguy and proud, without whom men would probably be more godly.

was a square outer garment of woollen goods, put on by women as well as men when going out. It came into use during the civil wars, but was forbidden by Augustus. Both sexes also wore in travelling a thick, long cloak without sleeves, called the *pænula*, and the men wore also over the toga a dark cloak, the *lacerna*.

On their feet the men wore slippers, boots, and shoes of various patterns. The *soccus* was a slipper not tied, worn in the house; and the *solea* a very light sandal, also used in the house only. The *sandalium* proper was a rich and luxurious sandal introduced from Greece and worn by women only. The *baxa* was a coarse sandal made of twigs, used by philosophers and comic actors; the *calcæus* was a shoe that covered the foot, though the toes were often exposed; and the *cothurnus*, a laced boot worn by horsemen, hunters, men of authority, and tragic actors, and it left the toes likewise exposed.

An examination of the mysteries of the dressing-rooms of the ladies of Rome displays most of the toilet conveniences that women still use. They dressed their hair in a variety of styles (see page 155), and used combs, dyes, oils, and pomades just as they now do. They had mirrors, perfumes, soaps in great variety, hair-pins, ear-rings, bracelets, necklaces, gay caps and turbans, and sometimes ornamental wigs.

The change that came over Rome during the long period of the kingdom and the republic is perhaps as evident in the table customs as in any respect. For centuries the simple Roman sat down at noon to a plain dinner of boiled pudding made of spelt (*far*), and fruits, which, with milk, butter, and vegetables, formed the chief articles of his diet. His table was plain, and his food was served warm but once a day

ARTICLES OF THE ROMAN TOILET.

When the national horizon had been enlarged by the foreign wars, and Asiatic and Greek influences began to be felt, hot dishes were served oftener, and the two courses of the principal meal no longer sufficed to satisfy the fashionable appetite. A baker's shop was opened at the time of the war with Perseus, and scientific cookery rapidly came into vogue.

We cannot follow the course of the history of increasing luxury in its details. Towards the end of the republic, breakfast (*jentaculum*), consisting of bread and cheese, with perhaps dried fruit, was taken at a very early hour, in an informal way, the guests not even sitting down. At twelve or one o'clock luncheon followed (*prandium*). There was considerable variety in this meal. The principal repast of the day (*cœna*) occurred late in the afternoon, some time just before sunset, there having been the same tendency to make the hour later and later that has been manifested in England and America. There were three usual courses, the first comprising stimulants to the appetite, eggs, olives, oysters, lettuce, and a variety of other such delicacies. For the second course the whole world was put under requisition. There were turbots and sturgeon, eels and prawns, boar's flesh and venison, pheasants and peacocks, ducks and capons, turtles and flamingoes, pickled tunny-fishes, truffles and mushrooms, besides a variety of other dishes that it is impossible to mention here. After these came the dessert, almonds and raisins and dates, cheese-cakes and sweets and apples. Thus the egg came at the beginning, and the apple, representative of fruit in general, at the end, a fact that gave Horace ground for his expression, *ab ovo usque ad* *mala,* from the egg to the apple, from the beginning to the end.*

The Roman dinner was served with all the ostentatious elegance and formality of our own days, if not with more. The guests assembled in gay dresses ornamented with flowers; they took off their shoes, lest the couch, inlaid with ivory, perhaps, or adorned with cloth of gold, should be soiled; and laid themselves down to eat, each one adjusting his napkin carefully, and taking his position according to his relative importance, the middle place being deemed the most honorable. About the tables stood the servants, dressed in the tunic, and carrying napkins or rough cloths to wipe off the table, which was of the richest wood and covered by no cloth. While some served the dishes, often of magnificent designs, other slaves offered the feasters water to rinse their hands, or cooled the room with fans. At times music and dances were added to give another charm to the scene.

The first occupation of the Romans was agriculture, in which was included the pasturage of flocks and herds. In process of time trades were learned, and manufactures (literally making with the hand, *manus,* the hand, *facere,* to make) were introduced, but not, of course, to any thing like the extent fa-

---

* The practical side of the Roman priesthood was the priestly *cuisine;* the augural and pontifical banquets were, as we may say, the official gala days in the life of a Roman epicure, and several of them form epochs in the history of gastronomy: the banquet on the occasion of the inauguration of the augur Quintus Hortensius, for instance, brought roast peacocks into vogue.—Mommsen. Book IV., chap. 12.

miliar in our times. There were millers and shoemakers, butchers and tanners, bakers and blacksmiths, besides other tradesmen and laborers. In the process of time there were also artists, but in this respect Rome did not excel as Greece had long before. There were also physicians, lawyers, and teachers, besides office-holders.*

When the Roman wished to go from place to place he had a variety of modes among which to choose, as we have already had suggested by Horace in his account of the trip from Rome to Brundusium. He might have his horse saddled, and his saddle-bags packed, as our fathers did of yore; he could do as one of the rich provincial governors described by Cicero did when, at the opening of a Sicilian spring, he entered his rose-scented litter, carried by eight bearers, reclining on a cushion of Maltese gauze, with garlands about his head and neck, applying a delicate scent-bag to his nose as he went. There were wagons and cars, in which he might drive over the hard and smooth military roads, and canals; and

* There were office-seekers, also, and of the most persistent kind, throughout the whole history of the republic, and they practised the corrupt arts of the most ingenious of the class in modern times. The candidate went about clad in a toga of artificial whiteness (*candidus*, white), accompanied by a *nomenclator*, who gave him the names of the voters they might meet, so that he could compliment them by addressing them familiarly, and he shook them by the hand. He "treated" the voters to drink or food in a very modern fashion, though with a more than modern profusion; and he went to the extreme of bribing them if treating did not suffice. Against these practices Coriolanus haughtily protests, in Shakespeare's play. Sometimes candidates canvassed for votes outside of Rome, as Cicero proposed in one of his letters to Atticus,

along the routes, there were, as Horace has told us, taverns at which hospitality was to be expected.

The Roman law was remarkable for embodying in itself "the eternal principles of freedom and of subordination, of property and legal redress," which still reign unadulterated and unmodified, as Mommsen says; and this system this strong people not only endured but actually ordained for itself, and it involved the principle that a free man could not be tortured, a principle which other European peoples embraced only after a terrible and bloody struggle of a thousand years.

One of the punishments is worthy of mention here. We have already noticed its infliction. It was ordered that a person might not live in a certain region, or that he be confined to a certain island, and that he be interdicted from fire and water, those two essentials to life, in case he should overstep the bounds mentioned. These elements with the Romans had a symbolical meaning, and when the husband received his bride with fire and water, he signified that his protection should ever be over her. Thus their interdiction meant the withdrawal of the protection of the state from a person, which left him an outlaw. Such a law could only have been made after the nation had become possessed of regions somewhat remote from its centre of power. England can now exile its criminals to another hemisphere, and Russia to a distant region of deserts and cold, but neither country could have punished by exile before it owned such regions.

XIX.

THE ROMAN READING AND WRITING.

IN the earliest times the education of young Romans was probably confined to instruction in dancing and music, though they became acquainted with the processes of agriculture by being called upon to practise them in company with their elders. It was not long before the elementary attainments of reading, writing, and counting were brought within their reach, even among the lower orders and the slaves, and we know that it was thought important to make the latter class proficient in many departments of scholarship.

The advance in the direction of real mental culture was, however, not great until after the contact with Greece. So long as the Romans remained a strong and self-centred people, deriving little but tribute from peoples beyond the Italian peninsula, and looking with disdain upon all outside that limit, there was not much to stimulate their mental progress; but when contrast with another civilization showed that there was much power to be gained by knowledge, it was naturally more eagerly sought. The slaves and other foreigners, to whom the instruction of the children was assigned, were familiar with the Greek language, and it had the great advantage over Latin of being the casket in which an illustrious literature was preserved. For this reason Roman progress in letters was founded upon that of Greece.

The Roman parent for a long time made the Twelve Tables the text-book from which his children were taught, thus giving them a smattering of reading, of writing, and of the laws of the land at once. Roman authorship and the study of grammar, however, were about coincident in their beginnings with the temporary cessation of war and the second closing of the temple of Janus. Cato the elder prepared manuals for the instruction of youth (or, perhaps, one manual in several parts), which gave his views on morals, oratory, medicine, war, and agriculture (a sort of encyclopædia), and a history entitled *Origines*, which recounted the traditions of the kings, told the story of the origin of the Italian towns, of the Punic wars, and of other events down to the time of his own death.* This seems to have originated in the author's natural interest in the education of his son, a stimulating cause of much literature of the same kind since.

The Roman knowledge of medicine came first from the Etruscans, to whom they are said to have owed so much other culture, and subsequently from the Greeks. The first person to make a distinct profession of medicine at Rome, however, was not

---

* See page 153. "Cato's encyclopædia . . . was little more than an embodiment of the old Roman household knowledge, and truly when compared with the Hellenic culture of the period, was scanty enough."—MOMMSEN, bk. IV., ch. 12.

an Etruscan, but a Greek, named Archagathus, who settled there in the year 219, just before the second Punic war broke out. He was received with great respect, and a shop was bought for him at the public expense; but his practice, which was largely surgical, proved too severe to be popular. In earlier days the father had been the family physician, and Cato vigorously reviled the foreign doctors, and like the true conservative that he was, strove to bring back the good old times that his memory painted; but his efforts did not avail, and the professional practice of the healing art not only became one of the most lucrative in Rome, but remained for a long period almost a monopoly in the hands of foreigners. Science, among the latest branches of knowledge to be freed from the swaddling-clothes of empiricism, received, in its applied form, some attention, though mathematics and physics were not specially favored as subjects of investigation.

The progress of Roman culture is distinctly shown by a comparison of the curriculum of Cato with that of Marcus Terentius Varro, a long-time friend of Cicero, though ten years his senior.* Varro obtained from Quintilian the title "the most learned of the Romans," and St. Augustine said that it was astonishing that he could write so much, and that

---

* Varro is said to have written of his youth. "For me when a boy there sufficed a single rough coat and a single undergarment, shoes without stockings, a horse without a saddle. I had no daily warm bath, and but seldom a river bath." Still, he utters warnings against over-feeding and over-sleeping, as well as against cakes and high living, pointing to his own youthful training, and says that dogs were in his later years more judiciously cared for than children.

one could scarcely believe that anybody could find time even to read all that he wrote. He was proscribed by the triumvirs at the same time that Cicero was, but was fortunate enough to escape and subsequently to be placed under the protection of Augustus. Cato thought that a proper man ought to study oratory, medicine, husbandry, war, and law, and was at liberty to look into Greek literature a little, that he might cull from the mass of chaff and rubbish, as he affected to deem it, some serviceable maxims of practical experience, but he might not study it thoroughly. Varro extended the limit of allowed and fitting studies to grammar, logic, rhetoric, geometry, arithmetic, astronomy, music, medicine, and architecture.

Young children were led to their first studies by the kindergarten path of amusement, learning their letters as we learned them ourselves by means of blocks, and spelling by repeating the letters and words in unison after the instructor. Dictation exercises were turned to account in the study of grammar and orthography, and writing was taught by imitation, though the "copy-book" was not paper, but a tablet covered with a thin coating of wax, and the pen a stylus, pencil-shaped, sharp at one end and flat at the other, so that the mark made by the point might be smoothed out by reversing the instrument. Thus *vertere stilum*, to turn the stylus, meant to correct or to erase.* The first school-book seems to have been an Odyssey, by one Livius Andronicus, probably a Tarentine, who was

* See illustrations on pages 23 and 219.

captured during the wars in Southern Italy. He became a slave, of course, and was made instructor of his master's children. He familiarized himself with the Latin language, and wrote dramas in it. Thus though he was a native of Magna Græcia, he is usually mentioned as the first Roman poet. It is not known whether his Odyssey and other writings were imitations of the Greek or translations, but it matters little; they were immediately appreciated and held their own so well that they were read in schools as late as the time of Horace. This first awakener of Roman literary effort was born at the time of Pyrrhus and died before the battle of Zama.

A few other Roman writers of prominence claim our attention. With some reason the Romans looked upon Ennius as the father of their literature. He, like Andronicus, was a native of Magna Græcia, claiming lordly ancestors, and boasting that the spirit of Homer, after passing through many mortal bodies, had entered his own. His works remain only in fragments gathered from others who had quoted them, and we cannot form any accurate opinion of his rank as a poet; but we know that his success was so great that Cicero considered him the prince of Roman song, that Virgil was indebted to him for many thoughts and expressions, and that even the brilliance of the Augustan poets did not lessen his reputation. His utterances were vigorous, bold, fresh, and full of the spirit of the brave old days. He found the language rough, uncultivated, and unformed, and left it softer, more harmonious, and possessed of a system of versification. He was born in

239 B.C., the year after the first plays of Andronicus had been exhibited on the Roman stage, and died just before the complete establishment of the universal empire of Rome as a consequence of the battle of Pydna.*

At the head of the list of Roman prose annalists stands the name of Quintus Fabius Pictor, at one time a senator, who wrote a history of his nation beginning, probably, like other Roman works of its class, with the coming of Æneas, and narrating later events, to the end of the second Punic war, with some degree of minuteness. He wrote in Greek, and made the usual effort to preserve and transmit a sufficiently good impression of the greatness of his own people. That Pictor was a senator proves his social importance, which is still further exemplified by the fact that after the carnage of Cannæ, he was sent to Delphi to learn for his distressed countrymen how they might appease the angry gods. We only know that his history was of great value from the frequent use that was made of it by subsequent investigators in the antiquities of the Roman people, because no manuscript of it has been preserved.

Titus Maccius, surnamed, from the flatness of his feet, Plautus, was the greatest among the comic poets of Rome. Of humble origin, he was driven to literature by his necessities, and it was while turning the crank of a baker's hand-mill that he began the work by which he is now known. He wrote three plays which were accepted by the managers of the public games, and he was thus able to turn his back

* See page 164.

upon menial drudgery. Born at an Umbrian village during the first Punic war, not far from the year when Regulus was taken,* he came to Rome at an early age, and after he began to write, produced a score or more of plays which captivated both the learned and the uneducated by their truth to the life that they depicted, and they held their high reputation long after the death of the author. Moderns have also attested their merit, and our great dramatist in his amusing *Comedy of Errors* imitated the *Menæchmi* of this early play-wright.†

Publius Terentius Afer, commonly known as Terence, the second and last of the comic poets, was of no higher social position than Plautus, and was no more a Roman than the other writers we have referred to, for he was a native of Carthage, Rome's great rival, where he was born at the time that Hannibal was a refugee at the court of Antiochus at Ephesus. In spite of his foreign origin, Terence was of sufficient ability to exchange the slave-pen of Carthage for the society of the best circles in Rome, and he attained to such purity and ease in the use of his adopted tongue that Cicero and Cæsar scarcely surpass him in those respects. His first play, the *Andria* (the Woman of Andros), was produced

* See page 133.

† Rude farces, known as *Atellanæ Fabulæ*, were introduced into Rome after the contact with the Campanians, from one of whose towns, Atella, they received their name. Though they were at a later time divided into acts, they seem to have been at first simply improvised raillery and satire without dramatic connection. The Atellan plays were later than the imitations of Etruscan acting mentioned on page 110.

in 166 B.C., the year before Polybius and the other Achæans were transported to Rome.* It has been imitated and copied in modern times, and notably by Sir Richard Steele in his *Conscious Lovers*. Andria was followed by *Hecyra* (the Stepmother), *Heautontimoroumenos*, (the Self-Tormentor), *Eunuchus* (the Eunuch), *Phormio* (named from a parasite who is an active agent in the plot), and *Adelphi* (the Brothers), the plot of which was mainly derived from a Greek play of the same title. This foreign influence is further shown in the names of these plays, which are Greek.

Cato, the Censor, found time among his varied public labors to contribute to the literature of his language. His *Origines* and other works have already been mentioned.† The varied literary productions of Cicero have also come under our notice,‡ but they deserve more attention, though they are too many to be enumerated. Surpassing all others in the art of public speaking, he was evidently well prepared to write on rhetoric and oratory as he did; but his general information and scholarly taste led him to go far beyond this limit, and he made considerable investigations in the domains of politics, history, and philosophy, law, theology, and morals, besides practising his hand in his earlier years on the manufacture of verses that have not added to his reputation. The writings of Cicero of greatest interest to us now are his orations and correspondence, both of which give us intimate information concerning life and

---

* See page 164 ; and portrait, page 141.
† See pages 153 and 239.   ‡ See page 202.

events that is of inestimable value, and it is conveyed in a literary style at once so appropriate and attractive that it is itself forgotten in the impressive interest of the narrative. The period covered by the eight hundred letters of Cicero that have been preserved is one of the utmost importance in Roman history, and the author and his correspondents were in the hottest of the exciting movements of the time.

When he writes without reserve, he gives his modern readers confidential revelations of the utmost piquancy; and when he words his epistles with diplomatic care, he displays with equal acuteness, to the student familiar with the intrigues of public life at Rome at the time, the sinuosities of contemporary statesmanship and the wiles of the wary politician, and the revelation is all the more entertaining and important because it is an unintentional exhibition. The orations of Cicero are likewise storehouses of details connected with public and private life, gathered with the minute care of an advocate persistently in earnest and determined not to allow any item to pass unnoticed that might affect the decision of his cause.

The learned Varro, already mentioned, deserves far more attention than we can afford him. He had the advantage at an early age of the acquaintance of a scholar of high attainments in Greek and Latin literature, who was well acquainted also with the history of his own country, from whom he imbibed a love of intellectual pursuits. During the wars with the pirates (in which he obtained the naval crown) and with Mithridates, he held a high command, and after supporting Pompey and the senate during the civil struggles, he was compelled to surrender to Cæsar (though he was not changed in his opinions), and passed over to Greece, where he was finally overcome by the dictator, and owed his subsequent opportunities for study to the clemency of his conqueror, who gave him pardon after the battle of Pharsalia. All the rest of his life was passed aloof from the storm that raged around him, the circumstances of his proscription and pardon being the only indication of his personal connection with it. He died in the year 28 B.C., after the temple of Janus had been closed the third time, when Augustus had entered upon the enjoyment of his absolute power.

Of nearly five hundred works that Varro is said to have written, one only has come down to our time complete, though some portions of another are also preserved. The first is a laboriously methodical and thorough treatise on agriculture. The other work (a treatise on Latin grammar) is of value in its mutilated and imperfect state (it seems never to have received its author's final revision), because it preserves many terms and forms that would otherwise have been lost, besides much curious information concerning ancient civil and religious usages. In regard to the derivation of words, his principles are sound, but his practice is often amusingly absurd. We must remember, however, that the science of language did not advance beyond infancy until after our own century had opened. The great reputation of Varro was founded upon a work now lost, entitled " Book of Antiquities," in the first part of which he discussed the creation and history of man, especially of man in Italy from the foundation of the city in 753 B.C. (which date he established), not omitting reference to Æneas, of course, and presenting details of the manners and social customs of the people during all their career. In a second part Varro gave his attention to Divine Antiquities, and as St. Augustine drew largely from it in his " City of God," we may be said to be familiar with it at second hand. It was a complete mythology of Italy, minutely describing every thing relating to the services of religion, the festivals, temples, offerings, priests, and so on. Probably the loss of the works of Varro may be accounted for by their lack of popular interest, or by their infelicities of style, which rendered them little attractive to readers.

Julius Cæsar must be included among the authors of Rome, though most of his works are lost, his *Commentaries* (mentioned on p. 226) being the only one remaining. This book is written in Latin of great purity, and shows that the author was master of a clear style, though the nature of the work did not admit him to exhibit many of the graces of diction. The Commentaries seem to have been put into form in winter quarters, though roughly written during the actual campaigns. Cæsar always took pleasure in literary pursuits and in the society of men of letters.

Valerius Catullus, a contemporary of the writers just named, was born when Cinna was Consul (B.C.

87), and died at the age of thirty or forty, for the dates given as that of his death are quite doubtful. His father was a man of means and a friend of Cæsar, whom he frequently entertained. Catullus owned a villa near Tibur, but he took up his abode at Rome when very young, and mingled freely in the gayest society, the expensive pleasures of which made great inroads upon his moderate wealth. Like other Romans, he looked to a career in the provinces for means of improving his fortune, but was disappointed, and like our own Chaucer, but more frequently, he pours forth lamentations to his empty purse. He was evidently a friend of most of the prominent men of letters of his time, and he entered freely into the debauchery of the period. Thus his verse gives a representation of the debased manners of the day in gay society. His style was remarkably felicitous, and it is said that he adorned all that he touched. Most of his poems are quite short, and their subjects range from a touching outburst of genuine grief for a brother's death to a fugitive epigram of the most voluptuous triviality. His verses display ease and impetuosity, tumultuous merriment and wild passion, playful grace and slashing invective, vigorous simplicity and ingenious imitation of the learned stiffness and affectation of the Alexandrian school. They are strongly national, despite the author's use of foreign materials, and made Catullus exceedingly popular among his countrymen.

Lucretius (Titus Lucretius Carus) was a native of Italy, whose birth is said to have occurred B.C. 95,

His death was caused by his own hand, or by a philtre administered by another, about 50 B.C., and very little is known about his life. His great work, entitled About the Nature of Things (*De Rerum Natura*), is a long poem, in which an attempt is made to present in clear terms the leading principles of the philosophy of Epicurus, and it is acknowledged to be one of the greatest of the world's didactic poems. He undertakes to demonstrate that the miseries of men may be traced to a slavish dread of the gods; and in order to remove such apprehensions, he would prove that no divinity ever interposed in the affairs of the earth, either as creator or director. The Romans were not, as we have had occasion to observe, inclined to philosophic pursuits, and Lucretius certainly labored with all the force of an extraordinary genius to lead them into such studies. He brought to bear upon his task the power of sublime and graceful verse, and it has been said that but for him "we could never have formed an adequate idea of the strength of the Latin language. We might have dwelt with pleasure upon the softness, flexibility, richness, and musical tone of that vehicle of thought which could represent with full effect the melancholy tenderness of Tibullus,* the exquisite ingenuity of Ovid,† the inimitable

---

* Albius Tibullus was a poet of singular gentleness and amiability, who wrote verses of exquisite finish, gracefully telling the story of his worldly misfortunes and expressing the fluctuations that marked his indulgence in the tender passion, in which his experience was extensive and his record real. He was a warm friend of Horace.

† Ovid (Publius Ovidius Naso) was born March 20, B.C. 43, and did not compose his first work, The Art of Love (*Ars Amatoria*), until

felicity and taste of Horace, the gentleness and high spirit of Virgil, and the vehement declamation of Juvenal, but, had the verses of Lucretius perished, we should never have known that it could give utterance to the grandest conceptions with all that sustained majesty and harmonious swell in which the Grecian Muse rolls forth her loftiest outpourings."

Caius Sallustius Crispus (Sallust) was born the year that Marius died (B.C. 86) of a plebeian family, and during the civil wars was a partisan of Cæsar, whom he accompanied to Africa, after having brought to him the news of the mutiny of his troops in Campania (B.C. 46).* Left as governor, Sallust seems to have pursued the methods common to that class, for he became immensely rich. Upon his return from Africa, he retired to an extensive estate on the Quirinal Hill, and lived through the direful days which followed the death of Cæsar. He died in the year 34 B.C., his last years being devoted to dilligent pursuits of literature. His two works are *Catilina*, a history of the suppression of the conspiracy of Catiline, and *Jugurtha*, a history of the war against Jugurtha, in both of which he took great pains with his style. As he witnessed many of the events he

he was more than fifty years of age. He wrote subsequently The Metamorphoses, in fifteen books; The Fasti, containing accounts of the Roman festivals; and the Elegies, composed during his banishment to a town on the Euxine, near the mouth of the Danube, where he died, A.D. 18. Niebuhr places him after Catullus the most poetical among the Roman poets, and ranks him first for facility. He did not direct his genius by a sound judgment, and has the unenviable fame of having been the first to depart from the canons of correct Greek taste.

* See page 245.

described, his books have a great value to the student of the periods. Roman writers asserted that he imitated the style of Thucydides, but there is an air of artificiality about his work which he did not have the skill to conceal. He has the honor of being the first Roman to write history, as distinguished from mere annals.

Livy (Titus Livius) was born in the year of Cæsar's first consulship (B.C. 59), at Patavium (Padua), and died A.D. 17. His writings, like those of Ovid, come therefore rather into the period of the empire. His great work is the History of Rome, which he modestly called simply *Annales*. Little is known of his life, but he was of very high repute as a writer in his own day, for it is said by Pliny that a Spaniard travelled all the way from his distant home merely to see him, and as soon as his desire had been accomplished, returned. Livy's history comprised one hundred and forty-two books, of which thirty-five only are extant, though with the exception of two of the missing books valuable epitomes are preserved. Though wanting many of the traits of the historian, and though he was of course incapable of looking at history with the modern philosophic spirit, Livy was honest and candid, and possessed a wonderful command of his native language. His work enjoyed an unbounded popularity, not entirely to be accounted for by the fascinations of his theme. He realized his desire to present a clear and probable narrative, and no history of Rome can now be written without constant reference to his pages.

Horace (Quintus Horatius Flaccus) was born on

the river Aufidus, in the year 65 B.C., and was son of a freeman who seems to have been a publican or collector of taxes. At about the age of twelve, after having attended the local school at Venusia, to which the children of the rural aristocracy resorted, he was taken to Rome, where he enjoyed the advantages of the best means of education. He studied Livius Andronicus, and Homer, and was flogged with care by at least one of his masters. He was accompanied at the capital by his father, of whom he always speaks with great respect, and because he mingled with boys of high rank, was well dressed and attended by slaves. The gentle watchfulness of the father guarded Horace from all the temptations of city life, and at the age of eighteen he went to Athens, as most well-educated Romans were obliged to, and studied in the academic groves, though for a while he was swept away by the youthful desire to acquire military renown under Brutus, who came there after the murder of Cæsar. Like the others of the republican army, he fled from the field of Philippi, and found his military ardor thoroughly cooled. He thenceforth devoted himself to letters. Returning to Rome, he attracted notice by his verses, and became a friend of Mæcenas and Virgil, the former of whom bestowed upon him a farm sufficient to sustain him. His life thereafter was passed in frequent interchange of town and country residence, a circumstance which is reflected with charming grace in his verses. His rural home is described in his epistles. It was not extensive, but was pleasant, and he enjoyed it to the utmost. His poetry is deficient in the highest properties of verse, but as the fresh utterances of a man of the world who was possessed of quick observation and strong common-sense, and who was honest and bold, they have always charmed their readers. The Odes of Horace are unrivalled for their grace and felicitous language, but express no great depth of feeling. His Satires do not originate from moral indignation, but the writer playfully shoots folly as it flies, and exhibits a wonderful keenness of observation of the ways of men in the world. His Epistles are his most perfect work, and are, indeed, among the most original and polished forms of Roman verse. His Art of Poetry is not a complete theory of poetic art, and is supposed to have been written simply to suggest the difficulties to be met on the way to perfection by a versifier destitute of the poetic genius. The works of Horace were immediately popular, and in the next generation became text-books in the schools.

Cornelius Nepos was a historical writer of whose life almost no particulars have come down to us, except that he was a friend of Cicero, Catullus, and probably of other men of letters who lived at the end of the republic. The works that he is known to have written are all lost, and that which goes under his name, The Biographies of Distinguished Commanders (*Excellentium Imperatorum Vitæ*), seems to be an abridgment made some centuries after his death, and tedious discussions have been had regarding its authorship. The lives are, however, valuable for their pure Latinity, and interesting for the lofty tone in which the greatness of the Roman people is celebrated. The life of Atticus, the friend and correspondent of Cicero, is the one of the biographies regarding which the doubts have been least. The work is still a favorite school-book and has been published in innumerable editions.

This brief list of celebrated writers whose works were in the hands of the reading public of Rome during the time of the republic, must be closed with reference to Virgil (Publius Vergilius Maro), the writer who stands at the head of the literature of Rome, sharing his pre-eminence only with his younger friend, Horace. Born on his father's small estate near Mantua, Virgil studied Greek at Naples, and other branches, probably, at Rome, where in time he became the friend of the munificent patron of letters, Mæcenas, with whom we have already seen him on the noted journey to Brundusium. It was at the instigation of Mæcenas that Virgil wrote his most finished work, the agricultural poem entitled *Georgica*, which was completed after the battle of Actium (B.C. 31), when Augustus was in the East. It had been preceded by ten brief poems called Bucolics (*Bucolica*, Greek, *boukolos*, a cowherd), noteworthy for their smooth versification and many natural touches, though they have only the form and coloring of the true pastoral poem. The Æneid, which was begun about 30 B.C., occupied eleven years in composition, and yet lacked the finishing touches when the poet was on his death-bed. His death occurred September 22, B.C. 19, at Brundusium, to which place he had come from Greece, where he had been in company with Augustus, and he was buried between the first and second milestones on the road from Naples to Puteoli, where a monument is still shown as his.

Though always a sufferer from poor health, and therefore debarred from entering upon an oratorical or a military career, Virgil was exceptionally fortunate in his friendships and enjoyed extraordinary patronage which enabled him to cultivate literature to the greatest advantage. He was fortunate, too, in his fame, for he was a favorite when he lived no less than after his death. Before the end of his own generation his works were introduced as text-books into Roman schools; during the Middle Age he was the great poet whom it was heresy not to admire; Dante owned him as a master and a model; and the people finally embalmed him in their folk-lore as a mysterious conjurer and necromancer. His *Æneid*, written in imitation of the great Greek poem on the fall of Troy, is a patriotic epic, tracing the wanderings, the struggles, and the death of Æneas, and vaunting the glories of Rome and the greatness of the royal house of the emperor.

Thus, through long ages the Roman wrote, and thus he was furnished with books to read. For centuries he had no literature excepting those rude ballads in which the books of all countries have begun, and all trace of them has passed away. When at last, after the conquest of the Greek cities in Southern Italy, the Tarentine Andronicus began to imitate the epics of his native language in that of his adoption, the progress was still quite slow among a people who argued with the sword and saw little to interest them in the fruit of the brain. As the republic totters to its fall, however, the cultivators of this field increase, and we must suppose that readers also were multiplied. At that time and during the early years of the empire, a Mæcenas surrounded himself with authors and stimulated them to put forth all their vigor in the effort to create a native literature.

On the Esquiline Hill there was a spot of ground that had been a place of burial for the lower orders. This the hypochondriacal invalid Mæcenas bought, and there he laid out a garden and erected a lofty house surmounted by a tower commanding a view of the city and vicinity. Effeminate and addicted to every sort of luxury, Mæcenas calmed his sometimes excited nerves by the sweet sound of distant symphonies, gratified himself by comforting baths, adorned his clothing with expensive gems, tickled his palate with dainty confections of the cook, and regaled himself with the loftier delights afforded by the companionship of the wits and virtuosi of the capital. Magnificent was the patronage that he dispensed among the men of letters; and that he was no mean critic, his choice of authors seems to prove. They were the greatest geniuses and most learned men of the day. At his table sat Virgil, Horace, and Propertius, besides many others, and his name has ever since been proverbial for the patron of letters. No wealthy public man has since arisen who could rival him in this respect.

XX.

THE ROMAN REPUBLICANS SERIOUS AND GAY.

IT is easier to think of the old Roman republicans as serious than gay, when we remember that they considered that their very commonwealth was established upon the will of the gods, and that no acts—at least no public acts—could properly be performed without consulting those spiritual beings, which their imagination pictured as presiding over the hearth, the farm, the forum—as swarming throughout every department of nature. The first stone was not laid at the foundation of the city until Romulus and Remus had gazed up into the heavens, so mysterious and so beautiful, and had obtained, as they thought, some indication of the fittest place where they might dig and build. The she-wolf that nurtured the twins was elevated into a divinity with the name Lupa, or Luperca (*lupus*, a wolf), and was made the wife of a god who was called Lupercus, and worshipped as the protector of sheep against their enemies, and as the god of fertility. On the fifteenth of February, when in that warm clime spring was beginning to open the buds, the shepherds celebrated a feast in honor of Lupercus. Its ceremonies, in some part symbolic of purification, were rude and almost savage, proving that they originated in remote antiquity, but they continued at least down to the end of the period we have considered, and the powerful Marc Antony did not disdain to clothe himself in a wolf-skin and run almost naked through the crowded streets of the capital the month before his friend Julius Cæsar was murdered.* It was a fitting festival for the month of which the name was derived from that of the god of purification (*februare*, to purify).

It was at the foot of a fig-tree that Romulus and Remus were fabled to have been found by Faustulus, and that tree was always looked upon with special veneration, though whenever the Roman walked through the woods he felt that he was surrounded by the world of gods, and that such a leafy shade was a proper place to consecrate as a temple. A temple was not an edifice in those simple days, but merely a place separated and set apart to religious uses by a solemn act of dedication. When the augur moved his wand aloft and designated the portion of the heavens in which he was to make his observations, he called the circumscribed area of the ethereal blue a temple, and when the mediæval astrologer did the same, he named the space a "house." On the Roman temple an altar was set up, and there, perhaps beneath the spreading branches of a royal oak, sacred to Jupiter, the king of the gods, or of an olive, sacred to Minerva, the maiden goddess, impersonation of ideas, who shared with him and his queen the highest place among the

* See page 248.

Capitoline deities, prayers and praises and sacrifices were offered.

When the year opened, the Roman celebrated the fact by solemnizing in its first month, March, the festivity of the father of the Roman people by Rhea Silvia, the god who stood next to Jupiter; who, as Mars Silvanus, watched over the fields and the cattle, and, as Mars Gradivus (marching), delighted in bloody war, and was a fitting divinity to be appealed to by Romulus as he laid the foundation of the city.* As spring progressed, sacrifices were offered to Tellus, the nourishing earth; to Ceres, the Greek goddess Demeter, introduced from Sicily B.C. 496, to avert a famine, whose character did not, however, differ much from that of Tellus; and to Pales, a god of the flocks. At the same inspiring season another feast was observed in honor of the vines and vats, when the wine of the previous season was opened and tasted.†

In like manner after the harvest, there were festivals in honor of Ops, goddess of plenty, wife of that old king of the golden age, Saturnus, introducer of social order and god of sowing, source of wealth and plenty. The festival of Saturnus himself occurred on December 17th, and was a barbarous and joyous harvest-home, a time of absolute relaxation and unrestrained merriment, when distinctions of rank were

---

* See page 19.

† This was the *Vinalia urbana* (*urbs*, a city), but there was another festival celebrated August 19th, when the vintage began, known as the *Vinalia rustica*, when lambs were sacrificed to Jupiter. While the flesh was still on the altar, the priest broke a cluster of grapes from a vine, and thus actually opened the wine harvest.

forgotten, and crowds thronged the streets crying, *Io Saturnalia!* even slaves wearing the *pileus* or skullcap, emblem of liberty, and all throwing off the dignified toga for the easy and comfortable *synthesis*, perhaps a sort of tunic.

Other festivals were devoted to Vulcanus, god of fire, without whose help the handicraftsmen thought they could not carry on their work; and Neptunus, god of the ocean and the sea, to whom sailors addressed their prayers, and to whom commanders going out with fleets offered oblations. Family life was not likely to be forgotten by a people among whom the father was the first priest, and accordingly we find that every house was in a certain sense a temple of Vesta, the goddess of the fireside, and that as of old time the family assembled in the atrium around the hearth, to partake of their common meal, the renewal of the family bond of union was in later days accompanied with acts of worship of Vesta, whose actual temple was only an enlargement of the fireside, uniting all the citizens of the state into a single large family. In her shrine there was no statue, but her presence was represented by the eternal fire burning upon her hearth, a fire that Æneas was fabled to have brought with him from old Troy. The purifying flames stood for the unsullied character of the goddess, which was also betokened by the immaculate maidens who kept alive the sacred coals. As Vesta was remembered at every meal, so also the Lares and Penates, divinities of the fireside, were worshipped, for there was a purification at the beginning of the repast and a libation poured upon the table or the hearth in their honor at its close. When one went abroad he prayed to the Penates for a safe return, and when he came back, he hung his armor and his staff beside their images, and gave them thanks. In every sorrow and in every joy the indefinite divinities that went under these names were called upon for sympathy or help.

In the month of June the mothers celebrated a feast called *Matralia*, to impress upon themselves their duties towards children; and at another they brought to mind the good deeds of the Sabine women in keeping their husbands and fathers from war.* This was the *Matronalia*, and the epigrammatist Martial, who lived during the first century of our era, called it the Women's Saturnalia, on account of its permitted relaxation of manners. At that time husbands gave presents to their wives, lovers to their sweethearts, and mistresses feasted their maids.

The *Lemuria* was a family service that the father celebrated on the ninth, eleventh, and thirteenth of May, when the ghosts of the departed were propitiated. It was thought that these spirits were wont to return to the scenes of their earthly lives to injure those who were still wrestling with the severe realities of time, and specially did they come up during the darkness of night. Therefore it was that at midnight the father rose and went forth with cabalistic signs, skilfully adapted to keep the spectres at a distance. After thrice washing his hands in pure spring water, he turned around and took certain black beans into his mouth, and then threw them

* See page 26.

behind him for the ghosts to pick up. The goodman then uttered other mystic expressions without risking any looks towards the supposed sprites, after which he washed his hands, and beat some brazen basins, and nine times cried aloud: "Begone, ye spectres of the house!" Then could he look around, for the ghosts were harmless.

Thus the Roman forefathers worshipped personal gods, but they did not, in the early times, follow the example of the imaginative Greeks, and represent them as possessing passions like themselves, nor did they erect them into families and write out their lines of descent, or create a mythology filled with stories of their acts good and bad. The gods were spiritual beings, but the religion was not a spiritual life, nor did it have much connection with morality. It was mainly based on the enjoyment of earthly pleasures. If the ceremonious duties were done, the demands of Roman religion were satisfied. It was a hard and narrow faith, but it seemed to tend towards bringing earthly guilt and punishment into relation with its divinities, and it contained the idea of substitution, as is clearly seen in the stories of Curtius, Decius Mus, and others.*

As time passed on the rites and ceremonies increased in number and intricacy, and it became necessary to have special orders to attend to their observance, for the fathers of the families were not able to give their attention to the matter sufficiently.

---

* "When the gods of the community were angry, and nobody could be laid hold of as definitely guilty, they might be appeased by one who voluntarily gave himself up."—MOMMSEN, Book I., chapter 12.

Thus the colleges of priests naturally grew up to care for the national religion, the most ancient of them bearing reference to Mars the killing god. They were the augurs and the pontifices, and as the religion grew more and more formal and the priests less and less earnest, the observances fell into dull and insipid performances, in which no one was interested, and in time public service became not only tedious, but costly, penny collections made from house to house being among the least onerous expedients resorted to for the support of the new grafts on the tree of devotion.

As early as the time of the first Punic war, a consul was bold enough to jest at the auspices in public. Superstitions and impostures flourished, the astrology of ancient Chaldea spread, the Oriental ceremonies were introduced with the pomps that accompanied the reception of the unformed boulder which the special embassy brought from Pessinus when the weary war with Hannibal had rendered any source of hope, even the most futile, inspiring.* Then the abominable worship of Bacchus came in, and thousands were corrupted and made vicious throughout Italy before the authorities were able to put a stop to the midnight orgies and the crimes that daylight exposed.

Cato the elder, who would have nothing to do with consulting Chaldeans or magicians of any sort, asked how it were possible for two such ministers to meet each other face to face without laughing at their own duplicity and the ridiculous superstition of

* B.C. 204. See page 153.

the people they deceived.* Cato was very much shocked by the preaching of three Greek philosophers: Diogenes, a stoic; Critolaus, a peripatetic; and Carneades, an academic, who visited Rome on a political mission, B. C. 155; because it seemed to him that they, especially the last, preached a doctrine that confounded justice and injustice, a system of expediency, and he urged successfully that they should have a polite permission to depart with all speed. The philosophers were dismissed, but it was impossible to restrain the Roman youth who had listened to the addresses of the strangers with an avidity all the greater because their utterances had been found scandalous, and they went to Athens, or Rhodes, to hear more of the same doctrine.

Thus in time the simplicity of the people was completely undermined, and while they became more cosmopolitan they also grew more lax. They used the Greek language, and employed Greek writers, as we have seen, to make their books for them, which, though bearing Greek titles, were composed in Latin. The public men performed in the forenoon their civil and religious acts; took their siestas in the middle of the day; exercised in the Campus Martius,

* It had been in early times customary to dismiss a political gathering if a thunder-storm came up, and the augurs had taken advantage of the practice to increase their own power by laying down an occult system of celestial omens which enabled them to bring any such meeting to a close when the legislation promised to thwart their plans. They finally reached the absurd extreme of enacting a law, by the terms of which a popular assembly was obliged to disperse, if it should occur to a higher magistrate merely to look into the heavens for signs of the approach of such a storm. The power of the priests under such a law was immeasurable. (See pages 236 and 247).

swimming, wrestling, and fencing, in the afternoon; enjoyed the delicacies of the table later, listening to singing and buffoonery the while, and were thus prepared to seek their beds when the sun went down. At the bath, which came to be the polite resort of pleasure-seekers, all was holiday; the toga and the foot-coverings were exchanged for a light Greek dressing-gown, and the time was whiled away in gossip, idle talk, lounging, many dippings into the flowing waters, and music. Pleasure became the business of life, and morality was relaxed to a frightful extent.

When we consider the gay moods of the Roman people we turn probably first to childhood, and try to imagine how the little ones amused themselves. We find that the girls had their dolls, some of which have been dug out of ruins of the ancient buildings, and that the boys played games similar to those that still hold dominion over the young English or American school-boy at play. In their quieter moods they played with huckle-bones taken from sheep, goats, or antelopes, or imitated in stone, metal, ivory, or glass. From the earliest days these were used chiefly by women and children, who used five at a time, which they threw into the air and then tried to catch on the back of the hand, their irregular form making the success the result of considerable skill. The bones were also made to contribute to a variety of amusements requiring agility and accuracy; but after a while the element of chance was introduced. The sides were marked with different values, and the victor was he who threw the highest value, fourteen, the numbers cast being each different from the rest. This throw obtained at a symposium or drinking party caused a person to be appointed king of the feast.

One of the oldest games of the world is that called by the Romans little marauders (*latrunculi*), because it was played like draughts or checkers, there being two sets of " men," white and red, representing opposed soldiers, and the aim of each player being to gain advantage over the other, as soldiers do in a combat. This game is as old as Homer, and is represented in Egyptian tombs, which are of much greater antiquity than any Grecian monuments. In this game, too, skill was all that was needed at first, but in time spice was given by the addition of chance, and dice (*tessera*, a die) were used as in backgammon; but gambling was deemed disreputable, and was forbidden during the republic, except at the time of the Saturnalia, though both Greeks and Romans permitted aged men to amuse themselves in that way.*

The games of the Romans range from the innocent tossing of huckle-bones to the frightful scenes of the gladiatorial show. Some were celebrated in the open air, and others within the enclosures of the circus or the amphitheatre. Some were gay, festive, and abandoned, and others were serious and tragic. Some were said to have been instituted in the earliest days by Romulus, Servius Tullius, or Tarquinius Priscus, and others were imported from abroad or

* A gambler was called *aleator*, and sometimes his implement was spoken of as *alea*, which meant literally gaming. When Suetonius makes Cæsar say, before crossing the Rubicon, " The die is cast," he uses the words *Jacta alea est !*

grew up naturally as the nation progressed in experience or in acquaintance with foreign peoples. The great increase of games and festivals and their enormous cost were signs of approaching trouble for the republic, and foretold the terrible days of the empire, when the rabblement of the capital, accustomed to be amused and fed by their despotic and corrupt rulers, should cry in the streets: "Give us bread for nothing and games forever!" It was gradually educating the populace to think of nothing but enjoyment and to abhor honest labor, and we can imagine the corruption that must have been brought into politics when honors were so expensive that a respectable gladiatorical show cost more than thirty-five thousand dollars (£7,200). If money for such purposes could not be obtained by honest means, the nobles, who lived on popular applause, would seek to force it from poor citizens of the colonies or win it by intrigue at home.

There were impressive games celebrated from the fourth to the twelfth of September, called the great games of the Roman Circus, but it is a disputed point what divinities they were in honor of. Jupiter was thought surely to be one, and Consus another, by those who believed the legends asserting that they were a continuation of those established by Romulus when he wished to get wives from the Sabines. Others think that Tarquinius Priscus, after a victory over the Latins, commemorated his success by games in a valley between the Aventine and the Palatine hills, where the spectators stood about to look on, or occupied stages that they erected for their separate use. The racers went around in a circuit, and it is perhaps on this account that the course and its scaffolds was called the circus (*circum*, round about). The course was long, and about it the seats of the spectators were in after times arranged in tiers. A division, called the *spina* (spine), was built through the central enclosure, separated the horses running in one direction from those going in the other.

A variety of different games were celebrated in the circus. The races may be mentioned first. Sometimes two chariots, drawn by two horses or four each (the *biga* or the *quadriga*), entered for the trial of speed. Each had two horsemen, one of whom, standing in the car with the reins behind his back to enable him to throw his entire weight on them, drove, while the other urged the beasts forward, cleared the way, or assisted in managing the reins. Before the race lists of the horses were handed about and bets made on them, the utmost enthusiasm being excited, and the factions sometimes even coming to blows and blood. The time having arrived, the horses were brought from stalls at the end of the course, and ranged in line, a trumpet sounded, or a handkerchief was dropped, and the drivers and animals put forth every exertion to win the prize. Seven times they whirled around the course, the applause of the excited spectators constantly sounding in their ears. Now and then a biga would be overturned, or a driver, unable to control his fiery steeds, would be thrown to the ground, and, not quick enough to cut the reins that encircled him

RUINS OF THE COLOSSEUM, SEEN FROM THE PALATINE HILL.

with the bill-hook that he carried for the purpose, would be dragged to his death. Such an accident would not stop the onrushing of the other competitors, and at last the victor would step from his car, mount the *spina,* and receive the sum of money that had been offered as the prize.

Another game was the Play of Troy, fabled to have been invented by Æneas, in which young men of rank on horses performed a sham fight. On another occasion the circus would be turned into a camp, and equestrians and infantry would give a realistic exhibition of battle. Again, there would be athletic games, running, boxing, wrestling, throwing the discus or the spear, and other exercises testing the entire physical system with much thoroughness. One day the amphitheatre would be filled with huge trees, and savage animals would be brought to be hunted down by criminals, captives, or men especially trained for the desperate work, who made it their profession.

For the purposes of these combats the circus was found not to be the best, and the amphitheatre was invented by Curio for the celebration of his father's funeral games. It differed from a theatre in permitting the audience to see on both sides (Greek *amphi,* both), but the distinctive name was first applied to a structure built by Cæsar, B.C. 46. The Flavian Amphitheatre, better known as the Colosseum, of which the ruins now stand in Rome, was the culmination of this sort of building, and affords a good idea of the general arrangement of those that were not so grand. That of Cæsar was, however, of wood, which material was used in constructing theatres also; the first one of stone was not erected until 30 B.C., when Augustus was consul.*

Variety was given to the exhibitions of the amphitheatre by introducing sufficient water to float ships, and by causing the same wretched class that fought the wild beasts to represent two rival nations, and to fight until one party was actually killed, unless preserved by the clemency of the ruler.

It must not be supposed that all these exhibitions were known in early times, for, in reality, they were mostly the fruit of the increased love of pleasure that characterized the close of the period of the republic, and reached their greatest extravagance only under the emperors.

The departure of a Roman from this world was considered an event of great importance, and was attended by peculiar ceremonies, some of which have been imitated in later times. At the solemn moment the nearest relative present tried to catch in his mouth the last expiring breath, and as soon as life had passed away, he called out the name of the departed and exclaimed "Vale!" (farewell). The ring had been previously taken from the finger, and now the body was washed and anointed by undertakers, who had been called from a place near the temple of Venus Libitina, where the names of all

---

* History gives an account of one edifice of this kind made of wood that fell down owing to imperfect construction, killing many thousand spectators, and of another that was destroyed by fire. Pompey's theatre of stone, built B.C. 55, has already been mentioned (page 231).

who died were registered, and where articles needed for funerals were hired and sold.*

A small coin was placed in the mouth of the deceased to pay Charon the ferryman who was to take it across the rivers of the lower world, the body was laid out in the vestibule, with its feet toward the door, wearing the simple toga, in the case of an ordinary citizen, or the toga *prætexta* in case of a magistrate, and flowers and leaves were used for decorations as they are at present. If the deceased had received a crown for any act of heroism in life, it was placed upon his head at death. We have already seen that cypress was put at the door to express to the passer-by the bereavement of the dwellers in the house. If the person had been of importance, the funeral was public, and probably it would be found that he had left money for the purpose; but if he had omitted to do that, the expenses of burial would devolve on those who were to inherit his property. These charges in case of a poor person would be but slight, the funeral being celebrated; as in the olden times of the republic, at night and in a very modest style.

The master of the funeral, as he was called, attended by lictors dressed in black, directed the ceremonies in the case of a person of importance. On the eighth day the body would be taken to its cremation or burial, accompanied by persons wearing masks, representing the ancestors of the deceased

* Libitina was an ancient Italian divinity about whom little is known. She has been identified with both Proserpina (the infernal goddess of death and queen of the domain of Pluto her husband) and with Venus.

and dressed in the official costumes that had been theirs, while before it would be borne the military and civic rewards that the deceased had won. Musicians playing doleful strains headed the procession, followed by hired mourners who united lamentations with songs in praise of the virtue of the departed. Players, buffoons, and liberated slaves followed, and of the actors one represented the deceased, imitating his words and actions. The couch on which the body rested as it was carried was often of ivory adorned with gold, and was borne by the near relatives or freedmen, though Julius Cæsar was carried by magistrates and Augustus by senators.

Behind the body the relatives walked in mourning, which was black or dark blue, the sons having their heads veiled, and the daughters wearing their hair dishevelled, and both uttering loud lamentations, the women frantically tearing their cheeks and beating their breasts. As the procession passed through the forum it stopped, and an oration was delivered celebrating the praises of the deceased, after which it went on through the city to some place beyond the walls where the body was burned or buried. We have seen that burial was the early mode of disposing of the dead, and that Sulla was the first of his gens to be burned.* In case of burning, the body was placed on a square, altar-like pile of wood, still resting on the couch, and the nearest relative, with averted face, applied the torch. As the flames rose, perfumes, oil, articles of apparel,

* See page 197.

and dishes of food were cast into them. Sometimes animals, captives, or slaves were slaughtered on the occasion, and, as we have seen, gladiators were hired to fight around the flaming pile.*

When the fire had accomplished its work, and the whole was burned down, wine was thrown over the ashes to extinguish the expiring embers, and the remains were sympathetically gathered up and placed in an urn of marble or less costly material. A priest then sprinkled the ashes with pure water, using a branch of olive or laurel, the urn was placed in a niche of the family tomb, and the mourning relatives and friends withdrew, saying as they went *Vale, vale!* When they reached their homes they underwent a process of purification, the houses themselves were swept with a broom of prescribed pattern, and for nine days the mourning exercises, which included a funeral feast, were continued. In the case of a great man this feast was a public banquet, and gladiatorial shows and games were added in some instances, and they were also repeated on anniversaries of the funeral.

The public buried the illustrious citizens of the nation, and those whose estates were too poor to pay such expenses; the former being for a long time laid away in the Campus Martius, until the site became unhealthy, when it was given to Mæcenas, who built a costly house on it. The rich often erected expensive vaults and tombs during their own lives, and some of the streets for a long distance from the city gate were bordered with ornamental

---

* See pages 158 and 210.

but funereal structures, which must have made the traveller feel that he was passing through unending burial-places. If a tomb was fitted up to contain

A COLUMBARIUM.

many funeral ash-urns, it was known as a columbarium, or dove-cote (*columba*, a dove), the ashes of the freedmen and even slaves being placed in niches covered by lids and bearing inscriptions. The Romans ornamented their tombs in a variety of ways, but did not care to represent death in a direct manner. The place of burial of a person, even a slave, was sacred, and one who desecrated it was liable to grave punishment—even to death,—if the bodies or bones were removed. Oblations of flowers, wine, and milk were often brought to the tombs by relatives, and sometimes they were illuminated.

Almost every country lying under a southern sun is accustomed to rejoice at the annual return of flowers, and ancient Rome was not without its May-day. Festivals of the sort are apt to degenerate morally, and that, also, was true of the Floralia, as these feasts were called at Rome. It is said that in the early age of the republic there was found in the Sibylline books a precept commanding the institution of a celebration in honor of the goddess Flora, who presided over flowers and spring-time, in order to obtain protection for the blossoms. The last three days of April and the first two of May were set apart for this purpose, and then, under the direction of the ædiles, the people gave themselves up to all the delights and, it must be confessed, to many of the dissipations of the opening spring. The amusements were of a varied character, including scenic and other theatrical shows, great merriment, feasting, and drinking. Dance and song added to the gay pleasures, and flowers adorned the scenes that met the eye on every hand. Probably no particular deity was honored at these festivals at first. They were simply the unbending of the rustics after the cold of winter, the rejoicings natural to man in spring; but finally the personal genius of the flowers was developed and her name given to the gay festival.

The rustic simplicity represented well the primal homeliness of the nation during the heroic ages; the orgies of the crowded city may be put for the growing decay of the later period when, enriched and intoxicated by foreign conquest and maddened by civil war, the republic fell, and the way was made plain for the great material growth of the empire, as well as for the final fall of the vast power that had for so many centuries been invincible among the nations of the earth;—a power which still stands forth in monumental grandeur, and is to-day studied for the lessons it teaches and the warnings its history utters to mankind.

INDEX TO THE TEXT AND THE NOTES.

A.

Achæa, province of, 166
Achæan League, the, revived, 163
Acting, Etruscan, 110
Actium, victory of Agrippa off, 268
Actors and masks, 231
Ædiles, election of, and duties of, 79
Æneas, fabled to have invented a game, 325; relics of, 14; story of, 4; Virgil's story of, 7; wanderings of, 8
Æneid, the, of Virgil, 309
Æquians, the, come down upon the city, 86; the, defeated, 87; war with, 90
Æsopus, Claudius, the tragic actor, 232
Ætolia ravaged by Rome, 162
Ætolians, the, claim the victory of Cynocephalæ, 161
Africa, Cæsar in, 245; contest between Rome and Carthage in, 132
African gold used at Rome, 176
Agamemnon, the Trojan hero, 2
Agrarian law, an, proposed, 119, 183, 184; of Cæsar, 226; of Caius Flaminius, 135; of Spurius Cassius, 83
Agrarian laws, the first and last, 82, 226
Agriculture, improvement in, 124; the first occupation, 289; Varro's work on, 301

Agrigentum taken by Rome, 130
Agrippa, Marcus Vipsanius, the general, 256; conquers the forces of Fulvia, 262; victory off Naulochus by, 264
Ahenobarbus, Cneius Domitius, the tribune, 183
Aix, Sertorius at the battle of, 199
Alba Longa founded, 10; chief of the Latin League, 34
Alban lake, the, drained, 95; rise of, 94
Alesia, siege of, 229
Alexander the Great, death of, 120; period of, 111
Alexander I., King of Epirus, helps the Tarentines, 120
Alexandria, Antony and Cleopatra at, 267; Rome sends ambassadors to, 123
Alexandrian library, the, burned, 245
Alexandrine war, the, 245
Allia, battle of the, 101; terrible days of the, brought to mind, 136
Allies, favoring the, legally opposed, 187; hope only for relief by revolution, 187; impatient for the franchise, 186; interests of, identical with those of Rome, 216; obtain concessions, 188; position of the, 124
Alps, the, crossed by Hannibal, 140

Amalthea, the Sibyl of Cumæ, comes to Tarquin the Superb, 59
Amphitheatre, invention of the, 325
Amulius takes his brother's throne, 11
Anchises, father of Æneas, 2
Ancus Martius, the fourth king, 37
Andria, the, of Terence, 298
Andronicus, Livius, the dramatist, 295; works of, 310
Antiochus the Great, allied with Philip V., 160; gives Hannibal an asylum, 148; war with, 161
Antiquities, the Book of, by Varro, 302
Antium, naval battle off, 116
Antony, Marc, at the Lupercalia, 313; chief man in Rome, 252; defeats Cassius, and takes the East as his domain, 261; endeavors to defame Cicero, 258; failing fortunes of, 263; flees to Cæsar, 232, 240; left in charge of Italy, 243; moves the people, 252; offers Cæsar the crown, 248; opposes the plans of Octavius, 257; oration over Cæsar's body, 251; papers of, burned, 270; possessed of Cæsar's moneys, 256; takes possession of Cæsar's papers, 251; warned against the wiles of Cleopatra, 267
Antony and Cleopatra, suicides of, 268
Apellicon of Teos, library of, 192
Apollo, shrine of, at Delphi, 60
Apollonia, Octavius at, 255
Apollonius of Alabanda, surnamed Molo, the rhetorician, 217
Appian Way, the, 124
Apii Forum, Horace at, 265
Appuleian laws, the, supported by Marius, 185

Appuleins, see Saturninus, 185
Apulia, war in, 117
Aquæ Sextiæ, victory of Marius over the Celts at, 181
Aqueducts, building of, 159
Aquitania, subjection of, 229
Arausio, rout of the Romans at, 184
Arcadia, land of innocence and virtue, 9
Arcadian happiness in the North, 98
Archagathus, the first physician, 294
Archimedes at the fall of Syracuse, 144
Ardea, the army before, 62
Arena, meaning of the word, 128
Aricia, Horace at the inn at, 265
Ariminum, an army sent to, 136; Cæsar's advance to, 240; situation of, 238
Ariovistus defeated by Cæsar, 227
Aristocracy, the, Pompey's rupture with, 212
Aristocratic character of the populus Romanus, 73
Aristocrats at head of government, 212; defined, 170
Aristotle, knowledge of, brought to Rome, 192
Armor of the different classes, 52
Army, the, largely composed of plebeians, 115
Arnold, Dr., on the second Punic war, 138; on the Roman character, 118
Arsia, battle at, 65
Art, backward in Rome, 71; not appreciated by Cicero, 204; theft of Verres of works of, 203
Art-rooms added to the house, 277
As, the unit of weight or measure, 51
Ascanius founds Alba Longa, 10
Asculum, battle at, 122; effect of, on Carthage, 123

INDEX TO THE TEXT AND THE NOTES. 335

Asia, province of, 166; conquered by Brutus and Cassius, 261; conquests of Rome in, 162; Pompey's power in, 220; the early home of the Gauls, 99
Asiaticus, a name of Scipio, 162
Assassination of Drusus, 186
Assemblies dispersed by the augurs, 319
Assembly, the National, formation of, 50
Astrology flourishes, 318
Astronomy, Cæsar's knowledge of, 247
Asylæus, the god, 20
Asylum, founding an, at Rome, 20
Atellanæ Fabulæ, the, 298
Ater, days marked, in the calendar, 85, 101, 283; the day of the defeat at Arausio, 184
Athenians, the, favor light ships of war, 131
Athens, besieged by Sulla, 190; commission sent to, 88
Atia, mother of Augustus, 255
Atlantic, blessed islands in the, 199
Atrium, the, 272, 274, 278
Attalus, king of Pergamos, an ally of Rome, 160; bequeaths his kingdom to the Romans, 166, 171
Atticus, life of, written by Nepos, 309
Atys, the old hero, 255
Aufidus, the river, 143
Augural banquets, luxury of, 289
Augurs, duplicity of, 319; examine the Sibylline Books, 59
Augury, the system of, 16
Augustine, St., makes use of Varro's work, 302
Augustus, parentage of, 255. (See Octavius.)
Auspices, become subjects of jests, 319; taking the, 16
Authorship, beginning of, 293
Autocracy, movements toward an, 198

Aventine Hill, the, 12; assigned to the plebeians, 37, 77, 88, 89

B

Bacchus, worship of, 319
Bachelors in early Rome, 21
Banquets, the augural, 289; luxury of the augural, 289
Barbarians threaten Rome, 181
Bathing in Rome, 277
Battles, sham, in the circus, 325
Bed, made of sheepskin, 280
Beginnings of nations, 5
Belgians, the, subjected by Cæsar, 227
Belly and members, apologue about, 78
Beneventum, battle near, 117; defeat of Pyrrhus at, 123; head of the Calydonian boar at, 13; Horace at, 265
Biga, the, in the races, 324
Birds, augury by, 17
Birth and party, 212
Black day, the, of the Cremara, 85; of the Allia, 101
Boarium, Forum, situation of, 136
Body and its members, the, apologue about, 78
Bohemia, Gauls in, 99
Bologna, meeting of Octavius, Antony, and Lepidus near, 258
Bona Dea, mysteries of, 223
Book-rooms added to the house, 277
Books, how made, 277
Boreas and his cold winds, 98
Boundaries, laws concerning, 30
Bovianum taken by the Romans, 117
Breakfast, luncheon, and dinner, 288
Brennus, leader of the Gauls, trusts in his sword, 100; burns Rome, 102; throws his sword into the scales, 104
Bribery, law against, 184

336 INDEX TO THE TEXT AND THE NOTES.

Bribes, in Rome, 176; Cæsar's use of, 227
Brides, customs regarding, 283
Bridge-builders, 32
Bridge, the wooden (*pons sublicius*), 32, 38; Gracchus flees over the, 174
Brindisi, 9
Britain visited by Cæsar, 228
Brundusium, on the Appian way, 124; besieged by Antony, 263; besieged by Cæsar, 243; Octavius at, 255
Bruttium, gladiators in, 211
Brutus and Cassius flee from Rome, 252; masters of the Eastern world, 260
Brutus, D. Junius, funeral of, 158
Brutus, great-grandson of Æneas, 6
Brutus, Lucius Junius, goes to Delphi, 60; swears to avenge Lucretia, 63; death and mourning for, 65-66
Brutus, Marcus Junius, plots against Cæsar, 249; suicide of, 261
Buffoonery instead of wit, 110
Buffoons at a dinner, 265
Burial of two couples alive in the Forum Boarium, 136
Burial-places sacred, 331

C.

Cædicius, Marcus, the tribune, hears a startling voice, 100
Cæpio, Quintus Servilius, ill-gotten gains of, 184
Cæsar, Caius Julius, birth and character of, 206; assassination of, 231; beneficent plans of, 246; builds the first amphitheatre, so called, 325; called Father of his Country, 246; captured by pirates, 217; clemency of, 243, 245, 249, 250; commentaries of, 302; crosses the Rubicon, 240; death of, announced to Octavius, 255; made dictator for ten years after Thapsus, 246; eclipses Pompey, 230; goes to Spain, 248; governor of Gaul, 226; in Asia, 245; in Greece, 244; intrigues against Pompey, 221; magical power of, 228; a Marian, 207; marries a relative of Pompey, 216; obsequies of, 251; offers to give up his command, 238; overcomes the Pompeians in Spain, 243; popularity with his army, 235; refuses the crown, 249; resists Sulla, 206; silent progress of, 224; will of, 252, 254
Calendar, the Roman, 32, 33; jugglery regarding, 236; the, reformed, 247
Camillus, Marcus Furius, dictator, 95; dictator the second time, 102; needed, 100; recalled from exile, 102; reaction against, 97; routs the Gauls, 104; saves the state a third time, 109; the second founder of Rome, 106
Campania inhabited by the Samnites, 114; servile insurrection in, 183
Campania and Capua regained, 144
Campus Martius, assembly of the centuries on, 54
Canal, the, at Tarracina, 265; travel by the, 290
Candidates for office, wiles of, 290
Cannæ, avenged at the Metaurus, 146; dark days after, 150; rout of the Romans at, 143
Canuleian Law, the, 92
Canuleius, Caius, urges the repeal of a marriage law, 92
Canusium, Hannibal at, 146; Horace at, 266
Canvassing for office, 290
Capital punishment, law regarding, 223
Capitol, the, burning of, 193

Capitoline Hill, citadel on the, 23; origin of name of, 59; temple of the, finished by Catulus, 208
Capua declares for Hannibal, 143; legions of Pompey and Cæsar sent to, 237; luxury at, 115; revolt at, 245; school of gladiators at, 209
Capua and Campania regained, 144
Carbo, Caius Papirius, friend of the Gracchi, 172
Carneades visits Rome, 319
Carrhæ, disaster at, 248; loss of Crassus at, 234
Carriages prohibited to women at a certain time, 150
Carthage, first notices Rome, 111; adds to its territory, 139; asks in vain for peace, 132; growth of, 126; meaning of the name, 127; commerce of, 127; congratulates Rome on the victory of Mt. Gaurus, 115; naval prestige of, destroyed, 131; on her guard against Rome, 129; recovers lost ground, 165; sends a fleet to help Rome, 123; tributary to Rome, 147
Carthaginians, defeated at the Metaurus, 146; expelled from Messana, 130; in Sicily, 123
Cassius and Brutus flee from Rome, 252; masters of the Eastern world, 260, 261
Cassius, Spurius, friend of the people, 82; popularity of, blasted, 84
Cassius, suicide of, 261; see Longinus, 249
Castor and Pollux, festival in honor of, 68; interfere for Rome, 67
Catilina, the work of Sallust, 305
Catiline, Lucius Sergius, conspiracy of, 205, 221; flees from Rome, 222; traits of, 204
Cato, Marcus Porcius, conservative views of, 152; eggs the Romans against Carthage, 165; intercedes for the captive Achæans, 164; manual of education of, 293; model of Brutus, 250; on foreign doctors, 294; on the care of children, 284; on the duplicity of the augurs, 319; opposes Scipio, 156
Cato, Marcus Porcius, of Utica, a determined enemy of Cæsar, 234; defeat and death of, 245; flees from Rome, 242; opposes Pompey, 221
Catulus and Hortensius defeated by Cicero, 219
Catulus, Quintus Lutatius, consul and aristocrat, 207; opposes the Cimbri, 182
Catullus, Valerius, writings of, 302
Caudine Forks, battle of the, 117
Celer kills a man, 20
Celeres, the body-guard of Romulus, 27
Celerity, Plutarch's derivation of, 20
Celts and Germans threaten Rome, 181
Censors, appointment of, 49; power of, limited by Sulla, 195; rank of, 93
Census, taken by consuls, 93; taking of, by Servius Tullius, 49
Centuries, the formation of the, 50
Ceremonies, increase of, 317
Ceres, goddess of agriculture, 79; the Greek Demeter, 314
Chaldea, astrology of, 319
Chance, games of, 320
Chariot-races, 323
Charon, coin to pay, 327
Charran, the city of Nahor, 234
Childhood, plays of, 320
Children and the control of them, 282
Chimneys not known, 279
China and Egypt, antiquity of, 4
Cicero, Marcus Tullius, traits of.

202; causes conspirators to be put to death, 223; correspondence of, 237; courted on account of his oratory, 216; courts Pompey, 221; exposes Catiline, 222; first oration before the people, 219; lauds Labienus, 242; leader of the senate, 251; outlawed, 224; proscription of, 260; prosecutes Verres, 204, 216; remarks of Froude concerning, 257; a rhetorical victory of, 219; says that he expected Curio to desert to Cæsar, 237; unmanliness of, 223; won by Octavius, 256; the works of, 299, 300

Cilicia, Verres in, 203
Cimbri, the, enter Central Europe, 181
Ciminian Hills, the, battle near, 119
Cincinnatus, Lucius Quintius, carcer of, 86; at his plow, 274
Cineas, the Thessalian, minister of Pyrrhus, 121; goes to Rome to sue for peace, 122
Cinna, Lucius Cornelius, takes part with Marius, 190; assassinated, 193; marches on Rome, 190
Circus Maximus, the, 44; great games of the, 322; origin of the word, 223; situation of, 136; the single one, 158
City, rites at the foundation of a, 18, 19
Class distinctions weakened, 212
Classes, of people in Italy, 124; the six, of Servius Tullius, 50
Claudia, daughter of Fulvia, renounced by Octavius, 262
Claudius, Appius, Sabinus Regillensis, 68; decemvir, 88; influence of, 89; origin of, 68; protests against peace with Pyrrhus, 122; wickedness of, 91

Clausus, Atta, founder of the Claudian house, 68
Cleopatra captivates Antony, 262; war against, by Octavius, 268; wins Cæsar, 244; with Antony in Syria, 267
Cloaca Maxima, the, built, 44; situation of, 136
Clodius, Publius, Pulcher, 224; intrigue of, 223
Cloth made by wives and daughters, 284
Clusium, attacked by the Gauls, 99; defeat of the Romans near, 136; Porsena, Lars, of, 66
Coccles, Horatius, defends the wooden bridge, 66
Cœlian Hill, the, assigned to the Albans, 36
Cœna, the Roman dinner, 288
Cohorts, the Marsic, meaning of, 187
Collatinus, husband of Lucretia, 62
Collections, penny, 318
Colline Gate, battle at the, 193, 199
Colonies, citizens in the, 124; in the West, relation of Sertorius to, 199; of Carthage, 128
Colosseum, the, 325,
Columbarium, the, 330
Comitia, election of consuls by, 64
Comitia Centuriata, formation of, 50
Comitia Curiata, rights of, 28, 223; not abolished by Servius Tullius, 52
Commentaries, the, of Cæsar, 226, 302
Commerce begins in Rome, 71; increase of, 124
Commons, a king from the, 48: rights of, swept away, 58
Concord, temple of, scene of Cicero's oratory, 258
Conference at Tarentum, 264
Confiscation of the property of Cicero, 224

Confiscations of Verres, 203
Confusion, year of, 248
Congiarium, the, of Sulla, 196
Conquest, consequences of, 333; meaning of, in the early times, 87
Conservatism, the, of Cato, 156
Consulate obtained by Octavius, 258
Consuls, choice of, after the banishment of the Tarquins, 64; endowed with dictatorial powers, 240; the first plebeian, 109
Consus, celebration in honor of, by Romulus, 21; festival of, 322
Copper found in Italian soil, 71
Corfinum chosen by the allies as capital of Italy, 187
Corinth, growth of, 39; taken by the Romans, sacked and pillaged, 164
Coriolanus, Caius Marcius, at Lake Regillus, 68; as an office-seeker, 290; banishment and death of, 82; origin of name of, 80
Cornelia, daughter of Scipio, 167; jewels of, 168; urges Gracchus to do some great work, 170
Cornelia, wife of Cæsar, 206
Cornelian gens bury their dead, 197
Cornelians, name of the veterans of Sulla, 196; the, headed by Catiline, 207
Correspondence, the, of Cicero, 299
Corruption in the provinces, 216; in the state, 174
Corsica and Sardinia taken from Carthage, 134
Corvus, Marcus Valerius, aided by a raven, 113; victorious at Mount Gaurus, 114
Cothurnus, use of, 286
Courses at dinner, 288
Crassus, Marcus Licinius, Dives, thrifty ways of, 200; makes peace with Pompey, 214; feasts the people, 216; jealous of Pompey, 214, 217; opposes Pompey, 221; rewarded by Cæsar, 226
Crassus and Pompey exterminate the gladiators, 211
Crassus, Cæsar, and Pompey, 232
Cremara, battle of the, 85
Cremation, the, of Sulla's body, 197
Cremation or burial, 327, 328
Cremona, colony at, 136
Crime, increase of, makes a prison necessary, 38
Critolaus visits Rome, 319
Crown, the oaken, awarded, 68
Crucifixion of gladiators, 211
Culina, the, 278
Cumæ, relics at, 14; the Sibyl of, 59
Cures, home of Numa, 29
Curio, Caius Scribonius, a partisan of Cæsar, 235; delivers a letter in Rome, 238; invents the amphitheatre, 325
Curses of the ambassadors from Veii fulfilled, 102
Curtius, idea of substitution involved in the story of, 317
Curtius, Marcus, 110
Curtius, Mettus, story of, 24
Cybele, the Idæan mother, 153
Cydnus, Cleopatra on the, 262
Cynocephalæ, Macedonians defeated at the, 160
Cypress, the, a sign of sorrow, 274
Cypselus, birth of, 40

D.

Dance and song at the Floralia, 331
Death and funerals, 326
Death, law regarding punishment of, 223
Debtor, a desperate, excites the people, 75

Debtors, release of, 78 ; trials of, 74
Debts, abolished to afford relief to the poor, 119 ; burdens of, after the burning of the city, 115 ; pressing heavily, 119 ; the, of Curio, 235
Decemvirs, take the place of other officers, 88 ; haughtiness of, 90
Deities, the, of early Rome, 72
Delayer, the (Fabius), 139.
Delphi, the oracle at, 39, 60 ; consulted about the rise of Alban Lake, 94
Demaratus goes to Tarquinii, 40
Demosthenes, Phillippics of, 257
Dentatus, see Sicinius, 90
Diana, temple to, on the Aventine, 48
Dice, games with, 321
Dictator, a, appointed, 67 ; office of, renewed by Sulla, 194 ; Fabius, chosen, 142
"Die is cast," the, exclamation of Cæsar, 241
Dining-room, the, 276
Dinner, the formal, 289 ; how served, 289 ; luncheon and breakfast, 288
Diogenes visits Rome, 319
Diomede, arms of, at Luceria, 14
Discus, throwing the, 325
Dishes at dinner, 289
Distinctions, political, between the two orders wiped out, 109
Dives, a name of Crassus, 22, 224
Dogs as guardians, 274
Dolls, the, of Roman girls, 320
Domestic slaves, 282
Domitian law, the, 183
Domitius, see Ahenobarbus, 183
Drains, the great, of Tarquin, 44
Drama, the earliest, 296 ; growth of the, 158
Dramatic exhibitions prohibited, 281
Dress among the Romans, 285

Drusus, Marcus Livius, the opponent of Gracchus, 174 ; attempts reform, 186 ; remark of, about his house, 187
Duilius, Caius, defeats the Carthaginians, 131
Duria, Hannibal in the valley of the, 140
Dwelling, an expensive, 200
Dwellings poor in early days, 71
Dyrrachium, defeat of Cæsar at, 244

E

Economus, point of departure of Regulus, 132 ; battle of, 132
Education, the early, in Rome, 292 ; efforts of Sertorius for, 199 ; the, of Horace, 307
Egeria, the nymph that Numa pretended to meet, 32
Egg to the apple, from the, 288
Egnatia, route of the road, 261
Egypt, ambassadors sent to, 123 ; antiquity of, 4
Elephants, introduced by Pyrrhus, 120 ; use of, by Xanthippus, 132
Elpenor, tomb of, 14
Elysium, the, of Plato, 200
Emigration, the, of Demaratus from Corinth, 40
Empire, establishment of, 270 ; material growth of the, 332 ; tendency towards an, 198
Ennius, works of, 296
Epeus, tools of, 13
Epicurus, philosophy of, exhibited by Lucretius, 304
Equites, the (knights), 28
Era, beginning of a new, 212, 270
Ercte, Mount, Hamilcar at, 134
Eryx, Hamilcar at, 134
Esquiline Hill, concentration of freedmen on, 168 ; house of Mæcenas on, 311
Etruria, customs derived from, 18 ; twelve cities of, 9 ; visit

of Gracchus to, and its results, 169
Etruscan acting, imitation of, 298.
Etruscans, civilization of, 42; names of the, 15; defeated at Lake Vadimonis, 117; in the Marsic war, 187; weakened by the Gauls, 99; Greek descent of the, 9; peace with the, 122; and Romans fight, 65; take sides with the Samnites, 117
Evander, the good king, 9
Exile, punishment of, 291
Exiles recalled by Antony, 254
Expediency, doctrine of, opposed by Cato, 319

F

Fabian family, the, cut off, 85
Fabii, the followers of Remus, 17; destruction of the, 101; the, overthow Cassius, 84
Fabius, Marcus, takes the part of the plebeians, 84
Fabius Maximus, see Maximus, 117; career of, 145, 146; looks askance at Scipio, 156; regains Campania, 144
Fabius, the Delayer, see Maximus, 139
Fables of early history, 5, 8
Family, Vesta, goddess of the, 315
Famine in Rome, 80
Farces, the early rude, 298
Father, autocratic authority of the, 71, 282
Father of his country, title borne by Camillus, Cicero, and Cæsar, 246
Faustulus finds Romulus and Remus, 12
Fawn, the white, of Sertorius, 199
Felix, the lucky, title assumed by Sulla, 195
Festivals, great cost of, 322; slow growth of, 158
Fidenæ mined, 94

Finances administered by the censors, 93
Fire and water, symbolical meaning of, 291
Flamens, the, 32
Flaminian road, the, 238
Flamininus, Lucius Quintus, commands the Roman army in Greece, 160
Flaminius, Caius, killed at lake Trasimenus, 142
Flogging in school, 307
Flora, festival of the goddess, 331
Floralia, the, 33
Food, Greek influence on, 287
Fortune, Feminine, temple to, 82
Forum, opening in the earth in the, 110; women in the, 152
Forum Romanum, meeting-place of Romans and Sabines, 26
Founding of Rome the second time, 106
Franchise, how obtained by allies, 188; restriction of the, by Gracchus, 168
Freedmen, and other citizens, difference between, 188; gathered on the Esquiline, 168; replaced by slaves in Sicilian fields, 166
Froude, James Anthony, on Cicero, 257
Fulvia, widow of Clodius and wife of Antony and Curio, 235; opposes Octavius and is defeated by his general, Agrippa, 262; wife of Antony, forgotten by him, 262; death of, 263
Funeral ceremonies, 326; fights of gladiators, 158, 210; oration over the body of Cæsar, 251
Funeral, the, of Sulla, 197
Furies, temple of the, 174

G

Gabii, schools at, 76
Gabinian law, the 218

Gabinius the tribune, 218
Gallia Cisalpina, boundaries of, 123; provincia, 166
Gambling, 321
Games, at the Circus Maximus, 44; celebrated by Romulus, 21, 22; the Roman, 321; of the children, 320; a law regarding, 150
Gastronomy, epoch in, 289
Gaul, assigned to Cæsar, 228; Cæsar governor of, 226; conquest of, 229
Gauls, aid the Etruscans against Rome, 118; alarmed by the approach of Roman settlers, 135; annihilated at Telamon, 136; attack Rome, 108; climb the Capitoline, 103; come to Italy, 99; flock to Hannibal, 140; habits of the, 98; havoc by increased hardships of poor debtors, 109; neglect Hannibal, 142; routed at Aquæ Sextiæ by Marius, 181; territory gained from the, 135
Gaurus, battle of Mount, 114
Germans and Celts threaten Rome, 181
Ghosts, exorcising the, 316
Gladiatorial exhibition, the first, 136; great cost of, 322
Gladiators at funerals, 158, 329; classes of, 209; fight at command of Cæsar, 246; fights of, 209; fights of, in Pompey's theatre, 232; rising of, under Spartacus, 210
Gods, Roman belief in, 312; honored in the farm-house, 281; traits of the, 317
Gold of Tolosa (ill-gotten gains), 184
Gold supposed to have been taken from Brennus, 243
Golden age, the, of Numa, 33
Government, stages of, in early Rome, 72
Governor, a provincial, 203, 222

Gracchi, the, 168; reforms of, apparently practicable, 184
Gracchus, Caius, death of, 174; misses an opportunity, 171; popularity of, 172
Gracchus, Tiberius, becomes husband of Cornelia, 167; goes to Africa, 168; murder of, 171; not understood, 172
Gradivus, Mars, delights in war, 314
Grœcia, Magna, contributes to Roman culture, 295, 296
Grain, distributed by Crassus, 216; free, promised by Lepidus, 208; Pompey pretends to seek supplies of, 227; price of, falls, 218; proposal to sell, at nominal prices, 185; rise of price of, 264; sold at low rates by Gracchus, 173; supply of, threatened, 217
Grammar, Varro's work on, 301
Greece, commission sent to learn about its laws, 88; decadence of, 158; fall of the liberties of, 165; influence of, 152; influence of, on Latin literature, 319; philosophy of, enters Rome, 319; a Roman province, 165; tyrranny in, 72
Grecian influence on food, 287; on mental culture, 292
Greek art not appreciated, 204
Greeks, names of the, 15
Gregorian calendar, the, 247
Guilds, institution of, by Numa, 31
Gymnasts in Pompey's theatre, 232

H

Hadrumentum, Hannibal asks terms at, 147
Hamilcar Barca, comes upon the stage, 133; defeated by Regulus off Economus, 132
Hannibal, appears, 137; demands war, 140; fate of, 148; great-

ness of, 138 ; neglected, 142 ;
policy of, 142 ; returns to Africa, 147 ; successes of, 143,
144 ; and Vercingetorix compared, 229
Hasdrubal, despatches of, intercepted, 146 ; tries to aid Hannibal, 146
Heating and lighting the houses, 279
Heautontimoroumenos, the, of Terence, 299
Helen, story of, 2
Heliodorus the Greek rhetorician, 265
Helvetii, the, conquered by Cæsar, 227
"Hercules, how cold are thy baths," 180
Hercules, weapons of, 13
Hercynian forests, the, 99
Herodotus goes to Phœnicia, 127
Heroes, the age of, 66
Hiero, king of Syracuse, 129 ; makes permanent peace with Rome, 130
Hills, the "Seven," 49
Hippodrome, the, at a villa, 281
History, fables of early, 5 ; made up of acts of fighting men, 271
Holidays, but one, 158
Holy of Holies, the, examined by Pompey, 221
Homer's story of Troy, 1
Horace and Virgil, journey of, 265
Horace (Quintus Horatius Flaccus), works of, 306 ; at Tarentum, 264
Horatii and Curiatii, the, 34
Horse-racing in the circus, 323
Horse, the wooden, of Troy, 2
Hortensian laws, 109, 119
Hortensius, Quintus, the orator, defends Verres, 204 ; augural dinner of, 289 ; defeated by Cicero, 219
Hospitality in the farm villa, 280
Hostilius, Hostus, champion of Rome, 24

Houses in Rome, 272
Huckle-bones, games with, 320
Hungary, Gauls in, 99
Hyperboreans, the, as depicted by the Greeks, 98

I

Icilian law, the, 88
Icilius, Lucius, affianced to Virginia, 90 ; stirs up the people, 91
Ideal, the, no leaning toward, at Rome, 158
Ides of March, the fatal, 250
Illyria added to Roman dominions, 135
Insurrections, servile, 175
Interest, rates of, 74 ; rate of, lowered, 270
Intermarriage, right of, 93
Islands of the blest, 199
Isthmian games, the, joy at, 161
Italia, early inhabitants of, 9
Italians, citizenship offered to the, 184 ; suffrage extended to, 173 ; lands to be divided among, 185
Italy and Persia contrasted by Livy, 112
Italy, early state of, 9 ; filled with complaints, 262 ; devastated by Pyrrhus, 122 ; laid waste by gladiators, 211

J

Janiculum Hill, secession to the, 92, 119 ; fortified, 37
January made the first month, 32
Janus, temple of, founded, 32 ; gates of, closed the second time, 134 ; third closing of, 270
Jewels, the, of Cornelia, 168
Jewish, temple examined by Pompey, 220
Judges, corruption of, 175
Jugerum, the standard of square measure, 71

Jugglery of the priests, 319
Jugurtha, the Numidian, at Numantia, 175; endeavors to gain control of Numidia, 176; war with, closed, 180
Jugurtha, the work of Sallust, 305
Julia, wife of Pompey, dies, 234
Julian calendar, the, 247
July named for Cæsar, 246
Junia, wife of Cassius, 250
Jupiter, prayer to, 19; among the deities, 314
Jupiter Stator, temple vowed to, 26
Jurisprudence, epoch in, 119
Justice and injustice confounded, 319
Justinian codifies Roman law, 246

K

King, suspicions that Cæsar wished to be, 249; name of, hated by the Romans, 69, 171, 236
Kings, characters of the seven, 70
Kitchen fire at Beneventum, described by Horace, 266
Kitchen, the Roman, 278

L

Labienus, Titus, deserts Cæsar, 242
Lacerna, the, 286
Lacus Curtius, origin of, 24
Lake, Alban, rise of, 94; Trasimenus, battle of, 142; Vadimonis, second battle near, 119; victory at, 117
Lanatus, Menenius Agrippa, treats with the plebeians, 78; death of, 79
Land, distributed among the people, 119; divided among patricians, 96; in the hands of the rich, 184
Landholders becoming few, 184
Lands, allotment of, to veterans, 261, 262; assignment of, stopped by the optimates, 174; derived from the Gauls divided among the people, 83, 135; distribution of, among the people, by Servius Tullius, 55; divided among the people by Numa, 30; another distribution of, 226; proposed division of, by Marius, 185; taken by the rich, 169; taken from the rich, 170; wealth derived from illegal use of, 83, 84
Language, improvement in, 159
Languages, education in the, 199
Lares and Penates, the, 315
Lateranus, Lucius Sextius. See Sextius, 109
Latin name, the, 125
Latins, dependent upon Rome, 116; determine to fight for equality, 115; invade the Roman territory, 37
Latinus, the Italian king, 10
Latium, leagues with the thirty cities of, 48; size of, 70
Latrunculi, game of (draughts), 321
Lavinia, wife of Æneas, 10
Lavinium, the town of Æneas, 10; penates of Æneas at, 14
Law, agrarian, the first, 83; beginning of the study of, 159; the Appuleian, 185; the Canuleian, 92; the Domitian, 183; the Gabinian, 217; the Hortensian, 109, 119; the Icilian, 88; the Licinian, 109; the Manilian, 219; the Oppian, 150; the Publilian, 109; the Sempronian, 173; proposal to codify, 246; principles of the Roman, 291
Law and punishment, 291
Laws, made by the rich oppressive to the poor, 74; mixed condition of, 88; sumptuary, enacted, 195

League, the Achæan, revived, 163
Lectisternium, the, performed the third time, 109
Legion, composition of the, 28
Legislation influenced by omens, 319
Lemuria, the, 316
Leniency of Cæsar, 243, 245
Lepidus, Marcus Æmilius, left in charge of Rome, 243; at head of the army, 251, 256; consul, favors the Marians, 207; ignored by the other triumvirs, 261; marches to Rome, 208; protests against Sulla's grand funeral, 197; put to flight, 208; retires to private life, 266
Letters, how taught to children, 295; patronage of, by Mæcenas, 311
Libitina, Venus, temple of, 326, 327
Library, the Alexandrian, burned, 245; the, of Apellicon, brought to Rome, 192
Libyssa, place of Hannibal's death, 148
Licinian Rogations, the, passed, 109; remembered by Gracchus, 169; reëstablished, 170
Life in Rome, 320; in a rural house, 280
Lilybæum, point of departure of Scipio, 146; siege of, 133
Literature, backward, 71; Cicero's works, 202; in Greece, 158; none in Rome, 158
Litter, travel in a, 290
Livy (Titus Livius), writings of, 306; history of Rome by, 7; account of a desperate debtor, 75; on the character of Alexander, 111; on Roman history, 13; on the second Punic war, 138; on stage plays, 110; story of Mettus Curtius, 25
Longinus, Caius Cassius, plots against Cæsar, 249

Lucania, entered by the Samnites, 117; overcome, 145
Lucanians and Tarentines, war between, 120
Lucca, conference at, 227
Lucius Tarquinius, birth of, 41; goes to Rome, 41
Lucomo (Lucius Tarquinius), 41
Lucretia, story of, 62; at her work, 71
Lucretius (Titus Lucretius Carus), works of, 303
Lucullus, Lucius Licinius, sent to Pontus, 218
Lupercalia, fatal feast of, 248, 312
Lupercus, feast of, 312
Lustration, the, 54
Lustrum, duration of a, 54
Luxury, increase of, 186; tendency towards, 152

M

Macedonia, king of, attacked by Pyrrhus, 120
Macedonian war, the first, 159, 160; the second, 162; the third (with Perseus), 163
Mæcenas, Caius Cilnius, at Tarentum, 264; builds a house on the Campus Martius, 329; in command at Rome, 268; patronizes Horace, 307; traits of, 311; villa of, 282
Magistrates, laws against peculation by, 184
Magna Græcia, decadence of, 117; growth of, 39; influence of, 152; Samnites enter, 114
Magnesia, Roman victory at, 162
Maleventum, old name of Beneventum, 117; change of name of, 123
Mamers, a form of "Mars," 129
Mamertine prison, the, built by Ancus Martius, 38; Jugurtha starved in, 180
Mamertines, call on Rome for assistance, 129; rise of the, 129

Mamilius, Octavius, of Tusculum, 58; aids Tarquin, 67
Manes, the, supposed to like blood, 158
Manilian law, the, 219, 220
Manlius, Marcus, hurled from the Tarpeian rock, 108; repels the Gauls, 103; takes the part of the plebeians, 108
Manners, refinement in, 156
Mantinœa, defeat of Sparta at, 163
Manufactures, beginning of, 289
March, Ides of, the, 250
March, the first month, 32
Marians, pursued by Pompey, 202; the, in Spain, 209
Marius and Sulla, traits of, 185
Marius, Caius, appearance of, on the stage, 175; appointed to command against Mithridates, 190; body of, cast into the Anio, 194; chosen consul, 178; chosen consul the fifth time, 182; death of, 190; goes to Gaul, 181; joins Cinna, 190; obliged to flee to Africa, 190; offers himself in vain, 184; retirement of, 185; returns to Rome to win office, 178; routs the Cimbri at Vercellæ, 182; the third founder of Rome, 182; triumph of, 180; vengeance of, 188
Marriage, ceremonies connected with, 282; between plebeians and patricians prohibited, 92; between members of the two orders permitted, 92
Mars, prayer to, 19; traits of, 314
Marsian war, the, 187
Masks worn by actors, 231
Massana taken by the Campanians (Mamertines), 129
Matralia, the feast of, 316
Matronalia, establishment of, 26; feast of, 316
Matrons, good works of, 154; a movement of the Roman, 149; appeal to Coriolanus, 81

Maximus, Fabius (Rullus), at the battle of Vadimonis, 117
Maximus, Quintus Fabius, 139; chosen dictator, 142
May-day, the Roman, 331
Medicine, knowledge of, 293
Memoirs, the, of Sulla, 196
Men, privileges of, as viewed by Cato, 152
Menæchmi, the, of Plautus, 298
Menenius Agrippa, see Lanatus, 78
Menenius, Titus, accused of treason, 85
Mésalliance, at Corinth, 39
Mesopotamia, Crassus in, 234
Metapontem, relics at, 13
Metaurus, defeat of the Carthaginians at the, 146
Metellus, Cæcilius, Numidicus, sent to Africa, 178
Metellus, Lucius Cæcilius, Creticus, opposes Cæsar's attempt to take posession of the sacred gold, 243
Miasma affects the Gauls, 104
Mile-stones erected by Gracchus, 173
Military tribunes with power of consuls, 93
Milton's way of writing English history, 5
Mistress and maid at work, 71
Mithridates, cut off and defeated, 220; first war with, 189; overcome by Sulla, 192; reckless ferocity of, 192; second war with, 218; succumbs to Lucullus, 218-219; third war with (the " great " war), 218
Mommsen, on Cato's encyclopædia, 293; on banquets, 289; on Roman religion, 317
Monarchical style of Pompey, 219
Monarchy, the, degenerates into tyranny, 72
Money-lending during the period of the republic, 74
Money, use of, for pleasure, 156; uses of, in early Rome 74

Months, the intercalary, 247; meaning of names of, 32
Moses on boundaries, 30
Mothers, feasts of the, 316
Mount Gaurus, battle of, 114
Mount Vesuvius, battle of, 115
Mucius, Caius Scævola, adventure of, 66
Mules, travel by, 265
Mulvian Bridge, battle at, 208
Munda, victory of Cæsar at, 248
Mus, Marcus Decius, at the battle of Vesuvius, 116
Mus, Publius Decius, devotes himself to the gods, 118; idea of substitution involved in the story of, 317
Music after dinner, 289; at funerals, 328
Mylæ, battle of, 131
Myrtle, the, a sign of rejoicing, 274
Mythology, the, of Greece, 72, 317

N.

Names, the, of the Romans, 14, 36
Naples, simply "New City," 127
Natura, de rerum, the, of Lucretius, 304
Naulochus, defeat of Pompeius Sextus at, 264
Navy, a, created by Rome, 131; lack of, by Rome, 130
Neapolis, league with, 116
Nepos, Cornelius, works of, 308
Neptunus, festival of, 315
New, as used in names of places, 127
New Carthage, 139; taken by Scipio, 144
Niebuhr, establishes the true character of the Gracchi, 171; lectures of, 67
Nomenclator, work of the, 290
Noricum, defeat of the Romans at, 181
Numa Pompilius, second king, 29; calendar of, 247; gives the people religious ceremonies, 30
Numantia taken by Scipio, 166
Numicius, the river, 10
Numidian war brought to a close, 180
Numitor, dispossessed of his throne, 11; replaced on his throne, 12

O

Oak, the, sacred to Jupiter, 313
Octavia, sister of Octavius, espoused by Antony, 263; desertion of, by Antony, 267
Octavius, at Apollonia with Cæsar's army, 255; at Tarentum, 264; chosen as successor of Cæsar, 248; in Asia, 268; takes possession of public funds, 256
Office, how used by provincial governors, 203; merely a means to gain wealth, 175
Office-holders and office-seekers, 290
Oligarchy, an, rules, 198; the, of time of Cicero, 207
Olive, the, sacred to Minerva, 313
Omens, at the foundation of Rome, 19; ill. after the fall of Veii, 97; system of, 319
Opimius, Lucius, convicted of receiving bribes, 178
Oppian law, argument for its repeal, 154; the, reason for, 150; restrictions of, 168
Ops, goddess of plenty, 314
Optimates, defined, 170; oppose Pompey and Cicero, 219; power of decreasing, 183; see the influence of Gracchus, 174; Sulla's adhesion to, 194; undermine the influence of Gracchus, 174
Oratory of Caius Gracchus, 173; of Cicero, 299, 300
Orders, union and severance of

348   *INDEX TO THE TEXT AND THE NOTES.*

the two, 73 ; a tie established between the two, by Corvus, 113 ; peace between, 109
Orgies and decay of simplicity, 332
Origines, the, of Cato, 153, 293
Ostia, colony founded at, by Ancus Martius, 37
Ovation of Crassus, 212
Ovicula, a name of Fabius, 139
Ovid (Publius Ovidius Naso,) writings of, 304 ; mentions calamitous Allia, 101 ; story of Celeres, 20
Outlawry, 291

P

Pænula, the, 286
Palæopolis (Old City), 116
Palace, origin of the word, 17
Palatine Hill, the, chosen for the site of Rome, 17 ; Evander's city at foot of, 10 ; residence of Romulus, 26
Pales, god of the flocks, 314 ; ceremonies connected with worship of, 18
Palestine, civil war in, 220 ; overrun by Pompey, 220
Palilia, feast of, 17
Palinurus Cape, defeat of the Romans off, 133
Pallantium, in Arcadia, 17
Pallium, the, 285
Panormus, Carthaginians defeated at, 133
Paris and Helen, story of, 2
Park, the, given by Cæsar to the people, 256
Parthia, a theatre for Crassus to act in, 232
Parthians, Antony wages war against, 266, 267 ; plans of Cæsar regarding, 248 ; pretended war against, 237
Paterculus, Caius Velleius, mention of Drusus, 186
Patricians, three tribes of, 28 ; choose censors from their own order, 93 ; irritated by measures of Cassius, 83
Patriotism, the, of Gracchus, 170
Paulus, Lucius Æmilius (Macedonicus), conqueror of Macedonia, 164
Peacocks come into vogue as delicacies, 289
Penny collections, 319
People, hope for the, 183 ; oppressed by the optimates, 174 ; power of increasing, 83 ; voice of the, made supreme law, 119
Pergamos falls into the hands of the Romans, 166
Peristylum, the, 276
Perseus, son of Philip V., at war with Rome, 163 ; defeated at Pydna, 163
Perusia, siege of, 262
Pharsalia, victory of Cæsar at, 244
Philip V., of Macedon, war with, 159 ; death of, 163 ; treats with Hannibal, 144
Philippi, defeat of Brutus and Cassius at, 261
Philippics, the, of Cicero, 257, 258
Philoctetes, tomb of, 13
Philopœmen revives declining spirit in Greece, 163
Phœnicia, citizens of, found Carthage, 126
Physician, the first, 293
Pictor, Quintus Fabius, writings of, 158, 297
Pirates, from Illyria, 135 ; increase of, 175 ; in the Mediterranean, 217
Pisistratus, tyranny of the family of, overturned, 73
Placentia besieged by Hasdrubal, 146 ; colony at, 136
Plague in Rome, 109
Plato's vision of Atlantis, 199
Plautus, Titus Maccius, writings of, 297 ; the first play-writer, 110
Players at funerals, 329

INDEX TO THE TEXT AND THE NOTES. 349

Plays begin to be written, 110, 158
Plebeian successions referred to by Valerius, 156
Plebeians, attempt to improve their political position, 82; become a part of the social organization, 36; continued distress of, 88; deprived of rights, 84; encouraged, 85; had no political rights, 28; increase of importance of, 51; learn their power, 76; number of, increased, 37; offices opened to, 93; oppression of, by the patricians, 73; refuse to enrol for war, 76; restless under a sense of injustice, 115; secede across the Anio, 77; second secession of, 92; and patricians reconciled, 109
Plutarch, on the effect of a shout, 161; on the foundation of Rome, 20; on the motives of Fabius, 145
Politician, defined, 40
Politics and social classes, 212
Polybius, on the complete establishment of Roman empire, 164; taken prisoner, 164
Pomœrium, the, of Rome, 19: enlargement of the, 49; extended by Sulla, 195
Pompeia, wife of Cæsar, 216
Pompeians in Spain, 248
Pompeius, Cneius Magnus, 202; acts in the East ratified, 226; defeated at Pharsalia, 244; denounced by Curio, 236; determined not to allow Cæsar to be consul, 235; does not go to Spain, 231; exterminates the pirates, 218; final defeat of, 245; flees from Rome, 242; given command in the East, 218; gives way to Sulla, 206; goes to Spain, 209; learns the art of war, 202; needs soldiers and does not get them, 241; statue of, 250; the principal citizen, 208, 214; triumph of, 212; villa of, 281
Pompeius, Magnus, Sextus, marauding expeditions of, and defeat, 264; peace with, 263
Pompey and Cæsar at war, 240
Pompey and Catulus oppose Lepidus, 208
Pompey and Crassus exterminate the gladiators, 212
Pons sublicius, building of the, by Ancus Martius, 38
Pontifex Maximus, 32
Pontiff, the chief, duties of, 183
Pontiffs, corruption of, 247
Pontius, Telesinus, leader of the Samnites, 193
Pontus, Cæsar in, 245
Poor and rich, struggle between, 74
Poor, the, growing poorer, 119; 186; mocked, 169
Poplicola (Valerius), consul, 65
Populares, attempt of Sulla to blot out, 194
Popularity of Pompey, 217
Population of Italy, classes of, 124
Populus Romanus, the, 73; organization of, 28, 36
Porsena, Lars, of Clusium, 66; losses by, repaired, 82
Porter, the, in the house 274
Portia, wife of Brutus, 250
Pourrières, village of, 182
Poverty, attempts to alleviate by laws, 83; increase of, 175
Præneste, siege of, 193
Prayer, rites of, established, 31; to Mars, 314
Priam's large family, 1
Priests, colleges of, 32, 319; colleges of, formed, 318; increase their power, 319
Prison, the Mamertine, 38
Private interests pushed, 214
Proculus, Julius, appearance of Romulus to, 27
Professions, the Roman, 290
Profligates flock to Lepidus, 207

Proletarii, the, 51
Property, instead of pedigree, the basis of rank, 50, 73 ; qualifications introduced by Servius Tullius, 51
Proscribed, estates of the, 200
Proscription by the second triumvirate, 260
Proscription, the, of Sulla, 194, 244
Provence, 166, 182, 226
Province, of Asia, 166 ; Greece becomes a Roman, 165 ; Sicily becomes the first Roman, 134
Provinces, the, of Rome, 166 ; corruption in the, 216 ; how governed, 203
Provincial governor, a, 222
Prusias, King of Bithynia, gives Hannibal an asylum, 148
Ptolemy Epiphanes applies to Rome for help, 160
Ptolemy II., surnamed Philadelphus, 123
Public opinion, change in, at Rome, 228
Publilian, laws, 85, 109
Publilius, Volero, favors laws friendly to the plebeians, 85
Pudding of spelt, 286
Punic war, the first, 129 ; end of the first, 134 ; the second, nature of, 139 ; the second, importance of, 138 ; the third begins, 165 ; one result of, 150
Punishment for law-breaking, 291
Puns, the, of Cicero, 204
Purification by fire, 18
Puteoli, Sulla retires to, 196
Pydna, battle at, 163
Pyrrhus, King of Epirus, enters Italy, 119 ; defeated at Maleventum, 123 ; goes to Sicily, 123 ; remark of, on leaving Sicily, 128 ; unsuccessful in Sicily, 123 ; victory of, much like defeat, 122

Q

Quæstor, office of, open to the plebeians, 93

Quintilii, the followers of Romulus, 17
Quirinal Hill, estate of Sallust on, 305 ; residence of Tatius, on, 26
Quirinalia, feast of, 28
Quirinus, the god representing Romulus, 27

R

Races and games in the circus, 323
Ravenna, ancient position of, 238 ; consultation of Curio and Cæsar at, 237
Records of Rome burned, 25
Reform needed, 168
Reforms, of the Gracchi, 184 ; the, of Servius Tullius, 52 ; the, of Sulla, 195
Regillus, Lake, battle at, 67
Regions, the four urban, 49 ; loss of ten, 67
Regulus, Marcus Atilius, determines to invade Africa, 132 ; heroic death of, 133 ; taken prisoner, 133
Religion, Ancus Martius regulates, 37 ; of the Romans, 312, 317 ; organized by Numa, 30 ; severe, 72 ; solemnities of, neglected by Flaminius, 142
Republic, end of, 254, 270 ; establishment of the, 64 ; fall of the, 332
Rhadamanthus, the yellow haired, 200
Rhea Silvia, mother of Romulus and Remus, 11
Rhegium, Mamertines driven from, by Hiero and the Romans, 130
Rhinoceros, a, exhibited in Pompey's theatre, 232
Rhodes allied to Rome, 160 ; Cæsar studies at, 206, 217
Rich, oppression of the, 73
Roads, communication with the capital by, 124 ; and bridges built by Gracchus, 173

Rogations, the, of Appuleius, 185; the Licinian, 109
Roma Quadrata, 30
Roman, characteristics, 69; law, Cæsar proposes to codify, 246; people, origin of the, 13; religion severe, 72
Romans, character of, 118; defeated at Lake Trasimenus, 142; earlier occupations of the, 71; ravage Africa, 147; routed by Hannibal, 140
Rome, architectural progress under Tarquin, 43; attacked at the north and south at once, 118; burned by Brennus, 102; burning of, 25; complete establishment of its power, 164; dismay in, 142; final success of, ensured, 115; for the Romans, a party cry, 186; grows in importance, 69; increasing power of, 111, 116; increase of wealth of, 124, 159; Jugurtha's opinion of, 176; Livy's history of, 7; loses territory, 67; menaced by Brennus, 101; not troubled by scruples, 130; outward appearance of the city, 272; power of, extended in Asia, 192; rebuilding of, after its burning by the Gauls, 106; seeking a site for, 16; takes Tarentum, 123; territory of, extended, 136, 221; territory of, in Asia enlarged, 162; threatened by Hannibal, 144; threatened by Pyrrhus, 122; threatened with ruin, 175;
Romulus and Remus thrown into the Tiber, 11
Romulus, gives the people warlike customs, 29; disappearance of, 27; sole ruler of Sabines and Romans, 27
Rostra, the, in the forum, 116; the, adorned with prows of ships, 132
Rubicon, the, becomes the border line of Roman territory, 123, 195; crossed by Cæsar, 240; difficult to identify, 238
Rumor, temple built in honor of, 107

S

Sabines, fight with the, 24; names of the, 15; war with, 90
Sacred Mount, the, 79; law of the, 89
Sacrifice of M. D. Mus, 116; of P. D. Mus, 118
Sacrifices, human, abolished, 31
Saddle, exercise in the, 281; travel in the, 290
Saguntum, siege of, 139
Salii, subordinate priests, 32
Sallust (Caius Sallustius Crispus), works of, 305
Samnites, allies of Rome, 115; in the Marsic war, 187; massacre of, by Sulla, 193; threaten to raze the city, 193; origin of, 113; overcome, 144; second war with, 116; third war with, 118
Samos, Octavius rests at, 270
Sandals and shoes, 286
Sardinia and Corsica taken from Carthage, 134
Saturn, Hill of, a name of the Capitoline, 24
Saturnalia, the, 314, 315; the women's, 316
Saturninus, Lucius Appuleius, rogations of, 185
Saturnus, god of social order, 314
Scævola, Mucius, adventure of, 66
Scandal, the game of, in history, 106
School-book, the first, 295
Science, slow growth of, 294
Scipio, Africanus Major, gives away his daughter, 167; investigated by Cato, 156; sent to Spain, 144; sets out for Africa, 146
Scipio, Lucius Cornelius, Asiaticus, at Magnesia, 162

352   INDEX TO THE TEXT AND THE NOTES.

Scipio, Publius Cornelius, 138
Scipio, Publius Cornelius, Nasica, defeated by Cæsar, 245
Scipio, Publius Cornelius Scipio Æmilianus, Africanus Minor, son of Æmilius Paulus, 164; becomes also "Africanus Minor," 165; becomes leader of the optimates, 172; marries Cornelia, daughter of Gracchus, 167; murder of, 172; restores peace in Spain, 165
Scylla and Charybdis, 129
Stylus, use of the, 295
Secession, of the plebeians, 77, 92; to the Janiculum, 119
Self-sacrifice of Mus, 118
Sempronian laws, the, 173
Senate, composition of, 28; deprived of the choice of chief pontiff, 183; enlarged by Sulla, 195; favors war with Philip V., 160; government by the, 29; opposes Drusus, 186; plebeians made eligible to the, 93; powers of, abridged, 173; powers of, restricted, 184; reluctantly forced to listen to a letter from Cæsar, 238; shut up in the capitol, 102
Senators, authorize Lepidus to make Cæsar dictator, 244; flee from Rome, 241; flee after murder of Cæsar, 250; murdered by the Gauls, 102
Sentium, battle near, 118
Sertorius, Quintus, bravery of, 199; assassinated, 209
Servants at dinner, 289
Servile insurrections, 175
Servius Tullius murdered, 56
Seven Hills, the, 49, 70
Sextus (see Pompeius Magnus Sextus), 263
Sextus, Lucius, first plebeian consul, 109
Shakespeare's version of the offer of the crown to Cæsar, 249
Ships, deficiency of, 130
Shoes and boots, 286

Sibyl, the, of Cumæ, visits Tarquin, 59
Sibylline books, the, 59, 72; burned, 193; the, consulted, 136; verdict of, by whom pronounced, 183
Sicily, becomes a Roman province, 134; career of Verres in, 203; colony of Carthage in, 128; result of a war in, 170; servile insurrection in, 166; taken from Lepidus by Octavius, 266; visited by Pyrrhus, 123
Sicinius, Lucius Dentatus, 90
Sidon, glass of, 127
Siege of Rome by the Gauls, 103
Siege of Veii, 95
Silvanus, Mars, traits of, 314
Silvanus, the god, determines a victory for the Romans, 65
Silvia, or Rhea Silvia, 11
Siris, battle of the river, 122
Slaves, domestic, 282; great increase of, 166; insurrection among, 183; occupations of, 200; punished for excesses, 199; their share in education, 292, traffic in, 74; working fields in chains, 169
Soldiers, not adapted to agriculture, 83; pay provided for, 83; rewarded by Octavius, 270; without homes, 169
Spain, assigned to Pompey, 228; Carthaginians in, 128, 139; mastered by Rome, 144; Pompeians in, 243, 248; Pompey in, 209; Sertorius in, 199; troubles in, 165
Spartacus, the gladiator, 210
Spectators in the theatres, 231
Spring-time festivities, 331
Spurius Cassius, 82
Stagirite, the, 192
Stola, use of the, 285
Stolo, Caius Licinius, see Licinius, 109
Stone, use of, in building, 326
Streets at Rome, 159

INDEX TO THE TEXT AND THE NOTES. 353

Substitution, the idea of, in Roman religion, 317
Suetonius on the crossing of the Rubicon, 241
Suffrage, extended to the Italians, 173, 184; offered to the allies who would lay down their arms, 188
Suggestum, the, 116
Sulla and Marius, traits of, 185
Sulla, Lucius Cornelia, character of, 176; after the Marsic war, 188; claims credit for capturing Jugurtha, 180; description of, 180; effects of his doings, 197; goes to Gaul with Marius; 181; in Asia, 190; legislation of, repealed by Pompey, 212; obtains command of the army, 190; resisted by Cæsar, 206; scatters his veterans through Italy, 196; retirement of, 196; threatens vengeance, 192
Sumptuary law, a, 150
Sumptuary laws enacted by Sulla, 195
Suovetaurilia, the, 54
Superstition increases, 319
Sybaris in Magna Græcia, 114
Syracuse, grain sent from, 80; taken, 144
Syria assigned to Crassus, 228
Square Rome, 30
Squatters on Roman lands, 83
Switzerland, Cæsar in, 227

T

Table-customs, 286
Tables, richness of, 289
Tacita, the nymph that Numa pretended to meet, 32
Talasia, the refrain of a marriage-song, 22, 283
Tanaquil, 55
Tarentines and Lucanians, war between, 120
Tarentum, in Magna Græcia, 114; conference at, 264; given up to pleasures, 121;
falls under the sway of Rome, 123; falls into the hand of Fabius, 145
Tarpeian Rock, the, 24
Tarpeia's fate, 24
Tarquinii, one of the cities of Etruria, 9
Tarquinius, Priscus, birth of, 41; goes to Rome, 41; progress of, 43; supposed to have established the great games of the circus, 322
Tarquinius, Superbus, endeavors to stir up a conspiracy, 64; flees to Cumæ, 68; intrigues for the crown, 56; great works of, 60; tyrrany of, 58
Tarquins, the, banished, 63
Tatius, proposes to attack Rome, 22; slain by people of Lavinium, 27
Telamon, Gauls defeated at, 136
Tellus, the nourishing earth, 314
Temple, the, at Jerusalem examined by Pompey, 220
Temples, dedicated to the honor of Cæsar, 246; the first Roman, 313
Ten Men, the, 89
Tennis, Mæcenas plays a game of, 265
Terence (Publius Terentius Afer), comedies of, 298
Terminalia, ceremonies of, 30
Terminus, worship of, 30
Territory of Rome, increased, 136; insignificant, 70
Terror, reign of, 194
Teuta, perfidious queen, 135
Thanksgiving for the victories of Cæsar, 227, 246
Thapsus, defeat of the followers of Pompey at, 245
Theatre, the, of Pompey, 231, 326
Theatres, at Tarentum shut up by Pyrrhus, 121; the Roman, characteristics of, 231
Thermopylæ, defeat of the Syrians at, 162

Thirty cities of Latium, the, 11
Thrace, native country of Spartacus, 211
Threshold, the bride lifted over, 283
Thunder-storm, influence of, on public meetings, 319
Thurii, relics at, 13
Tiber overflows its banks, 110
Tibullus Albius, poetry of, 304
Ticinu: battle of the, 140
Toga, the, use of, 285; exemplified in the case of Cincinnatus, 86
Tolosa, gold of, 184
Torquatus, Titus Manlius, slays a Gaul, 113
Towns built on hills, 70
Trades learned, 289
Trasimenus, battle of Lake, 142
Travel, modes of, 290
Traveller, hospitality to the, 280
Treaties with Carthage, 115, 128
Treaties with neighbors, 82
"Treating" by office-seekers, 290
Trebia, battle of the, 140
Tribes, citizens of the, 124; divisions of the, 28; ten new, formed, 188; the thirty, 49
Tribunes of the people, the first, 79; Coriolanus opposed to, 81; power of, restricted by Sulla, 195; restored by Pompey, 212; military, chosen, 93
Triclinium, the, 276
Triremes and quinquiremes, 130
Triumph, the, defined, 36; description of, 212; instituted by Tarquin, 44; of Camillus, 96; of Cincinnatus, 87; of Fabius, 146; of Marius at Rome, 180, 182; of Octavius, for victories of Actium and Egypt, 270; of Pompey, 202, 212, 221; of Sulla, 194, 195
Triumvirate, the first, so-called, 224; the second, 258; extension of the second, 266
Triumvirs, reconciliation of two, 263; the three, each striving

for the ascendency, 232; proscription by, 260
Trojan origin of Albans and Romans, 34
Troy, the play of, 325; beginnings of the British race in, 6; date of fall of, 4; names of the heroes of, fixed on Italian places, 13; story of, 1
Tullia, the wicked daughter of Servius Tullius, 55
Tulliarium, the, Mamertine prison, 180
Tullius, Servius, sixth king, 46
Tullus Hostilius, the king, 33; offends the gods and dies, 37
Tunes, age of, 127
Tunnel under Veii, constructed, 96
Turchina, the remains of Tarquinii, 41
Turnus, the early Italian king, 10
Tusculum hills, the, 124
Twelve tables, laws of the, 89, 90; used as a text-book, 293
Tyrant, a, 58, 236
Tyre, antiquity of, 127; inhabitants of, 126

U

Ulysses, relics of, 14
Urn, the funeral, 329
Utica, antiquity of, 127; Scipio at, 146

V

Vadimonis, Lake, victory at, 117; second battle near, 119
Valerian laws, 78
Valerius, Lucius, champion of the women, 153
Valerius, Publius, the people's friend, 65
Valerius, see Corvus, Marcus Valerius, 113
Varro, Marcus Terentius, on education, 294; describes life in a rural house, 280; on the care of children, 284; writings of, 300

Varro, Terentius, champion of the popular party, 143
Vaults, burial, 329
Vegetables, a diet of, 287
Veii, one of the Etrurian cities, 9; siege of, 94; stones brought from, to build Rome, 107
Velian Hill, house of Valerius on the, 65
Veni, vidi, vici, expression of Cæsar, 245
Ver Sacrum, sacrifice of, described, 114
Vercellæ, rout of the Cimbri at, 182
Vercingetorix, character of, 229; opposes Cæsar, 228
Verres, Caius Licinius, traits of, 202; flees from Rome, 204
Verrucosus, name of Fabius, 139
Vesta, goddess of the fireside, 315
Vestal virgins, the, 32
Vestibule, use of, 275
Vesuvius, battle of Mount, 115; gladiators in, 211
Veterans, allotment of land to, 261, 262
Veto, senate deprived of, 119
Via, Appia, course of, 124; Egnatia, route, of, 261; Latina, course of, 124; Ostiensis, course of, 124; Sacra, 212; Saleria, route of, 124; Valeria, course of, 124
Vice, increase of, 175
Villa, adornments of the pleasure, 281; the farm, 279; the pleasure, 279; of Cicero, given over to destruction, 224
Vinalia, feasts of, 314
Violence and bloodshed, familiarity with, 185
Virgil (Publius Vergilius Maro), works of, 309; joins Horace on a journey, 265; story of Æneas, 7
Virginia, death of, 91
Virginius, Lucius, commands against the Æquians, 90
Voice, temple built to, 107

Volero (see Publilius), 85
Volscians, the, threaten Rome, 81; overcome, 116
Votes, solicitation of, by women, 150, 153
Vulcanus, festival of, 315
Vultures, augury by, 17

W

Walls and floors, 278
War, civil, consequences of, 333; in early times, traits of, 87; engines of, 95; precautions neglected in, 101; prosperity by, 125
Wars add to Roman prestige, 94
Wealth, increase of, 150, 185; how obtained by Crassus, 200; of private citizens, 235; of Sallust, 305
Wedding ceremonies, 283
Windows and shutters, 279
Wives wanted in early Rome, 21
Women, corruption of, 284; customs regarding, at Rome, 149; dress of the, 285; good works of, for the state, 153; movement of the Roman, 149; the Sabine, bring peace, 26; toilet articles of, 286; 287; want of, in early Rome, 21
Woods, the first temples in the, 313
Workmen, importance of, 51

X

Xanthippus, the Spartan, aids Carthage, 132

Y

Year, the, lengthened by Cæsar, 247; the pontiffs lengthen or shorten, 236; the Roman, 32
Yoke, the, passing under, 87, 117

Z

Zama, rout of the Carthaginians at, 147; soldiers of Macedonia at, 160
Zela, Cæsar's victory at, 245

The Story of the Nations.

MESSRS. G. P. PUTNAM'S SONS take pleasure in announcing that they have in course of publication, in co-operation with Mr. T. Fisher Unwin, of London, a series of historical studies, intended to present in a graphic manner the stories of the different nations that have attained prominence in history.

In the story form the current of each national life is distinctly indicated, and its picturesque and noteworthy periods and episodes are presented for the reader in their philosophical relation to each other as well as to universal history.

It is the plan of the writers of the different volumes to enter into the real life of the peoples, and to bring them before the reader as they actually lived, labored, and struggled—as they studied and wrote, and as they amused themselves. In carrying out this plan, the myths, with which the history of all lands begins, will not be overlooked, though these will be carefully distinguished from the actual history, so far as the labors of the accepted historical authorities have resulted in definite conclusions.

The subjects of the different volumes have been planned to cover connecting and, as far as possible, consecutive epochs or periods, so that the set when completed will present in a comprehensive narrative the chief events in the great STORY OF THE NATIONS; but it is, of course, not always practicable to issue the several volumes in their chronological order.

The "Stories" are printed in good readable type, and in handsome 12mo form. They are adequately illustrated and furnished with maps and indexes. Price, per vol., cloth, $1.50. Half morocco, gilt top, $1.75.

The following volumes are now ready (March, 1895):

THE STORY OF GREECE. Prof. JAS. A. HARRISON.
" " " ROME. ARTHUR GILMAN.
" " " THE JEWS. Prof. JAMES K. HOSMER.
" " " CHALDEA. Z. A. RAGOZIN.
" " " GERMANY. S. BARING-GOULD.
" " " NORWAY. HJALMAR H. BOYESEN.
" " " SPAIN. Rev. E. E. and SUSAN HALE.
" " " HUNGARY. Prof. A. VÁMBÉRY.
" " " CARTHAGE. Prof. ALFRED J. CHURCH.
" " " THE SARACENS. ARTHUR GILMAN.
" " " THE MOORS IN SPAIN. STANLEY LANE-POOLE.
" " " THE NORMANS. SARAH ORNE JEWETT.
" " " PERSIA. S. G. W. BENJAMIN.
" " " ANCIENT EGYPT. Prof. GEO. RAWLINSON.
" " " ALEXANDER'S EMPIRE. Prof. J. P. MAHAFFY.
" " " ASSYRIA. Z. A. RAGOZIN.
" " " THE GOTHS. HENRY BRADLEY.
" " " IRELAND. Hon. EMILY LAWLESS.
" " " TURKEY. STANLEY LANE-POOLE.
" " " MEDIA, BABYLON, AND PERSIA. Z. A. RAGOZIN.
" " " MEDIÆVAL FRANCE. Prof. GUSTAVE MASSON.
" " " HOLLAND. Prof. J. THOROLD ROGERS.
" " " MEXICO. SUSAN HALE.
" " " PHŒNICIA. Prof. GEO. RAWLINSON.
" " " THE HANSA TOWNS. HELEN ZIMMERN.
" " " EARLY BRITAIN. Prof. ALFRED J. CHURCH.
" " " THE BARBARY CORSAIRS. STANLEY LANE-POOLE.
" " " RUSSIA. W. R. MORFILL.
" " " THE JEWS UNDER ROME. W. D. MORRISON.
" " " SCOTLAND. JOHN MACKINTOSH.
" " " SWITZERLAND. R. STEAD and Mrs. A. HUG.
" " " PORTUGAL. H. MORSE STEPHENS.
" " " THE BYZANTINE EMPIRE. C. W. C. OMAN.
" " " SICILY. E. A. FREEMAN.
" " " THE TUSCAN REPUBLICS. BELLA DUFFY.
" " " POLAND. W. R. MORFILL.
" " " PARTHIA. Prof. GEORGE RAWLINSON.
" " " JAPAN. DAVID MURRAY.
" " " THE CHRISTIAN RECOVERY OF SPAIN. H. E. WATTS.
" " " AUSTRALASIA. GREVILLE TREGARTHEN.
" " " SOUTHERN AFRICA. GEO. M. THEAL.
" " " VENICE. ALETHEA WIEL.
" " " THE CRUSADES. T. S. ARCHER and C. L. KINGSFORD.
" " " VEDIC INDIA. By Z. A. RAGOZIN.

Heroes of the Nations.

EDITED BY
EVELYN ABBOTT, M.A., FELLOW OF BALLIOL COLLEGE, OXFORD.

A SERIES of biographical studies of the lives and work of a number of representative historical characters about whom have gathered the great traditions of the Nations to which they belonged, and who have been accepted, in many instances, as types of the several National ideals. With the life of each typical character will be presented a picture of the National conditions surrounding him during his career.

The narratives are the work of writers who are recognized authorities on their several subjects, and, while thoroughly trustworthy as history, will present picturesque and dramatic "stories" of the Men and of the events connected with them.

To the Life of each "Hero" will be given one duodecimo volume, handsomely printed in large type, provided with maps and adequately illustrated according to the special requirements of the several subjects. The volumes will be sold separately as follows:

Cloth extra	$1 50
Half morocco, uncut edges, gilt top . . .	1 75
Large paper, limited to 250 numbered copies for subscribers to the series. These may be obtained in sheets folded, or in cloth, uncut edges	3 50

The first group of the Series comprises the following volumes:

Nelson, and the Naval Supremacy of England. By W. CLARK RUSSELL, author of "The Wreck of the Grosvenor," etc.

Gustavus Adolphus, and the Struggle of Protestantism for Existence. By C. R. L. FLETCHER, M. A., late Fellow of All Souls College, Oxford.

Pericles, and the Golden Age of Athens. By Evelyn Abbott, M.A., Fellow of Balliol College, Oxford.

Theodoric the Goth, the Barbarian Champion of Civilisation. By THOMAS HODGKIN, author of "Italy and Her Invaders," etc.

Sir Philip Sidney, and the Chivalry of England. By H. R. FOX-BOURNE, author of "The Life of John Locke," etc.

Julius Cæsar, and the Organisation of the Roman Empire. By W. WARDE FOWLER, M.A., Fellow of Lincoln College, Oxford.

John Wyclif, Last of the Schoolmen and First of the English Reformers. By LEWIS SERGEANT, author of "New Greece," etc.

Napoleon, Warrior and Ruler, and the Military Supremacy of Revolutionary France. By W. O'CONNOR MORRIS, sometime Scholar of Oriel College, Oxford.

Henry of Navarre, and the Huguenots in France. By P. F. WILLERT, M.A., Fellow of Exeter College, Oxford.

Cicero, and the Fall of the Roman Republic. By J. L. STRACHAN DAVIDSON, M.A., Fellow of Balliol College, Oxford.

Abraham Lincoln, and the Downfall of American Slavery. By NOAH BROOKS.

Prince Henry (of Portugal) the Navigator, and the Age of Discovery. By C. R. BEAZLEY, Fellow of Merton College, Oxford.

Julian the Philosopher, and the Last Struggle of Paganism against Christianity. By ALICE GARDNER, Lecturer on Ancient History in Newnham College.

Louis XIV., and the Zenith of the French Monarchy. By ARTHUR HASSALL, M.A., Senior Student of Christ Church College, Oxford.

To be followed by:

Saladin, the Crescent and the Cross. By STANLEY LANE-POOLE.

Joan of Arc. By Mrs. OLIPHANT.

The Cid Campeador, and the Waning of the Crescent in the West. By H. BUTLER CLARKE, Wadham College, Oxford.

Charlemagne, the Reorganiser of Europe. By Prof. GEORGE L. BURR, Cornell University.

Moltke, and the Founding of the German Empire. By SPENSER WILKINSON.

Oliver Cromwell, and the Rule of the Puritans in England. By CHARLES FIRTH, Balliol College, Oxford.

Alfred the Great, and the First Kingdom in England. By F. YORK POWELL, M.A., Senior Student of Christ Church College, Oxford.

Marlborough, and England as a Military Power. By C. W. C. OMAN, A.M., Fellow of All Souls College, Oxford.

Frederic the Second, the Wonder of the World. By A. L. SMITH, of Balliol College, Oxford.

Charles the Bold, and the Attempt to Found a Middle Kingdom. By R. LODGE, M.A., Fellow of Brasenose College, Oxford.

Alexander the Great, and the Extension of Greek Rule and of Greek Ideas. By Prof. BENJAMIN I. WHEELER, Cornell University.

G. P. PUTNAM'S SONS

www.ingramcontent.com/pod-product-compliance
Lightning Source LLC
Chambersburg PA
CBHW021338300426
44114CB00012B/988